S0-AQJ-964

The Complete Freezer Cookbook

Madeline Fraser

OCTOPUS

This edition published 1977 by
Octopus Books Limited
59 Grosvenor Street
London W1

© 1976 Hennerwood Publications Limited

ISBN 0 7064 0851 9

Printed in England by Jarrold & Sons Ltd

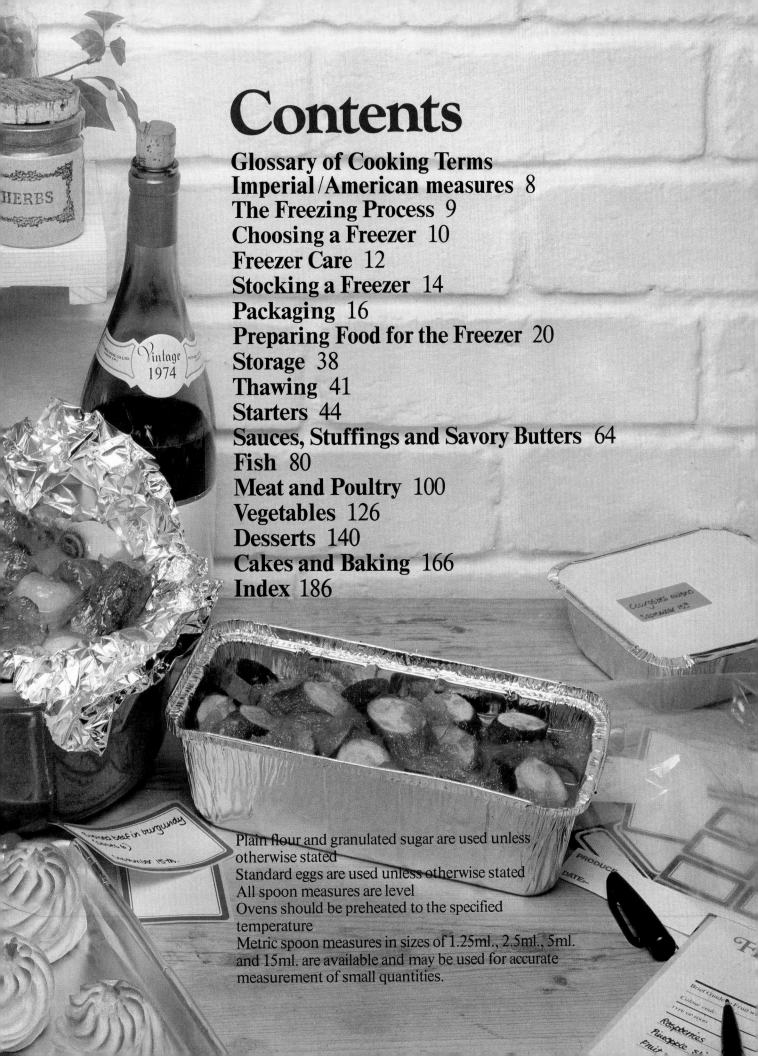

Contents

Plain flour and granulated sugar are used unless
otherwise stated
Standard eggs are used unless otherwise stated
All spoon measures are level
Ovens should be preheated to the specified
temperature
Metric spoon measures in sizes of 1.25ml., 2.5ml., 5ml.
and 15ml. are available and may be used for accurate
measurement of small quantities.

Glossary of Cooking Terms

British	American
BEEF CUTS	
braising steak	beef flank or round steak
fillet steak	tenderloin steak
lean stewing beef	lean beef chunk or plate of beef
minced beef	ground beef
ribs of beef	short rib roast
silverside of beef	beef heel or round
sirloin steak	porterhouse steak
skirt steak	London broil
topside of beef	rolled rump roast
VEAL	
leg of veal	veal centre leg roast
veal knuckles	veal hindshanks or foreshanks
PORK	

(N.B. In Britain pork is fresh meat, ham or bacon is cured and salted)

British	American
belly of pork	pork arm steak
gammon	smoked ham, centre slice
back bacon	Canadian style bacon
fillet of pork	pork tenderloin
leg of ham	salted shank of ham
leg of pork	fresh ham, shank half
pig's trotter	pig's feet
salted belly of pork	pork butt
sausagemeat	minced pork
slipper of ham	use smoked ham or salted shank
unsalted pork	fresh ham
LAMB	
lamb chops	lamb rib chops
leg of lamb	leg of lamb, shank half
shoulder of lamb	square cut shoulder
FISH AND POULTRY	
bream	none
hake	use cod or halibut
kippers	kippered herrings
plaice	use dab or flounder
prawns	jumbo shrimp
sole	use dab or flounder
turbot	if not available use halibut
pigeon	squab
VEGETABLES	
aubergine	eggplant
broad beans	Java beans
beetroot	beets
chicory	endive
cos lettuce	Romaine lettuce
courgettes	zucchini
endive	chicory
French beans	snap or green beans
haricot beans	white beans
marrow	summer squash
pickling onions	small white onions
Spanish onion	Bermuda onion
spring onions	scallions
FRUITS AND NUTS	
cooking apples	green apples
glacé cherries	candied cherries
hazelnuts	filberts
sultanas	seedless white raisins

Imperial/American Measures

Imperial	American
FLOUR	
Plain	**All-purpose**
½ oz	3 tablespoons
1 oz	¼ cup
2 oz	½ cup
4 oz	1 cup
1 lb	4 cups
Cornflour	**Cornstarch**
1 oz	4 tablespoons
2 oz	½ cup less 1 tablespoon
4 oz	1 cup
SUGAR	
Castor/granulated	**Granulated**
2 oz	¼ cup
4 oz	½ cup
6 oz	¾ cup
8 oz	1 cup plus 3 tablespoons
1 lb	2¼ cups
Icing	**Sifted confectioners**
2 oz	½ cup
4 oz	1 cup
5 oz	1½ cups
6 oz	1½ cups
1 lb	4½ cups
Light and Dark Brown	
1 oz	2 tablespoons, packed
4 oz	½ cup, firmly packed
6 oz	1 cup, lightly packed
8 oz	1 cup plus 2 tablespoons, packed
1 lb	2¼ cups
BUTTER, LARD, SHORTENING – HARD OR MELTED	
½ oz	1 tablespoon
2 oz	¼ cup
4 oz	½ cup
8 oz	1 cup
CREAM	
Double and single	**Heavy and light**
3 tablespoons	¼ cup
2 fl. oz	¼ cup
4 fl. oz	½ cup
8 fl. oz	1 cup
¼ pint (5 fl. oz)	⅔ cup
Sour	
1 × 5 oz carton	½ cup
CHEESE	
Grated hard	
½ oz	1 tablespoon
2 oz	½ cup
4 oz	1 cup
Parmesan, grated	
6 oz	1 cup
Cottage	
6 oz	1 cup
SOFT FRUITS	
1 lb	4 cups or 1 quart
APPLES, PEELED AND SLICED	
1 lb	3 cups

Imperial	American
DRIED FRUITS	
Currants, raisins, white raisins etc	
2 oz	⅓ cup
6 oz	1 cup, packed
Prunes, stoned	
6 oz	1 cup
Dried apricots	
8 oz	1½ cups
PULSES	
Haricot beans	**White beans**
6 oz	1 cup
Kidney beans	
11 oz	1 cup
Lentils	
6 oz	1 cup
RICE	
Long grain, uncooked	
4 oz	½ cup
8 oz	1¼ cups
1 lb	2½ cups
Cooked	
5-6 oz	1 cup
Short grain or pudding	
8 oz	1 cup
YEAST	
1 oz fresh yeast	1 cake compressed yeast
½ oz dried yeast	1 packet active dry yeast
BREADCRUMBS	
1½-2 oz fresh	1 cup fresh
1 oz fresh	½ cup fresh
6 oz dried	1 scant cup dried
2½ oz dried	½ cup dried
NUTS	
Most chopped nuts	
4 oz	¾ cup
Most whole nuts	
4 oz	1 cup
Ground almonds	
2 oz	scant ½ cup
Blanched whole almonds	
4 oz	1 cup
HONEY, JAM, SYRUP, PRESERVES	
8 oz	¾ cup
12 oz	1 cup
1 lb	1⅓ cups
LIQUID MEASUREMENTS	
½ fl. oz or 1 tablespoon	½ fl. oz
2 fl. oz or 4 tablespoons	¼ cup
¼ pint or 5 fl. oz	½ cup plus 2 tablespoons
½ pint or 10 fl. oz	1¼ cups
1 pint or 20 fl. oz	1¼ pints or 2½ cups
1 quart or 40 fl. oz	2½ pints or 5 cups
A British pint is 20 fl. oz	An American pint is 16 fl. oz

The Freezing Process

Freezing is one of the easiest and safest methods of preservation, and one which preserves the food closest to its original state, with minimum loss of colour, freshness or texture. If correctly prepared and stored in the freezer, frozen food will be indistinguishable from its fresh counterpart.

How freezing preserves food

The basic principle of freezing is to reduce the temperature of the food to a point where chemical changes are reduced and micro organisms become inactive.

Frozen food, as long as the temperature of the freezer is maintained at $-18°C/0°F$ or less, will remain in a similar state as when it first went into the freezer (see storage times pages 38–40 for different foods). As soon as the food is thawed, deterioration will start up again.

Freezing will not improve the quality of any food. Food to be frozen must be of the highest quality prepared in hygienic conditions, correctly packaged and stored at the recommended temperature.

What is meant by fast freezing

The quality of frozen food is partly determined by the rate at which it is frozen. To achieve good results food must be frozen fast to a very low temperature to preserve its original colour, flavour and texture.

All foods are made up of animal or vegetable tissue which in turn are composed of cells, each of which contains and is surrounded by a fluid holding mineral salts, proteins and vitamins. This fluid, like water, freezes at a temperature of $0°C/32°F$, and ice crystals are formed in and around each cell.

If food is frozen slowly large ice crystals form. These expand during freezing, puncture cell walls and destroy surrounding tissue. On thawing those valuable nutrients are lost through the punctured cells, making the food flabby and discoloured. So the faster the food is frozen, the smaller the ice crystals and the more perfect is the structure of the food.

But there is another good reason for fast-freezing. Fresh food, even if cooled, has a certain warmth or temperature of its own. When put into the freezer containing already-frozen food it will cause a rise in temperature of both the cabinet and the packages of food. Large ice crystals will start to form as a result of this fluctuation in temperature which, if allowed to continue, will affect the storage condition of the rest of the frozen food. (Opening the freezer too often or for too long has the same effect.) To combat this, there is a special control called the fast-freeze switch.

The fast-freeze switch Known also as auto-freeze, super-freeze or super-cold, the fast-freeze switch enables the freezer motor to override the thermostat, the vital piece of equipment that tells it how cold to keep the cabinet. Consequently, the temperature continues to fall so that fresh food can be frozen solid *without* raising the temperature of the already-frozen food present. It does not in fact freeze food faster as such.

Some freezers have a separate compartment for fast-freezing, its size governing how much fresh food can be put in without affecting the temperature of the food elsewhere in the cabinet.

If there is no separate fast-freeze compartment, put fresh food in the coldest part of the freezer and away from frozen packages. In a chest freezer the coldest part is against the sides; in an upright it is also against the sides unless the freezing coils are within the shelves.

Set the fast-freeze control 2–5 hours before you start freezing fresh food; the instructions for your particular freezer will give you guidance as to exactly how long is necessary.

How long fast-freezing of food takes is impossible to specify; so much depends on the make of freezer, the size, density and shape of packages, the type of food, and how much is already stored. But, as a rule, liquids, thin slices of bread, meat or poultry, dairy products, sliced vegetables or fruit, or small cakes take about 1 hour per $\frac{1}{2}$ kg./1 lb. and bulkier, more solid foods like prepared meals, fish, joints of meat and dishes with a high sugar content take about 2 hours per $\frac{1}{2}$ kg./1 lb.

As soon as all packs in any one batch of food are frozen hard, turn off the fast-freeze switch so that the cabinet can return to its normal setting – this can take up to 10 hours. Although very little extra electricity is used when the fast-freeze switch is on, too long a time is wasteful and uneconomic and might cause the motor to overheat. So be guided by the manufacturer's instructions.

How much fresh food can be frozen at any one time in 24 hours is called the daily freezing capacity, and it is important not to exceed this capacity for the reasons given above. The recommended capacity for your freezer can be found in the manufacturer's instructions and on the rating plate which is either on the side or at the back of the cabinet. In general, it is usually about 10% of the freezer's total capacity.

Star symbols

It is important to distinguish between a refrigerator and a freezer. They are *not* interchangeable. Neither is a conservator, which is merely a cabinet for storing already-frozen food at $-18°C/0°F$ for whatever its storage life may be. A refrigerator will keep perishable foods fresh and safe only for a short period of time and will store or conserve already-frozen foods in its freezer compartment according to the obligatory British Standards star markings. Check the storage recommendation given on the packaging of commercially frozen foods. As a guide, a refrigerator with one black star will store frozen food for up to 1 week and ice cream for 1 day; with two black stars the refrigerator will store frozen food up to 1 month and ice cream for 2 weeks, and with three black stars frozen food may be stored for up to 3 months and ice cream for 1 month.

Only a freezer has the ability quickly to freeze fresh food to a minimum temperature of $-18°C/0°F$ within 24 hours, and to store it in perfect condition for several months and sometimes longer. The British Standards white star in front of the three-star refrigerator symbol denotes a freezer.

Choosing a Freezer

Once you have made the decision to buy a freezer, the type you choose will be determined largely by the services expected of it, the range of produce you intend to freeze, the size of the family, the space available and the amount of money you can afford to spend.

Whatever your needs, think big. It is a common complaint to underestimate the size required. Many freezer owners often wish they had chosen a larger model when they realise the storage space is below their requirements. Remember the life of a freezer is long and reliable, and as the housewife becomes more and more freezer-conscious, her storage needs may well outgrow the capacity of the freezer long before the end of its useful life. Therefore choose the largest you can afford and have space available for. A rough guide is to allow 85–113l./3–4cu.ft. for each member of the household. A 350l./12cu.ft. model is the smallest you should consider for a family of four.

Remember that each 28l./1cu.ft. of freezer space will only store between 9–11kg./20–25lb. of food and you will need extra capacity if you intend to freeze large quantities of fruit and vegetables in season or to take advantage of economical prices when buying in bulk.

There is a large choice of freezers on the market. Basically they fall into three categories:
1 The upright type
2 The chest type
3 The combination refrigerator/freezer type

Time should be spent comparing prices in as many shops and discount houses as you can before buying.

Remember you are more likely to get reliable after-sales service from large reputable manufacturers.

The chest freezer

The chest freezer gives the maximum storage for any given capacity and is particularly useful for storing large, bulky or awkwardly shaped packages. It takes up twice as much floor space as an upright model of the same capacity and many householders find that the larger models will not fit into the average kitchen. So consider housing a chest freezer under the stairs, in a garage or in a suitable outbuilding. However, there are many sizes to choose from, starting at 113l./4cu.ft. but the most popular range is between 255–400l./9–14cu.ft.

Most chest freezers have a counter-balanced lift-up insulated lid which will stay open in any position and thus leave your hands free for packing. The top can provide a useful temporary work surface, but you cannot use it as a permanent storage space. There is very little temperature fluctuation when the lid is raised because cold air is dense and falls to the bottom and warm air, which rises, only penetrates a very small distance below the top. Running costs are therefore very economical and a chest freezer requires less defrosting than other types.

Check before you buy a chest freezer that you can reach the bottom of the cabinet. The most inaccessible part is the bottom on the side farthest from the lock. The depth of the storage compartment may be as much as 75cm./30in., a considerable reach for a small person, particularly when packing and cleaning the freezer.

A methodical storage system is essential for the chest freezer because top layers have to be taken out before a package can be retrieved further down. Wire partitions which fit at the bottom of the freezer and baskets or trays which slide sideways across the top are invaluable for keeping the smaller items together and will make packing and selection of food much easier. Many manufacturers now supply these baskets ready fitted, and additional baskets can be bought. But check that you can fit these baskets easily when fully loaded.

The upright freezer

The upright freezer resembles a refrigerator in appearance and will take up a similar amount of floor space. It has a front-opening door, several shelves, often adjustable and/or pull-out baskets, so that the food can be seen and easily removed. Some have shelves fitted on the door to hold small packages.

Some models have a special fast-freeze shelf, drawer or compartment, while in others any shelf can be used for fast-freezing. Again, there is a wide range of sizes from around 57l./2cu.ft., intended to stand on top of an existing work surface of refrigerator, up to 566l./20cu.ft.

The upright freezer is usually considered to be less economical to run than the chest freezer. Each time the door is opened cold air is lost throughout, and moisture-laden warm air entering produces extra frosting on the walls. Running costs will, therefore, be slightly higher than the chest type, and defrosting needs to be more frequent. However the temperature recovery of a modern upright is quite rapid so this is not a serious drawback.

Some uprights are filled with separate spring-hinged doors or flaps to each shelf, while larger models can have two doors; all help to minimise the loss of cold air.

The combination refrigerator/freezer

Some manufacturers produce 'Twin-Units', which are two separate front-opening models combining refrigerator and freezer, the refrigerator usually having the same litre/cubic capacity as the freezer. These may be designed to stand on top of each other or side by side. The upright combination is particularly suitable for limited kitchen space.

The freezer unit has a separate temperature control which can be lowered for fresh and precooked foods, but the freezing capacity is usually fairly small, up to about 198l./7cu.ft. and capable of storing a maximum of 63kg./140lb. of frozen food; only very small amounts of fresh food can be fast-frozen at any one time. The combination freezer unit is better suited to long-term storage of commercially frozen food, or for the person who does not intend to freeze his own produce on a large scale.

Buying second-hand

Take care when buying a second-hand freezer. First check that spare parts and service are still available for that particular model. 'Bargain' freezers can often go wrong without hope of being repaired.

Useful extras

When choosing a freezer, look for the following extra features.

Interior light An interior light is particularly important if the freezer is housed in a garage or outbuilding. The light should come on when the door or lid is opened.

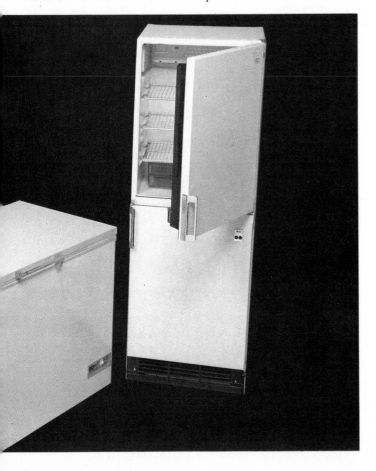

Ease of movement Castors or skid rails can be fitted to the freezer, which will protect your floor and permit easy movement for cleaning.

Locks Most large models are fitted with a lock, a particularly important safety feature if you have small children. Prevent tragedy by having a lock fitted, if possible, and keep the key out of the way of tiny fingers.

Alarm system An alarm system, either in the form of a light or buzzer, will indicate a rise in temperature or if there is a fault in the electrical system.

Running costs

The amount of electricity used in running the freezer depends to a large extent on the number of times and for how long the door or lid is opened, the amount of food that is in the cabinet, the temperature of fresh food when put in and the siting of the freezer.

Running costs can be kept down by siting the freezer in a cool dry place, keeping it well stacked with food so that no electricity is wasted chilling surplus air, and only opening the door or lid when necessary.

Most manufacturers will give you an idea of the amount of electric units likely to be consumed by each model. As an approximate guide, a freezer will use between $1\frac{1}{2}$ and 2 units of electricity per 15l./$\frac{1}{2}$cu.ft. per week. There is very little difference between the three basic types although a large chest freezer usually works out as the most economic. Maintenance and repair charges are usually very low.

Siting

If the freezer is in constant use, the kitchen is obviously the most convenient place. A refrigerator/freezer or upright model will occupy the minimum of floor space and can be more readily accommodated in a small kitchen. However, the freezer can be stored virtually anywhere, as long as the floor is strong enough to support it. A spare bedroom, pantry, under the stairs, in an outbuilding or garage – all are suitable providing there is an earthed electrical outlet – ideally independent – and the freezer can stand in a cool, dry and well-ventilated position. It will then give best performance and lowest running costs.

It is important that there is a good circulation of air around the freezer. Tucking it snugly into a cupboard or in a warm kitchen may seem a good idea, but can result in the condenser over-heating and force the motor to labour to maintain zero temperature. Remember that a freezer actually warms the atmosphere around it by transferring heat to the air.

If the freezer is stored in a garage or basement, damp may be unavoidable, and this will damage both the exterior and the motor. Therefore the freezer should be protected as much as possible. Support it on wooden blocks so that it is not in contact with the floor, and polish the exterior regularly with a good silicone polish to guard against rusting. Some models have a special tough external finish and undersealing, which may be worth considering at the time of purchase.

One of the disadvantages of having the freezer in a garage or outbuilding is that it is probably visited infrequently. If anything goes wrong it may not be detected in time. So it is advisable to have the freezer fitted with a warning light or bell, connected into the house, which will operate in the event of a breakdown.

Three types of freezers

Freezer Care

When your new freezer is first installed, before you do anything else, read the manufacturer's instructions for the care and maintenance of that particular model.

Cleaning the freezer

Wash out the interior thoroughly before switching on with a solution of 15 ml./1 level tablespoon of bicarbonate of soda to 1.2 l./2 pints of warm water and wipe completely dry. Only then can the freezer be connected to a properly earthed power socket, ideally one that is used only for the freezer. Where a socket is used for other appliances as well there is always the possibility that the freezer can be switched off by mistake so take the precaution of taping over the plug and switch. However, you can no longer switch off at the mains when you go on holiday unless the freezer is installed on a separate circuit.

Switch on the freezer and check with the manufacturer's instructions that the temperature control has been properly set. Leave the freezer on for 12 hours before putting in any food. This ensures that the correct temperature has been reached and that the appliance is in full working order. The freezer should not be filled in one go other than with fully frozen foods; how much fresh food is put in at a time will depend on its daily freezing capacity.

General maintenance of the freezer is comparatively simple; it should be professionally serviced once a year, and there should be a daily emergency service available. So find out what service facilities are offered by the retailer before the model is purchased.

The exterior surface of the freezer is easily kept clean by wiping down with a damp cloth and a little liquid detergent and to keep the freezer sparkling it needs only an occasional polish with a soft cloth and silicone polish.

If you use the top of the freezer as a work surface, protect it with wipe-over contact paper. This will prevent scratching and staining and many people forget that if they sell their freezer the overall appearance could make a big difference to the selling price.

Defrosting

Study the instructions in your instruction book on how to defrost your particular model as many freezers require different methods.

Frost will build up on the walls and refrigerated surfaces of the freezer when in use. A thick layer of frost and ice will hinder the efficiency of the freezer and make it difficult to remove baskets and shelves. The capacity will be reduced, and the freezer will have to work harder, which in turn will increase the running costs. Most manufacturers recommend that the frost from the walls of the freezer should be scraped off once a month.

As a guide line, defrosting should take place when frost is $\frac{1}{2}-1$ cm./$\frac{1}{4}-\frac{1}{2}$ in. thick and particularly if there is a layer of ice. Once or twice a year is normal, but upright models may need to be defrosted more frequently.

Some freezers have an automatic defrosting device and there will be no need to empty the contents of the food compartment in order to defrost. But the interior will need to be cleaned once a year if only to remove stray packages.

Try to plan a time for defrosting when the stock of frozen food is at its lowest. If there is room, some of the food can be stored in the refrigerator, but remember to set the refrigerator at its coldest setting first. Larger packages should be wrapped in several layers of newspaper or thick foil and packed into boxes as closely together as possible; the more compactly they are stored the colder the packages will remain. Cover the boxes with heavy blankets to minimise the circulation of air and store in a cool place. They should stay frozen for up to 2 hours.

Turn the temperature switch to defrost or switch off the freezer and check that the power supply has been disconnected. Leave the freezer open to let warm air circulate. To hasten defrosting place bowls of hot water in the bottom of the freezer and close the door for 15 minutes. Remove the bowls and spread towels or newspapers in the bottom of the cabinet to catch the frost and to save time mopping up.

Remove as much frost as possible by scraping down the sides of the freezer with a wooden or plastic spatula. Never use a sharp knife or a metal tool which could damage the interior walls. Large pieces of ice can be picked up and thrown away as they fall and a dustpan is useful for scooping up the remaining ice. Do wear gloves to protect your hands.

If there is a drain at the base of the compartment, then warm water can be poured over the refrigerated surfaces which will help speed up the melting of any ice. *Do not use hot water* as this could damage the refrigeration system.

When the cabinet is free from ice and frost remove the towels and newspapers and wipe out with a solution of bicarbonate of soda and warm water to remove grease and smells. If there is still an odour do not use soap or detergents which could impart a soapy flavour to the frozen food, but use a solution of 15 ml./1 tablespoon vinegar to 1 l./$1\frac{3}{4}$ pints of warm water. Finally rinse again with fresh warm water and dry thoroughly with an absorbent cloth. Leave the door open until the cabinet is thoroughly dry. Wash and dry baskets or shelves and return them to the freezer. Close the door, restart the freezer and leave for 1 hour before repacking with frozen food. Set aside for immediate use any food which has begun to thaw (see opposite page).

The whole defrosting operation should take no longer than 2 hours, and is an excellent opportunity for stock-taking, especially if the record-keeping has been allowed to lapse.

Power failure

Freezers have a good working life and most will give years of trouble-free service. It is important, however, to be well prepared for a freezer emergency, particularly as the replacement value of a full freezer is considerable both in terms of cash and time spent in the preparation of the food.

If you have a battery-operated alarm system fitted to the freezer, check the battery regularly.

If the freezer suddenly stops working check that the switch has not been accidently turned off (it is worth covering the plug with tape to prevent this from happening). Or the cause may be a fuse blown in the plug or at the fuse box.

If it is an external power failure, find out from your local Electricity Board how long it will be before power will be restored. Food in a well-stocked freezer will remain frozen for at least 24 hours provided you resist the temptation to open the freezer constantly to see if the food is thawing. Reduce the surrounding air temperature as much as possible by keeping the room well ventilated.

If the fault is in the freezer ring a Service Agent

immediately. Save time and panic by having the telephone number and address readily to hand. The address can usually be found on the instruction leaflet or guarantee card issued at the time of purchase. The Electricity Board may also have a list of local service agents.

Leave the food in the freezer, unless the engineer requires it to be removed. If it has to be removed for a short while only (up to 2 hours), food will remain frozen if wrapped in newspaper and covered with a thick blanket. But if the repairs are to take longer, then most firms will provide an emergency service either providing a temporary freezer or offering storage space.

If, after a failure, the temperature has risen above 0°C/32°F the food will be thawing and a decision has to be made as to what to do with the food. If the packages are still frozen solid, the food can be safely returned to the freezer.

If thawing is complete, but the food still feels cold, then raw foods like meat, fish and poultry can be refrozen provided they are first cooked. All pre-cooked dishes – cooked meat, cooked fish, cooked poultry – and either raw or cooked vegetables should not be refrozen but should be kept chilled and eaten within 24 hours and they must be thoroughly reheated to stop any possible bacteriological action: warming is *not* sufficient. All ice cream or puddings made with fresh

cream must be thrown away, but breads and cakes can be refrozen. Most fruit can be refrozen but it will have lost flavour and juice, sometimes colour as well.

All thawed foods which do not feel cold and have an unpleasant appearance and/or smell should be thrown away without tasting them as they could be a potential danger to health.

Insurance
A freezer is an expensive item to buy and stock, therefore it is well worthwhile increasing your own household policy to cover the contents or taking out a separate insurance policy against damage or deterioration of frozen food due to the freezer being out of action. The policy will not, however, normally cover power failure due to strikes or accidental switch-off. The premium will obviously depend on the age of the freezer and whether it is still under the maker's guarantee.

Moving house
When moving house check with the removal firm that the freezer can be moved still fully loaded. If the move takes place within a day, then the food will remain frozen providing the door is not opened. Arrange for the freezer to be the last item in the van and the first off. Make provisions for power to be on at the mains, that there is someone to switch on the freezer when it arrives, and that the plug will fit the new socket.

If the move takes longer than a day, then plans should be made to run down or dispose of the food supply.

Tape over the switch and plug for the freezer so that it cannot be disconnected or switched off by mistake

Stocking a Freezer

Bulk buying

Buying in bulk will entail a large initial outlay, so the household budget will need to be reorganised.

Many items can be bought in bulk at a considerable discount off normal retail prices. It is important, however, to ensure that any item in a bulk pack is up to the same standard as in a smaller pack. Always compare price lists before buying, for both quality and price vary. Buy items which have been tried out by your family on a small scale first before embarking on a large order.

A few firms will operate a home delivery service by refrigerated van, but they stipulate a minimum order value, and someone will have to be at home to receive the goods. This service has largely been replaced by cash and carry firms and freezer centres which offer lower prices in general than normal retail outlets.

Many butchers specialise in preparing cuts of meat especially for the freezer and at very competitive prices. But buying a whole or half carcass is not necessarily the economy it seems to be. It is vital to have a reliable supplier who will prepare a carcass to your personal requirements if you are to 'bulk-buy' wisely.

Few of us are experienced in butchery and apart from the financial outlay, you won't want to have a freezer full of cuts of meat which your family do not like and which you would not normally buy. Catering packs, consisting of ready-to-use cuts of meat are often economical in price, but the quality of the meat may not be as good value.

Batch cooking

This is the answer if you want to cut down on day-to-day cooking and fuel bills. You can have a grand cook-in and stock up for school holidays, weekend guests or leisure days. Food can be prepared at a time most convenient to you or, when preparing a main meal, treble the quantities so that you can eat some now and freeze the rest for a later date. Batches of sauces and pastry, for example, can be made and drawn upon to add variety to meals, to dress up convenience foods and to save time when recipes ask for a quantity of sauce or pastry to be made up.

It is certainly a good idea when batch baking to enlist the help of either a friend who has a freezer or perhaps husbands and wives who both go out to work can team together on a non-working day and prepare a large number of meals at one go.

The single person will find cooking one batch particularly useful. No longer will he or she have to eat the same meal three nights running to use it up. Shopping expeditions can be limited to once a month, meals can be prepared in bulk and then frozen in single servings or larger quantities for entertaining, and there will always be a variety of interesting meals to hand.

Special uses for the freezer

A freezer can be regarded as an extension to a store cupboard, its advantages being that food can be kept much longer, therefore enabling you to have reserves of food in the event of an emergency or any special situation.

Special diets Salt free, fat free or diabetic diets can all be catered for. Selected dishes can be prepared in bulk and then frozen in individual portions. Dishes can be made more varied and interesting and lengthy preparation of duplicate cooking at each meal time can be avoided.

Baby foods Puréed or sieved meat, fish, fruit and vegetables suitable for a baby can be prepared in quantity and packed in sterilised pots with no nutritional loss. It is particularly important when you prepare baby food to observe a high standard of hygiene: food must be quickly cooled before storage and thoroughly reheated before serving.

Packed meals Whether for work, school or picnics, packs containing individually wrapped sandwiches, small cakes, pastry and individual portions of fruit or pudding, can all be made in one session for freezing, thus avoiding last-minute preparations. Choose items which do not need reheating and simply leave to thaw in the packaging.

Complete meals A busy mum who perhaps has a job outside the home or a hobby to pursue can take time off from the kitchen by providing individually frozen meals which can be reheated by the family in her absence. The meals can be specially prepared, or, when you are cooking, build in extra portions which can be frozen in foil trays. Any meat or fish must be covered with sauce or stock to prevent drying out on reheating. Exclude as much air as possible from the packaging and provide simple instructions on thawing and reheating the food. Pack the meals together in a polythene bag and store them in the freezer where they can be most easily found.

Entertaining The freezer is invaluable when it comes to entertaining and preparing for special occasions such as Christmas or Easter. The problems of bank holidays with lots of meals to provide and shops being shut can also be solved. Whatever you are planning, whether a dinner party, a children's party or for weekend guests, the preparation is very time-consuming. With planning, the work load can be spread over a number of days, or weeks. Always remember that adequate time must be allowed for thawing and reheating the frozen food.

Time-saving items to freeze

Below is a list of what a well-stocked freezer could contain. It is not suggested that you store them all for this will depend on your individual needs, and experience will show you which foods from the freezer are of most value to you and your family. Storage times are given with each item where this is not included in the charts on pages 38–40.

Bread

Sliced bread can be toasted straight from the freezer. Foil-wrapped rolls or French loaves may be reheated from frozen in a hot oven for approximately 10–15 minutes for rolls, 30–40 minutes for loaves.

Breadcrumbs

Will remain fresh and separate if stored in a polythene bag. They can be used frozen in puddings, sauces and stuffings which are to be cooked, but thaw at room temperature for 30 minutes before using for coating.

Cheese

Hard cheese: grate and pack into usable quantities.

When preparing a dish, double or treble the quantities for the freezer

Chocolate curls
Give a professional touch to cakes and cold desserts; open freeze then pack in rigid containers. (Storage: 2 months.)

Concentrated coffee
Freeze in ice-cube trays for iced coffee; remove cubes from the trays when frozen and pack in polythene bags. (Storage: 3 months.)

Cream
Whipped cream containing 40% or more butter fat. Can also be frozen piped into rosettes, etc. (see page 20).

Croûtons
Fried bread croûtons or shapes for canapés or snacks can be reheated from frozen in a hot oven for 5–10 minutes. (Storage: 3 months.)

Eggs
Either raw whole, *out* of their shells, or separated and packed individually (see page 20).

Fresh herbs
Wash, wrap and freeze sprigs and use whole or crumble while still frozen to save time chopping. Chopped herbs can be mixed with a little water and packed into ice-cube trays.

Ice cubes
A ready supply for drinks.

Lemon and orange juice
Freeze in small containers or ice-cube trays and use for drinks, cakes, dressings and sauces.

Lemon or orange rind
Grate rind from orange and lemon halves, store in small quantities, closely wrapped in foil and use for flavouring. (Storage: 1 year.)

Lemon and orange slices
Open freeze first then pack in polythene bags; handy for garnishing food and serving with drinks. (Storage: 1 year.)

Mixed vegetables
Packs of diced vegetables, for use in soups and stews, save time in preparation.

Pastry
Either frozen before use – puff, short, flaky, or after use, baked or unbaked in pies, quiches, tarts and flans.

Sauces
Batches of sweet or savoury sauces are handy to store in usable quantities (see pages 76–77).

Savoury butters
Give a luxury touch to grilled meat, fish or vegetables (see pages 66–67).

Seville oranges
Buy when they are cheap and plentiful and freeze whole until you are ready to make marmalade. (Storage: 1 year.)

Stock
Make stock whenever you have a chicken carcass or meat bones available. Freeze concentrated in small quantities for convenience (see page 68).

Packaging

The importance of effective packaging, especially for long periods of storage, is to maintain the food in the freezer in as perfect condition as possible, to eliminate as much air as possible, and to seal food so it is protected from contamination when taken from the freezer to thaw. Failure to do so will result in heavy deposits of frost on the *inside* of the packaging and a general loss of colour and flavour.

The following changes to food during storage can also be caused by inadequate packaging or excessive fluctuations in temperature.

Dehydration will inevitably start to take place if food is stored for too long. It will also occur very quickly if as much air as possible is not excluded from the package or if it is insufficiently wrapped. Moisture and natural juices are lost, resulting in the food becoming dry and tough when cooked. It is essential to protect food from contact with air during freezing.

Freezer burn appears as brown or greyish-white patches on the surface of frozen food. This is caused by extreme dehydration and is most often seen on meat, poultry and fish where it causes the tissues to go tough and spongy.

Oxidation may occur particularly in meats and fish with a high fat content. Oxygen penetrates the animal tissues causing the fat to oxidise and go rancid. This gives the food an unpalatable flavour and sometimes an unpleasant 'off' smell. Salt in fatty foods such as bacon and butter will also cause this and they therefore have short storage lives.

Ice crystals The larger these form, the greater the loss of quality and texture in frozen foods. You must, therefore, avoid fluctuations in temperature and also inadequately filled containers where a layer of ice crystals can form in the extra air space. In dishes to be reheated, such as soups and sauces, the extra moisture can be absorbed with little effect. But in, for example, fruit and vegetables it can be more noticeable and cause a deterioration in colour and texture.

Cross-flavourings Highly flavoured foods, or those containing onions, garlic, etc. can, if not properly wrapped, transfer their smell and flavour to other items in the freezer. So always overwrap such foods either in heavy-duty foil or by placing in a polythene bag.

The ideal packaging material must be strong, yet easy to manage, and must suit both the type and quantity of food to be frozen. It must be able to stand up to being handled in preparation and in the freezer, and maintain its protective properties at low temperature. It must be moisture-proof and resistant to odours so that the food neither loses its flavour nor is tainted by other foods in the freezer; and the packaging itself should have no odour.

Valuable freezer space can be wasted by using bulky or awkwardly shaped packages, whereas uniform shapes like square or rectangular containers take up less room.

All food must be completely cold before it is placed in the freezer. Cooked food should be cooled quickly by standing the container of food in iced or very cold water.

All packaging of fresh food must be sealed tightly to expel as much air as possible (see page 19). The exception to this rule is pre-frozen food (i.e. items which have already been open frozen) and liquids which expand on freezing and so a small headspace must always be left (see below).

Liquids may be packed in a polythene bag placed inside a rigid container as a preformer

Liquids, such as sauces, soups or juices should be packed in rigid containers (not glass which can crack), boiling bags or preformed foil or polythene packages (see opposite page). It is essential to leave room for liquids to expand slightly on freezing: allow 1–2 cm./$\frac{1}{2}$–1 in. headspace per 600 ml./1 pint liquid. For ease of thawing, make sure that any container or preformer will fit into a large heavy-based saucepan so that the frozen block can be reheated easily.

Solids-plus-liquids, such as stews or fruit in syrup should be packed in rigid containers or preformed foil or polythene packages. A headspace of approximately 1 cm./$\frac{1}{2}$ in. should be allowed and the solids should be below the surface of the liquid. A layer of crumpled greaseproof or waxed paper can be placed over the surface to keep solids below the liquid. Crumpled greaseproof or waxed paper should also be used if it is impossible to keep solids below the liquid level or if the container is not completely filled.

Solids, fruits in dry sugar packs are best accommodated in rigid containers while most vegetables can be packed in polythene bags. Ready-cooked foods can be packed in foil dishes ready for reheating from frozen in the oven, so freeing cookware for other uses (see also page 18).

Unless you are going to eat a lot of one particular food at one time, it is far better to package in small usable quantities; the food will freeze more quickly and therefore give better eating. It is virtually impossible – even if you have a special freezer knife or saw – to divide up a large frozen block of food, so separate individual helpings such as chops, fish fillets, etc. with waxed paper, then overwrap or store in polythene bags or containers to economise on space.

A selection of packaging materials

Packaging materials

There is a bewildering range of packaging materials available, varying greatly in quality and price. Buy a small selection to begin with so that you can ascertain which packaging materials are most suited to your needs.

Packaging materials can be roughly divided into three types, in each case the materials designed for the freezer should be used

Sheet wrapping	(aluminium foil, polythene wrap, waxed, or moisture-vapour-proof freezer paper).
Bags	(polythene, boilable plastic, foil or waxed freezer paper).
Rigid containers	(waxed, plastic, polythene, toughened glass or ceramic ware, aluminium foil).

Rigid containers

Waxed containers Handy to have but foil or polythene are better. Waxed containers cannot be reused unless already specially lined and should never be filled with anything hot which will melt the wax. Extra sealing with freezer tape can be necessary.

Polythene or plastic containers Although expensive to buy initially, these are virtually indestructible, and can be washed and reused almost indefinitely. Many have snap-on lids which make them airtight, and all can be used to freeze almost any kind of food; particularly useful for fragile foods.

Foil dishes, plates and trays There is a wide variety of shapes and sizes available for pies, tarts, puddings and casseroles. The advantage of a foil container is that it is light, space saving, reusable and easy to clean. When filled the contents should be covered with a foil-lined lid, often supplied with the dish, then overwrapped with foil or put in a polythene bag before freezing. Vinyl-coated foil basins are especially useful for fruity puddings and prevent possible pitting of the foil due to fruit acids.

Bags

Polythene bags These are one of the cheapest and easiest freezer wrappings for most kinds of food. Only heavy-duty (120–200 gauge) polythene bags are suitable for freezing, and should be bought in moisture-vapour-proof weights. They come in a wide range of sizes, colours, or combinations of stripes of colour-and-clear for simple storage coding; some have special gussets for large quantities, others have a built-in label or are self-sealing.

Polythene bags can be reused, providing they are sound and untainted; wash in warm soapy water, rinse well and turn inside out to dry thoroughly.

Polythene bagging by the yard is also available – simply cut to size required; however, a special heat-sealing machine is needed for effective sealing.

Only use polythene bags for liquids if preformed by placing inside a rigid container, filling with the liquid and then freezing; when solid the polythene-covered shape can be removed from the preformer and packed in the freezer.

Boiling bags These are usually polythene, sometimes foil, bags which have been specially heat-treated so that cooked foods in sauces or soups can be taken straight from the freezer and plunged into boiling water to thaw and reheat. They are more expensive than plain polythene but very convenient to use.

Sheet wrapping

Polythene film or waxed paper These are strong, moisture-proof and can be used to wrap bulky or irregularly shaped parcels. Small sheets can be used to separate individual portions of meat or fish for easy removal without the need to thaw the whole package. Both need sealing with wire ties or freezer tape.

Rolls of very thin clearfilm are also available; this is self-sealing and moulds snugly round food, making it easy to eliminate air. It is not suitable for external wrapping on its own.

Aluminium foil Aluminium foil is completely impermeable to moisture, vapour and oxygen thus making it virtually indispensable for wrapping all kinds of food for the freezer. It can be used to line dishes before freezing, folded double for lids, or moulded easily to give extra protection to irregularly shaped foods such as chicken, without needing any further closure. It can also be used to cook certain items straight from the freezer.

Ordinary household (thin gauge) aluminium foil is not recommended for long-term storage, unless used doubled or overwrapped with a polythene bag or cotton stockinette. Heavy-duty freezer foil is more robust and can therefore be used without additional covering.

A new addition to the foil range is foil bags lined with polythene for storing liquids.

Improvised packaging

There are many items in everyday use in the kitchen which can be used for freezing.

Casserole dishes Make sure ovenproof glassware is at room temperature before placing in an oven, otherwise it may crack. If it is not convenient to have a casserole out of

Casserole dishes can be lined with foil

How to wrap

The individual packing of each item of food will be covered in more detail in the chapter on preparation of food.

There are two basic methods of wrapping meat, fish, baked goods and irregularly shaped foods.

Butcher's wrap Place the food diagonally close to one corner of a large sheet of your chosen freezer wrap; fold this corner up and over the food. Give the package a complete turn, then bring the sides over the centre of the package and continue to roll the package to the opposite corner. Seal the edges with freezer tape.

Druggist's wrap Place the food in the centre of a sheet of your chosen freezer wrap, allowing enough to cover it, plus an 8–10cm./3–4in. overlap. Bring the longest edges together over the food, then fold the edges over and over down towards the food so the wrapping is folded tightly against the food. Fold in the shortest ends and seal all the edges with freezer tape.

Parcels with sharp edges or irregularly shaped should be overwrapped with cotton stockinette, foil or placed in a polythene bag.

Sealing

Efficient sealing is essential if you are to preserve your frozen food in the freezer. Elimination of air is important when packing and sealing food for the freezer. Air inside a package can cause discoloration and will slow down the freezing process. The exceptions are liquids and fruit in syrup which expand when they freeze and headspace should be left in the container to allow for expansion. There are several methods of sealing packages.

Butcher's wrap; Druggist's wrap (below)

circulation while it is in the freezer, line the dish with foil before adding the food, freeze and when solid the foil package can be removed, sealed, labelled and returned to the freezer. Alternatively, freeze the unlined filled casserole dish and when hard, dip quickly in hot water to free the frozen block. Wrap it, seal, label and return to the freezer. When required, the foil can be removed and the food returned to the same casserole for reheating.

Glass jars or bottles Unless you know these are specially toughened to withstand low temperature, always test first. Fill with water, allowing a 2cm./1in. headspace, place inside a polythene bag, just in case it cracks, and freeze. To be on the safe side, always pack glass containers in polythene before freezing.

Choose jars or bottles with wide necks so that the food can be removed easily, and check that the lids are airtight and rust-proof.

Plastic cartons for free Any plastic container that has held cream, yoghurt, fats, cottage cheese, ice cream, honey, mousses, trifles, etc. can be reused for freezing providing it is scrupulously clean. They are useful for storing small quantities of food such as grated cheese, breadcrumbs, baby foods (sterilise cartons first in Milton's), herbs, etc.

Baking tins Cakes, bread and pastry can be frozen in their baking tins, providing they are satisfactorily covered with a moisture-vapour-proof wrapping. If the tin is likely to rust, it should be lined with greaseproof paper first.

Tarts and mince pies can be open frozen in their tins and when quite hard, can be removed – a sharp bang is usually sufficient to free them – and packed into boxes. Uncooked pastry cases, however, must be returned, while still frozen, to their original containers before thawing and baking.

Ice-cube trays These are handy for freezing herbs, citrus rinds, and concentrated stock in cubes. Open freeze, then when the cubes are solid they can be tipped out, placed in polythene bags and returned to the freezer.

Sealing and eliminating air from bags Plastic or paper-covered wire tags are ideal for polythene bags; they are simple to use and inexpensive. Fill the bag and press it gently, from the bottom upwards, to exclude as much air as possible; twist the neck of the bag securely, fold over the top and twist the wire tie around firmly, then twist the ends together and label.

An equally effective way to exclude air is by lowering the full bag into a bowl of cold water so that the water pressure forces the air up and out. Remember to dry the bag before freezing or else you'll have to chip it out!

Film wrappings or polythene bags may be heat-sealed, using a special sealing iron or press or a cool domestic iron. Protect the wrapping from direct heat with two pieces of tissue or brown paper, and iron along the clean, open edges.

Some freezer bags or wrappings like foil are self-sealing; if in doubt, secure with freezer tape. Avoid using rubber bands as seals whenever possible as they can perish.

Rigid containers Screw-on or snap-on lids require no extra sealing. Other lids should be sealed with freezer tape.

Freezer tape This has a special adhesive, unlike ordinary adhesive tape, so that it does not come off at sub-zero temperatures. Use for wrapped packages, waxed or other containers whose lids are not airtight, or for extra security.

Labelling

Every package should be clearly labelled before freezing, so that it can be quickly located and identified when required. The method of labelling will depend on the packaging material used, but every label should show the following information:

1 Kind of food and variety

All packaging must be securely sealed

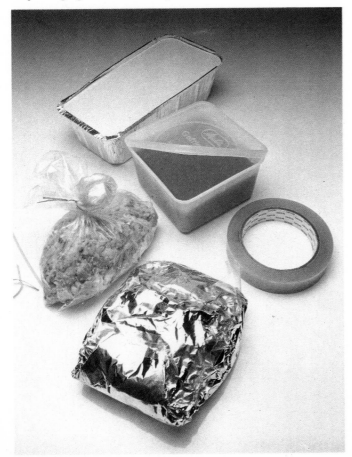

It is essential to label every item clearly

2 Quantity or number of portions
3 Date of freezing
4 Any special instructions relating to thawing, heating or seasoning

Wax or chinagraph pencils or waterproof felt pens write best directly onto almost anything, and their wide range of colours help to code packages. Ordinary writing inks are not water-resistant, and pencil quickly fades. Self-adhesive labels suitable for freezing are also available. Use different-coloured labels for the different types of food, e.g., red for meat, green for vegetables, blue for fish, etc., to provide a quick method of identification.

For film or polythene bags the label can be slipped inside just before sealing or fixed to the outside of the package with a strip of transparent freezer tape.

Keeping a record

An up-to-date record of the foods in the freezer is vital to ensure that the food is used in correct rotation and not left in longer than the recommended storage time. You can now buy freezer record books but it is also quite simple to make your own.

Use an exercise book and divide it into sections for the various types of food. List the food frozen, the quantity or number of portions and the date it was put into the freezer. When you remove a package cross it off the list. You may find it useful for future reference to leave a section in the record book for comments on the method of freezing used and the results obtained.

Know exactly what your freezer contains by making a chart to hang nearby, showing where the different types of food are to be found. This is only effective if you have methodically packed the freezer. Divide up the cabinet with baskets or cardboard boxes, or group packaged foods of the same kind into coloured string or polythene bags, using a different colour for each group. This will save rummaging about trying to find a package, and the loss of valuable cold air while the lid or door is open.

19

Preparing Food for the Freezer

This chapter deals primarily with the methods of preparing different foods for freezing. For full instructions on thawing, refer to the chapter on thawing.

The basic rules for successful freezing

Observe the basic rules of hygiene The general rule for looking after all food is: keep it cool, keep it clean and keep it covered. All raw food should be prepared separately from cooked ready-to-eat food. A high standard of hygiene in the kitchen at all times is extremely important particularly when food is being prepared for freezing. Work quickly when preparing food to be frozen.

Freeze only top-quality food Freezing cannot improve food and it is a waste of valuable freezer space to store poor quality food. Freeze when the food is at its peak of condition.

Cool foods quickly Cool all food to room temperature or below before putting it into the freezer for the sake of the food already frozen. Cooked food, particularly, should be cooled quickly by placing the container of food into iced or very cold water. Freeze quickly in the coldest part of the freezer or use the fast-freeze control.

Fatty foods Remove surplus fat from foods before freezing; all fried foods must be thoroughly drained on absorbent paper to prevent soggy results.

Good packaging Only use packaging materials which are guaranteed to be moisture-vapour-proof. Keep a selection of several different types of packaging materials at hand so that all types of precooked and prepared dishes may be adequately packed. Whatever packaging material is used, it is very important that as much air is excluded as possible before sealing. Moisture and exposure to air will damage the frozen goods. With liquids, however, a small headspace must be left.

Label and date packages Label all packages clearly so that the food can be quickly located. Dating will enable you to arrange a sensible turnover. A record of the contents of the freezer will ensure that the food is eaten at its best and that no package is forgotten.

Observe the recommended storage times Do not keep frozen food for longer than the recommended storage time. The period will vary with the type of food stored, but all frozen food should be stored at a temperature of -18°C/0°F or lower. Plan your freezing so that all the frozen foods are eaten by the time they are in season again.

Thaw according to directions Follow the recommended thawing procedure, and pack foods in usable quantities. It is a waste of food to thaw more than is required at one meal.

Open freezing

This method is excellent for delicate foods and for any items, e.g. raspberries, which you wish to keep separate so that they are free flowing when packed. Place the items to be frozen on plastic trays or foil-lined baking sheets, spreading them out so that they do not touch. Fast-freeze until solid. Remove from the freezer, pack quickly into polythene bags or rigid containers, seal, label and return to the freezer.

Dairy produce

As most dairy products can be stored for quite some time in a refrigerator, it hardly seems worth storing these items in the freezer. However, you may find it useful to have a small reserve of eggs, butter and cheese to draw on in an emergency.

Butter and other fats should be overwrapped in polythene bags, foil or freezer wrap.

Cheese Hard cheeses tend to crumble if stored too long; they are best grated and sealed in small plastic pots for future use in cooking. Blue cheeses may also be frozen; wrap securely in freezer film or foil, and overwrap in polythene.

Cream Only freeze cream with a butterfat content of 40% or more. This is known as double or heavy cream. Single or pouring cream or some whipping creams, which have a lower butterfat content will separate when thawed. Clotted and Jersey creams also freeze well, though the latter must be very fresh.

The most successful way of freezing double cream is to chill it, then whip it and either spoon into plastic tubs, cover, seal and freeze or pipe into rosettes which should be open frozen until hard and then packed in a rigid container. Use the rosettes while still frozen – they take about 10 minutes to thaw at room temperature – to decorate puddings, cakes, etc.

If you like, a little sugar – 5 ml./1 teaspoon per 150 ml./$\frac{1}{4}$ pint – can be added to the whipped cream, which will prevent the likelihood of its separating on thawing.

Eggs Whole eggs cannot be frozen in their shells, as expansion during freezing will crack them. 45 ml./3 tablespoons whole egg equals 1 egg. Several whole eggs may be frozen together, providing they are mixed lightly together with 2.5 ml./$\frac{1}{2}$ teaspoon of salt or sugar to 6 eggs. Pack the prepared eggs in small rigid containers or in a plastic ice-cube tray. Label carefully to indicate the number of eggs used. If an ice-cube tray is used, open freeze, then remove the cubes when they are frozen, pack them in a polythene bag, seal, label and return to the freezer.

Egg whites can be successfully frozen just as they are. Separate the eggs, lightly beat the whites and place in a small rigid container or ice cube tray (see above) in usable quantities of 2, 3 or 4, clearly labelled to show the contents. As a rough guide 30 ml./2 tablespoons egg white equal 1 egg white.

Allow 2 – 3 hours for the egg whites to thaw and use in the normal way.

Egg yolks will coagulate during freezing, but the addition of either salt or sugar, as a stabiliser, will prevent this happening.

To every 6 egg yolks beat in 2.5 ml./$\frac{1}{2}$ teaspoon of salt for savoury dishes or 2.5 ml./$\frac{1}{2}$ teaspoon of sugar for sweet dishes.

Pack into small rigid cartons or ice-cube trays (see above), labelling the contents clearly with the quantity and whether for sweet or savoury dishes; 15 ml./1 tablespoon of egg yolk equals 1 egg yolk.

Eggs should be thawed in their unopened container at room temperature for about 40 minutes to 1 hour. Thawed whole eggs and egg yolks should be used immediately after thawing, but egg whites will keep satisfactorily for up to 2 days if they are stored in the refrigerator.

Ice cream Bought ice cream which is to be stored in the freezer can stay in its original container. Overwrapping is rarely necessary.

Home-made ice cream is best made with pure flavourings rather than synthetic ones and should be placed in a mould or plastic box in quantities you can use at one time. Always freeze as quickly as possible.

Do not attempt to re-freeze ice cream once it has thawed.

Pastry

All types of pastry will freeze satisfactorily either raw or baked. Raw pastry such as shortcrust or flaky may be made in bulk, but it should be packaged in usable quantities (e.g. ½ kg./1 lb.) so that thawing time is fairly short.

Form the weighed quantities of pastry into rectangular blocks, wrap in polythene or foil and seal securely.

It may be more convenient to shape raw pastry into pie lids, vol-au-vent, patty or flan cases and plate pies before freezing.

To freeze baked or unbaked flan cases and open tarts Freeze raw or baked flan cases and open tarts in foil-lined tins. When hard, they can be removed stacked with a piece of waxed paper between; then wrapped in foil. Pack in a rigid container for added protection. For baking, remove the wrapping while the pastry is still frozen. Peel off the foil lining and return to the baking tin, prick the base of the pastry after it has started to thaw, and bake in the usual way.

Thaw baked flan cases at room temperature for 1 hour, if they are to be served cold, or reheat from frozen.

To freeze unbaked pies Pies may be prepared with or without a bottom crust. A little cornflour added to sugar helps thicken fruit juices and so prevent a bottom crust going soggy. Open freeze until solid in foil dishes, then overwrap with foil, seal and freeze. Bake the pie unthawed in preheated oven, cutting a vent for steam to escape, and allowing longer cooking time than for fresh pies.

Plate pies can be made up with the desired filling, or for a crisper pie, freeze two circles of dough to fit a pie plate. Freeze together on a metal or foil plate separated with a piece of waxed paper. The pastry should be thawed before use and the filling added just before baking.

To freeze baked pies Pies can be baked in the usual way, but in a foil dish, cooled quickly and frozen. Wrap in foil, seal, label and freeze.

Thaw 2–4 hours at room temperature or reheat from frozen in a moderate oven (180°C/350°F or Gas Mark 4).

Bread and rolls

Fresh-baked bread and rolls freeze well. Home-made bread is one of the most satisfying things to keep in your freezer and making a larger than usual batch takes very little longer.

Yeast products are particularly susceptible to dehydration and therefore need extra care when packaging.

Wrap cooled breads and rolls in polythene or foil and overwrap in a polythene bag. The bread should be thawed in its wrapping for 3–6 hours, but if loaves are wrapped in foil, they can be reheated, from frozen, in the oven.

Bought bread can be stored in its waxed paper wrapping, but place the loaf in a polythene bag to give extra protection.

Sandwiches Sandwiches may be prepared in bulk for parties or packed lunches. Prepare the sandwiches in the usual way, but leave the crusts on, wrap tightly together, keeping flavours separate, in usable quantities in polythene or foil and seal securely.

Open freezing raspberries

The sandwiches should be thawed unwrapped, the crusts can be trimmed off and the sandwiches cut to size just before serving.

When making sandwiches, avoid using moist fillings such as jam which will make them soggy, salad vegetables which will become mushy during thawing, mayonnaise or sandwich spreads containing mayonnaise because they will curdle.

Open sandwiches can be open frozen, then interleaved with freezer paper and packed in a rigid container. Thaw on the serving dish at room temperature.

Biscuits

The most satisfactory biscuit mixtures for the freezer are those rich in fat but low in moisture.

Uncooked biscuit mixture gives light crisp results when baked from frozen. The mixture should be frozen in cylinder shapes and wrapped in foil. When thawing, leave the dough in its wrapping until it begins to soften, when it can be cut into slices and baked.

Baked biscuits will store equally well in an airtight tin if freezer space is short; but if you wish to freeze a batch of home-made baked biscuits, pack them in a rigid container with waxed paper or foil between each layer, and crumpled paper in the air spaces of the container to prevent breakage. They must be fully thawed before unwrapping.

Cakes

Undecorated cakes may be frozen baked or unbaked, and most recipes for cakes are satisfactory for freezing, providing synthetic flavourings are omitted and top-quality ingredients are used. All cakes should be cold before packaging.

Plain and fruit cakes should be packaged in polythene bags, or foil, with as much air as possible excluded before sealing.

If the cake is large, it can be sliced before freezing and individual portions wrapped in waxed paper. They can then be taken from the freezer as required for picnics or packed lunches.

Sandwich cakes unfilled can be packaged together with a layer of waxed paper between the layers, then packed in a rigid container.

Sandwich cakes filled with buttercream will freeze satisfactorily but fruit, jam, custard cream and any very moist fillings should be avoided because they make them soggy. In any case there is very little advantage in filling the cake before freezing, for this can easily be done on thawing.

Swiss rolls should be rolled up in cornflour, not sugar, if they are being frozen unfilled.

Small undecorated cakes can be packed together in a polythene bag in usable quantities.

Decorated cakes should be open frozen to prevent the decoration becoming spoilt. Only buttercream, or decorations containing a proportion of fat, will freeze satisfactorily. Fondants, glacé icing, royal icing and boiled icings do not freeze. When frozen the cake can be wrapped in foil or polythene, then placed in a rigid container and returned to the freezer. It is important to remove the wrappings before the cake starts to thaw to stop them from sticking to the surface.

Raw cake mixture can be packed into plastic tubs which have tight-fitting lids. On thawing the mixture can then be transferred to baking tins and baked in the usual way.

Meat

Choose only top-quality meat in prime condition for freezing. The carcass must be chilled and hung for the correct length of time. The 'ageing' process is very important, and develops the flavour and tenderises the meat, so it pays to find a reliable butcher. If he is given prior warning of the type and quantity required, he should be able to supply you with meat correctly frozen or in just the right condition for freezing yourself.

The meat must be cut into joints ready for cooking before freezing, and particular attention must be given to the correct packaging. Overwrap where necessary for long periods and exclude as much air as possible from the packages before sealing and freezing.

Always keep a detailed record of what you have stored, to ensure a regular turnover.

Steaks, chops and cutlets Trim off any excess fat and pack in usable quantities.

Place a double thickness of waxed paper or freezer film between each portion of meat so that they may be easily separated on thawing. Overwrap in a polythene bag, seal securely and label with the contents and quantity.

Meat for stews and casseroles Trim off excess fat and skin, and cut into cubes. Weigh out the meat and pack into polythene bags in quantities suitable for your family's needs at one meal. Seal securely and label.

Minced meat Home minced meat should be trimmed of as much fat as possible before putting it through a mincer. Weigh out the meat and pack compactly into polythene bags, seal securely and label. Never re-freeze mince made from thawed raw meat unless it has been cooked. Minced meat may be shaped into hamburgers and meat balls which should be frozen in small quantities with each portion wrapped in waxed paper, and sealed in polythene bags or a rigid container.

Offal This must be very fresh for freezing and it must be packaged and frozen as quickly as possible. Clean the offal thoroughly, trim off any attached skin and blood vessels, wash thoroughly in cold water, and dry well. Extra care must be taken when freezing offal as it is more prone to developing 'off' flavours.

Weigh the offal and pack into polythene bags. Liver and heart may be frozen whole or sliced and interleaved with waxed paper before packing in a polythene bag.

Sausages Pack sausages in ½ kg./1 lb. quantities in polythene bags, seal securely and label.

Ham and bacon These quickly go rancid, particularly unsmoked kinds, and the best results are obtained by freezing vacuum-packed joints, rashers or steaks. The milder the cure, the less salty it will taste and the less likelihood of it developing an 'off' flavour. Never store any kind of bacon or ham, or salted meats in general for very long.

Joints Make sure the joints you buy are cut to a usable size before freezing.

Trim off any excess fat and gristle, protect sharp edges and bones with a double thickness of foil or waxed paper to avoid puncturing the wrapping. Shank, brisket and flank which are to be used for stews or casseroles should be boned to make packing easier and to save freezer space. Bones and scraps of meat can then be used to make stock which can be frozen.

Weigh the joint and wrap in a polythene bag or foil, seal and label.

Poultry

ALL RAW POULTRY MUST BE THOROUGHLY THAWED BEFORE COOKING

Whole chicken should be thoroughly cleaned, drained and made as compact as possible for freezing. Tie the legs close together and cover or remove any sharp bones to avoid

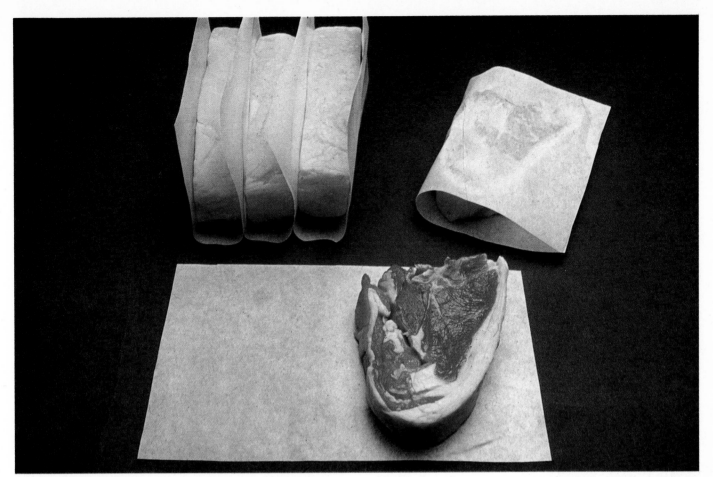

Use waxed paper to keep individual portions separate

puncturing the wrapping. Lay the wings close to the body and truss securely ready for cooking. Pack the bird in a polythene bag, removing as much air as possible before sealing. Label with the type and weight of bird frozen.

Do not stuff the bird before freezing as stuffings have a shorter storage life.

Giblets These have a shorter freezer storage life and should not be frozen with the bird, but stored separately in a polythene bag.

The giblets should be washed, dried and chilled before packing. Chicken livers, which can be turned into pâté, can be packed separately in small plastic tubs.

Chicken portions These take up less space in the freezer than whole birds. If you are freezing several chickens, it is a good idea to pack similar-sized joints in the same wrapping, for example, chicken legs together for picnics, breasts of chicken for special dinner party menus, wings of chicken for a paella.

To joint, cut the bird in half, through the breast bone and back bone and cut each half into two or three pieces. Either wrap individually in waxed or freezer paper for easy separation when thawing, or pack the joints in usable quantities on plastic or foil trays and overwrap securely with foil or place in a polythene bag.

Because of the risk of freezer burn, jointed poultry must be well packaged to exclude as much air as possible.

Turkey This is prepared for the freezer in the same way as chicken.

Remember that a turkey will take up a lot of freezer space and is therefore only worth freezing if you have freezer space to spare.

Duckling Use ducklings for roasting and old birds for braising, casseroles, etc. Prepare and freeze as for chicken.

Game

Game birds must be hung before freezing to tenderise the flesh for the same time you would allow when used fresh. This varies according to personal preference but is generally between 5 and 8 days.

After hanging, prepare game for cooking; pluck and draw as for a domestic bird, then wash and drain the body cavity.

Place in a polythene bag, seal and label with the type of bird and its weight. Then freeze. It is advisable to pluck and draw waterfowl as soon as possible after shooting, so that the flesh does not become contaminated.

Rabbit and hare A rabbit should be frozen completely fresh. Skin, eviscerate and clean. The carcass can be frozen whole for roasting, or cut into joints. Each joint should be wrapped separately in freezer paper. Pack in a polythene bag, seal, label and freeze.

A hare is usually sold ready hung and prepared, but to do it yourself, it should be hung 5–7 days before freezing and bled. Any blood should be frozen separately in a small plastic container, so that it can be used to thicken the gravy for jugged hare, or added to the gravy when the hare is roasted. Skin and draw it and leave whole or joint. Pack as for rabbit.

Fish

Fish must be fresh. If freshly caught fish straight from the sea or river is not available, buy only from a reliable fishmonger with a good source of supply, and turn into a made-up fish dish before freezing, or buy commercially frozen fish products.

Freeze fish as quickly as possible and pay particular attention to the packaging to prevent dehydration. Wrap well in doubled foil or polythene and always seal securely with freezer tape.

Freezing fish whole Round fish should be washed under cold running water, then remove the scales and gut the fish by cutting along the entire length of the belly and removing the viscera. Remove the head, fins and tail. Wash again under cold water, drain and dry on absorbent paper.

For flat fish, cut off the fins and trim round the edges with a kitchen scissors. Gut the fish, wash and dry on absorbent paper.

Wrap the fish in freezer paper or foil and overwrap in a polythene bag. Seal and freeze.

Whole salmon to be served 'dressed', should be gutted, well washed and dried, then stuffed with freezer paper to preserve the shape, before wrapping.

Whole fish may be glazed to give them extra protection. Open freeze whole fish, then when frozen solid dip it into a bowl of ice-cold water, so a thin coating of ice forms, and return to the freezer. Repeat the process, dipping and returning to the freezer, several times until the fish has a hard ice glaze all over. Wrap the fish in freezer paper or aluminium foil, seal the edges securely with freezer tape and return to the freezer.

Fish steaks or fillets Cut the cleaned fish into steaks or fillets and skin them if preferred.

Several fillets may be packed together to suit the family's needs. Each piece should be wrapped separately in freezer paper and then packed together in usable quantities. Overwrap in polythene bag and seal.

Stews and casseroles

When making stews and casseroles, it is an economy on time to double the recipe and freeze half for later use.

It is important to omit ingredients which go mushy during freezing such as potatoes and other root vegetables, pasta and rice; they can always be added after freezing.

The fat content should be as low as possible to avoid rancidity. When a dish has been cooked and cooled, surplus fat should be removed before freezing.

There should be sufficient liquid in the stew or casserole so that the meat is completely covered. If this is not done the meat may dry out. All cooked meat dishes must be cooled thoroughly and quickly.

Pack stews and casseroles in foil dishes for easy reheating, or use foil-lined dishes (see page 18). If frozen in cartons or heavy-duty polythene bags, the stew or casserole can be transferred to an ovenware dish (check sizes before packing for freezing) or reheated in a heavy-based pan over direct heat. When reheating in a saucepan, stir occasionally to prevent sticking. Ensure that the food is thoroughly heated and served piping hot.

Pâtés

Pâtés should be prepared and cooked ready for eating, before freezing. Pack in individual pots for serving, or freeze in foil-lined loaf tins, foil dishes or terrines and turn out when frozen. Overwrap with foil or place in a polythene bag, seal securely and return to the freezer. If the whole pâté is not required at one meal, it can be cut into slices divided by waxed paper and reformed into a loaf for freezing. Slices can then be

All food to be frozen should be cooled quickly

removed and thawed as required. Thaw in its wrapping overnight in refrigerator, or under cool conditions for a maximum of 6 hours.

Soups

Nearly all soups will freeze well. The exceptions are those containing starchy ingredients such as pasta, rice, barley and chopped potatoes which become mushy when frozen in a liquid and should be added on thawing.

When using milk, cream and egg yolks to thicken a soup, add them to the soup when reheating (where possible) to avoid the danger of curdling.

Cool soups immediately after cooking by placing the saucepan over ice or in cold running water, and remove any surplus fat as this will separate during storage and may cause rancidity.

Pack in usable quantities in rigid containers or boiling bags; allow 1 cm./½ in. headspace for wide-topped containers and 2 cm./1 in. headspace for narrow-topped containers. Larger quantities of soup may be frozen in preformed packs, and stacked like bricks.

Stock, to save freezer space, can be reduced before freezing by boiling, and the concentrated liquid frozen in ice-cube trays.

Sauces

It is worth making larger than usual quantities of sauce for the freezer which can be drawn upon when required.

Most sauces will freeze satisfactorily providing ingredients which are known to freeze badly are avoided: sauces containing a small amount of fat freeze better than those with a high fat content, and egg-based sauces such as mayonnaise must be avoided as they will curdle on thawing.

Basic sauces can be adapted after thawing according to the recipe you are following.

Make the sauces in bulk and pack into 150 ml./$\frac{1}{4}$ pint, 300 ml./$\frac{1}{2}$ pint and 600 ml./1 pint containers or in usable quantities to suit your needs. Once the sauce has been made up it should be cooled quickly and stirred frequently to prevent a skin forming on the surface. Pack in boiling bags or rigid containers, allowing a 2 cm./1 in. headspace for expansion. Seal securely and label with the type and quantity.

Fruit

The luxury of having an all-the-year round supply of seasonal fruits is one of the great pleasures of owning a freezer.

If you grow your own produce, the fruit should be picked and frozen as quickly as possible, preferably within 2 hours of picking.

If you purchase the fruit from a shop, check that the fruit is of high quality, fully ripe and free from bruises and blemishes.

There are four basic methods of preparing fruit for the freezer:
1 Free flow pack
2 Dry sugar pack
3 Syrup pack
4 Puréed

The method you choose to prepare the fruit, will depend not only on the type and quality, but its subsequent use after freezing.

Soft fruits which make their own juice are best packed in dry sugar, or open frozen. They can then be used still partially frozen for all types of desserts.

Firm-textured fruits such as peaches, apples and apricots (where the juice does not flow liberally and which have a tendency to discolour) should be frozen in a syrup to which ascorbic acid has been added. The fruit can either be thawed and used for fruit salads, pies or tarts, or heated from frozen and served hot in its syrup.

Free flow pack This method is particularly suitable where you want to preserve fruit separate.

Open freeze the prepared fruit on trays lined with foil or waxed paper, until frozen solid. It can then be packed into polythene bags, sealed, labelled and returned to the freezer.

The advantage of this method is that the fruit remains separated, so you need only remove a small amount when required without having to thaw the whole quantity. In the case of fruit such as raspberries (or vegetables such as beans or Brussels sprouts) the food retains a better shape.

Packing with dry sugar This method is suitable for soft, juicy, whole or sliced fruit. The juice which flows from the fruit combines with the sugar to make a natural syrup. Wash and drain the fruit only if necessary and prepare in the normal way. Place the fruit in a large shallow dish and sprinkle over the sugar; allow to stand for a few minutes until the fruit juice begins to flow and the sugar dissolves. The amount of sugar used will vary with the tartness of the fruit and personal tastes. Approximately $\frac{1}{2}$ kg./1 lb. of caster sugar should be used for every 2 kg./4 lb. of fruit.

Stir the fruit gently until evenly coated with sugar syrup and pack in rigid containers, allowing 1 cm./$\frac{1}{2}$ in. headspace.

An alternative method of dry sugar packing for small quantities of fruit, is to place a little fruit in the container and sprinkle with sugar, add more fruit and then sugar and continue layering until the container is filled. Leave room for 1 cm./$\frac{1}{2}$ in. headspace. In thawing the fruit and sugar will make its own syrup.

Packing in sugar syrup This is the most satisfactory method for non-juicy fruits and for those fruits which discolour quickly during preparation and storage.

The syrup can be heavy, medium or light. The choice of an appropriate syrup will depend on the sweetness of the fruit and personal taste. A medium syrup normally suits most tastes, but a light syrup should be used for delicately flavoured fruit, or the taste of the sugar will predominate.

The water must be heated to dissolve the sugar, therefore the syrup should be made a day in advance, so that it is quite cold before using.

Syrup strengths for freezing fruit

Type	Approximate percentage of sugar in syrup	Weight of sugar	Quantity of water
Light	20%	225 g./$\frac{1}{2}$ lb.	1.2 l./2 pints
Medium	30%	$\frac{1}{2}$ kg./1 lb.	1.2 l./2 pints
Heavy	45%	1 kg./2 lb.	1.2 l./2 pints

Allow approximately 300 ml./$\frac{1}{2}$ pint of syrup per $\frac{1}{2}$ kg./1 lb. of fruit.

The amount of syrup used will depend on the type of fruit, and on the shape and size of the container used.

Pack the prepared fruit into rigid containers and pour over the cold syrup, allow 1–2 cm./$\frac{1}{2}$–1 in. headspace. It is important that the fruit is fully submerged in the syrup. If the fruit floats in the syrup, the top layer may not remain completely covered and will therefore discolour. To prevent this happening, press a piece of crumpled greaseproof or waxed paper down into the syrup before sealing the container.

Purées Puréeing fruit is a useful method of utilising well ripened or slightly damaged fruit; it will take up less space in the freezer, and it is convenient to have a selection of fruit purées to use for flavouring, mousses, ice cream and fools.

Wash and dry the fruit. Cooking soft fruits such as strawberries and raspberries is not necessary but harder fruits such as apples will need to be lightly cooked first. Sieve and add sugar according to taste, approximately 50–100 g./2–4 oz. of sugar per $\frac{1}{2}$ kg./1 lb. of fruit.

Pack into rigid containers, allowing 1 cm./$\frac{1}{2}$ in. headspace and seal securely.

Discoloration Some fruits such as peaches, pears, apples and apricots, discolour during preparation.

This discoloration can be prevented by adding ascorbic acid – better known as Vitamin C – to the syrup. You can purchase ascorbic acid powder or crystals at chemists. 2.5 ml./$\frac{1}{2}$ teaspoon of powder should be dissolved in a little cold water before adding to 600 ml./1 pint of syrup.

The juice of one lemon added to 1 l./1$\frac{3}{4}$ pints of water will also give good results. The fruit should be sliced into the solution and allowed to steep for 15 minutes prior to packing. Rinse the fruit before packing into containers with sugar or syrup.

Note: All fruits and methods of freezing will keep for up to 1 year unless otherwise specified.

APPLES

Preparation
Choose ripe apples with a good flavour. Discard any that are bruised. Peel, core, slice or chop. For purée, cook in the minimum of water with or without sugar. Sieve and allow to cool.

Packing
1. Steep chopped or sliced apple in a solution of the juice of 1 lemon added to 1 l./1¾ pints water for 15 minutes. Dry on absorbent paper. Open freeze and pack in polythene bags.
OR
2. Steep slices in lemon solution, as above. Dry and pack in light syrup, in rigid containers. Allow 1 cm./½ in. headspace.
OR
3. Pack purée into rigid containers. Allow 2 cm./1 in. headspace. (Storage: 6 months.)

To use
Thaw in the unopened containers. For pies and tarts thaw enough to separate the slices for stewing. Tip frozen into a saucepan and stew gently.
Purées should be thawed in their containers and used for mousses, soufflés and sauces.

APRICOTS

Preparation
Choose firm ripe fruit with golden skin. Wipe and leave whole, or skin fruit by plunging it in boiling water for 30 seconds, rub off skins, stone, halve or slice.
OR
Cook the fruit in a little water until tender, stone and purée, sweeten to taste.

Packing
1. Cover prepared fruit in a heavy sugar syrup to which ascorbic acid has been added and pack in rigid containers, fill headspace with crumpled waxed paper.
OR
2. Pack cooked purée in rigid containers, allowing 1 cm./½ in. headspace.

To use
Thaw in their containers for 3 hours at room temperature and serve cold.
OR
Tip frozen apricots in syrup into a saucepan and reheat gently. (Storage: Sugar syrup packs – 1 year; purée – 4 months.)

BLACKBERRIES

Preparation
Pick on a dry day for best results. Avoid blackberries with large woody pips. Wash in iced water. Dry well and remove stalks.

Packing
1. Pack in dry sugar in rigid containers, allowing 1 cm./½ in. headspace.
OR
2. Open freeze and pack when frozen in polythene bags.
OR
3. Pack blackberries in a medium syrup in rigid containers.

To use
Allow to thaw in their containers. Use while partially frozen to serve cold or in pies.
Tip blackberries in syrup while frozen into a saucepan and reheat gently.

CHERRIES

Preparation
Choose ripe sweet cherries. The red varieties are better for freezing than the black. Wash and dry well, remove stalks and stone.

Packing
1. Open freeze and when frozen pack into polythene bags.
OR
2. Pack in a medium sugar syrup in rigid containers. Allow 2 cm./1 in. headspace.

To use
Thaw unopened in their containers for 3 hours at room temperature for pies and fruit salads.
OR
Tip frozen cherries into a saucepan and reheat gently in their own syrup.

CURRANTS – RED, BLACK AND WHITE

Preparation
Choose ripe firm fruit. Blackcurrants have the best flavour for freezing. Remove from stalks, wash, dry well, top and tail and leave whole. If preferred, freeze currants on the stalks which can be removed when thawing.
OR
Stew in the minimum of water, sweeten to taste. Cool.

Packing
1. Open freeze and pack into polythene bags with or without sugar.
OR
2. Pack in a light syrup in rigid containers. Allow 1 cm./½ in. headspace.
OR
3. Pack purée into rigid containers, allow 1 cm./½ in. headspace.

To use
Thaw unopened in their containers for 3 hours at room temperature for pies and cold desserts.
OR
Tip frozen currants in syrup into a saucepan and heat gently in their own syrup.

Different methods of freezing fruit

DAMSONS

Preparation
Wash, dry and cut in halves. Remove the stones, which can flavour the fruit.

Packing
1. As skins tend to toughen during freezing, stew in sugar syrup, then cool, pack in rigid containers, allowing 1 cm./$\frac{1}{2}$ in. headspace.

OR

2. Pack cooked purée into rigid containers, allowing 1 cm./$\frac{1}{2}$ in. headspace.

To use
Thaw unopened in the container for 3 hours at room temperature. For use in jams and pies, or sauces and mousses.

GOOSEBERRIES

Preparation
Choose ripe berries, wash and drain, top and tail and leave whole, or stew in the minimum of water, sweetened or unsweetened. Sieve and cool.

Packing
1. Pack without sugar in a polythene bag.

OR

2. Pack in a medium syrup in a rigid container, allow 1 cm./$\frac{1}{2}$ in. headspace.

OR

3. Pack cooked purée in rigid containers, allow 1 cm./$\frac{1}{2}$ in. headspace.

To use
Thaw unopened in the container for 4 hours at room temperature before using in jams or pies.

OR

Tip frozen into a saucepan and stew gently.
Use partially thawed purée – thaw overnight in refrigerator – in fools and mousses.

Pears should be poached in sugar before freezing

GRAPES

Preparation
Choose firm ripe fruit with tender skins. Wash and drain, halve and remove pips. Seedless varieties may be packed whole.

Packing
Pack whole or halved grapes in a medium syrup. Pack in rigid containers, allow 1 cm./½ in. headspace.

To use
Thaw unopened in the container for about 2 hours at room temperature, and use while still partially frozen for pies and fruit cocktails.

LEMONS

Preparation
Wipe over the fruit and leave whole or cut into slices.
OR
Grate peel, or extract juice.

Packing
Freeze whole wrapped closely in a polythene bag. Open freeze lemon slices, when frozen pack into polythene bags.
Peel: grate before extracting juice, pack in small cartons.
Juice: freeze sweetened or unsweetened in rigid containers or ice-cube trays. Pack cubes in polythene bags.

To use
Thaw in wrappings for about 3 hours at room temperature and use as required. Lemon slices can be used frozen in drinks.

MELON

Preparation
Choose melons which are fully ripe. Peel, cut in half and remove the seeds. Slice, cube or cut into balls.

Packing
1. Pack in dry sugar, in a rigid container, leave 2½ cm./1 in. headspace.
OR
2. Cover with a medium syrup and pack into rigid containers; allow 2 cm./1 in. headspace.

To use
Thaw unopened in the container for about 3 hours at room temperature. Serve while still frosty.

ORANGES

Preparation
Scrub skins and dry. Only leave Sevilles whole (the bitter type used for marmalade), as whole citrus fruits tend to go bitter during freezing. Peel, remove pith and cut into segments or slices. Remove membrane and pips.

Packing
1. For whole fruit, wrap closely in polythene bags.
OR
2. Cover sliced fruit with a light syrup, pack into rigid containers. Allow 1 cm./½ in. headspace. Fill headspace with crumpled greaseproof paper.
OR
3. Pack alternate layers of sliced fruit and sugar into rigid containers.

To use
Use whole fruit frozen for marmalade. Sliced fruit should be thawed in its container for about 3 hours and served chilled.

PEACHES

Preparation
Choose firm ripe fruit. Peel with a knife or plunge into boiling water for 30 seconds and then into cold water, this will loosen the skin. Cut in halves or slices and remove stone.

Packing
Pack in a heavy syrup with ascorbic acid or lemon juice added to prevent discoloration. Pack in rigid containers. Allow 1 cm./½ in. headspace.

To use
Thaw in the container unwrapped for about 4 hours at room temperature. Serve chilled.

PEARS

Preparation
Choose just ripe pears. Wash, peel and core. Halve or slice. These are best frozen lightly cooked as they tend to lose flavour and crispness if frozen raw.

Packing
Poach for 1½ minutes in heavy syrup, to which has been added ascorbic acid or lemon juice to prevent discoloration. Cool then pack in rigid containers with poaching syrup. Allow 2 cm./1 in. headspace and cover with crumpled greaseproof paper to submerge fruit.

To use
Thaw in the container unwrapped for about 4 hours at room temperature.

PINEAPPLE

Preparation
Choose ripe fruit. Peel, core and slice or dice.

Packing
1. Pack pieces, covered with medium sugar syrup, in rigid containers. Allow 1 cm./½ in. headspace, covering with crumpled greaseproof paper.
OR
2. Mix raw fruit with dry sugar (½ kg./1 lb. sugar to 1½ kg./3 lb. fruit). Pack in polythene bags or rigid containers. Allow 2 cm./1 in. headspace.

To use
Thaw unwrapped in containers for 3–4 hours at room temperature. Serve well chilled.

PLUMS

Preparation
Choose fully ripened fruit with no blemishes. Wash, freeze whole although skins will toughen and stones will give fruit an almond flavour, so best to halve and remove stones.

Packing
1. Cover with medium syrup and pack in rigid containers, allow 2 cm./1 in. headspace.
OR
2. Freeze without sugar and syrup. Do not keep longer than 3 months. Pack in polythene bags.
OR
3. Stew stoned fruit gently, cool, then pack in rigid container. Allow 1 cm./½ in. headspace.

To use
If used in pies, thaw for about 3 hours at room temperature before using. Otherwise tip frozen into a pan and stew gently in their own syrup, or reheat.

RASPBERRIES

Preparation
Choose firm, ripe fruit, Discard any blemished fruit. Wash in iced water and dry gently and leave whole.
OR
Sieve fruit to a purée.

Packing
1. Open freeze, when hard pack in polythene bags or rigid containers, allowing 1 cm./½ in. headspace.
OR
2. Cover with a medium syrup and pack in rigid containers, allow 1 cm./½ in. headspace.
OR
3. Pack in dry sugar and pack as above.

To use
Thaw unopened in their containers for 3 hours at room temperature; use just before the fruit has completely thawed out.

RHUBARB

Preparation
Choose firm but tender stalks. Wash and cut into required lengths.

Packing
Blanch in boiling water for 1 minute. Drain and pack in polythene bags or rigid containers without sugar. Allow 1 cm./½ in. headspace.

To use
Allow to thaw partially at room temperature in containers. Use for pies.
OR
Tip frozen fruit into a saucepan with enough water just to stop it catching, add sugar to taste and reheat gently.

STRAWBERRIES

Preparation
Choose firm dry fruit, remove stalks. Wash in iced water and dry gently on kitchen paper. Leave whole or purée with sugar to taste if preferred.
Note: Frozen whole strawberries do show a loss of texture and flavour on thawing. They are best used for decoration or in recipes such as fruit salad.

Packing
1. Open freeze and pack when frozen in polythene bags or rigid containers.
OR
2. Pack in dry sugar in rigid containers.
OR
3. Pack in a medium sugar syrup in rigid containers and allow 2 cm./1 in. headspace.
OR
4. Pack purée into small waxed or polythene containers and allow 2 cm./1 in. headspace.

To use
Thaw in unopened containers for about 3 hours at room temperature and use just before fruit has completely thawed.

Vegetables

Most vegetables can be frozen raw except those with a high water content like salad greens, tomatoes, white cabbage, or potatoes which must be cooked before freezing. You should, however, blanch vegetables for long-term storage (i.e. more than 2 weeks); this is necessary to stop enzymes working, which cause spoilage and loss of flavour and colour, even when frozen. Blanching will have partially cooked vegetables, so it is only necessary to 'quick cook' the vegetables before serving; all vegetables should be cooked from frozen.

Vegetables can also be puréed and frozen, and this method is excellent for soups, sauces and baby foods. Puréed asparagus, carrots, peas and spinach are particularly successful.

Prepare and cook the vegetables in the normal way, sieve or blend to a smooth purée and pack into rigid containers, allowing 1 cm./½ in. headspace. Seal and freeze immediately.

For baby foods, the purée can be frozen in ice-cube trays, and one cube should be sufficient for a young baby's appetite.

Vegetables must be packed in rigid containers or polythene bags. They must be packed as tightly as possible without squashing, to exclude as much air as possible.

Blanching Wash the vegetables thoroughly in cold water, prepare according to their specific needs, or sort into similar sizes, rejecting imperfect vegetables.

For the best results, only blanch ½ kg./1 lb. vegetables at a time. Bring a large saucepan of water to a fast boil: 4.5 l./1 gallon of water is required to blanch ½ kg./1 lb. of vegetables, although the same water can be used for 6–7 consecutive batches.

Put each batch of prepared vegetables into a wire basket or muslin bag and completely immerse in the fast boiling water. Cover with a lid and start timing from the minute the water comes *back* to the boil; this is very important if vegetables are not to go mushy. Carefully follow the chart for individual blanching times of vegetables. While blanching, shake the basket or bag to ensure that the vegetables are all equally heated.

Immediately the blanching time has been completed, drain the vegetables and plunge them at once into ice-cold water, adding extra chunks of ice to keep it cold or place under cold running water. Vegetables must be cooled for as long as the blanching time again to ensure they are cooled right through or else the cooking process will continue. Drain well, open freeze on trays until solid, then pack in polythene bags or rigid containers in usable quantities, seal, label and return to the freezer.

Note: Recommended maximum storage lives for vegetables is 1 year unless otherwise specified.

ARTICHOKES, GLOBE

Preparation	Blanching time	Packing	To use
Remove outer leaves, trim and wash.	Up to six at a time – 7 minutes.	In polythene bags or rigid containers, leaving 1 cm./½ in. headspace.	Thaw over night in refrigerator or 4 hours at room temperature. Eat cold with vinaigrette dressing.

Preparing a carrot purée to be frozen

ARTICHOKES, JERUSALEM

Preparation
Only worth freezing as a purée. Scrub, peel, then simmer in water until tender. Sieve or liquidise. Cool.

Blanching time
Nil.

Packing
In rigid containers, leaving 2 cm./1 in. headspace. (Storage: 3 months.)

To use
Reheat gently from frozen with a little milk to prevent it catching, or use for soup.

ASPARAGUS

Preparation
Clean, trim off woody ends. Grade by thickness of stems. Cut to fit container, but don't tie.

Blanching time
Thin   – 2 minutes.
Medium – 3 minutes.
Thick   – 4 minutes.

Packing
Pack closely in rigid containers head to tail to save space or tie in bundles and freeze in a polythene bag.

To use
Plunge in boiling salted water for 5–8 minutes.

AUBERGINES

Preparation
Wash and cut in 1 cm./½ in. slices. Blanch immediately to avoid discoloration.

Blanching time
4 minutes.

Packing
Open freeze, pack in polythene bag.

To use
Plunge in boiling salted water for 3–5 minutes.

BEANS, BROAD

Preparation
Choose small young beans. Shell and grade into sizes.

Blanching time
2 minutes.

Packing
Open freeze, then pack into polythene bags.

To use
Plunge in boiling salted water for 5–10 minutes.

Vegetables should be blanched in fast boiling water, then cooled for the same time as they were blanched

BEANS, FRENCH AND RUNNER

Preparation	Blanching time	Packing	To use
Choose young tender stringless beans. Cut off ends and tips. Leave whole if small, or cut into 2 cm./1 in. lengths.	Whole or cut – 2 minutes.	Open freeze, then pack into polythene bags.	Plunge in boiling salted water for 8–12 minutes.

BEETROOT

Preparation	Blanching time	Packing	To use
Choose young beetroot not more than 7 cm./3 in. in diameter. Twist off tops leaving about 5 cm./2 in. attached. Cook in boiling water for 25–45 minutes or until tender.	Nil.	Skin, dice or slice or leave whole. Pack into polythene bags or rigid cartons leaving 1 cm./½ in. headspace. (Storage: 6 months.)	Thaw in refrigerator and use in salads or reheat gently in a sauce to serve hot.

BROCCOLI

Preparation	Blanching time	Packing	To use
Choose compact heads, cut off woody stalks and trim to an even length.	Thin stalks – 3 minutes. Thick stalks – 4 minutes.	Pack head to tail in polythene bags or rigid containers, or open freeze, then pack as above.	Plunge frozen into boiling salted water and cook for 5–8 minutes.

BRUSSELS SPROUTS

Preparation	Blanching time	Packing	To use
Choose small even sized sprouts. Trim off outside leaves.	Small – 3 minutes. Medium – 4 minutes.	Open freeze. Then pack in polythene bags.	Plunge frozen into boiling salted water and cook for 5–8 minutes.

CABBAGE, RED

Preparation	Blanching time	Packing	To use
Wash and shred.	1½ minutes.	Pack in polythene bags. (Storage: blanched, 1 year; braised, 6 months.)	Plunge in boiling salted water for 3–5 minutes or braise, when it can be re-frozen.

CABBAGE, WHITE

Preparation	Blanching time	Packing	To use
Wash and shred.	1½ minutes.	Pack as for red cabbage.	Plunge in boiling salted water for 3–5 minutes.

CARROTS

Preparation	Blanching time	Packing	To use
Choose small young carrots. Scrub and leave whole. If using large carrots scrape and slice or dice.	Small, whole – 5 minutes. Diced or sliced – 3 minutes.	Pack in polythene bags or rigid containers. Allow 1 cm./½ in. headspace.	Plunge frozen into boiling salted water and cook for 5–10 minutes.

CAULIFLOWER

Preparation	Blanching time	Packing	To use
Choose compact white cauliflower. Break into florets of an even size not larger than 2 cm./1 in. across.	3 minutes.	Open freeze, then pack in polythene bags. (Storage: 6 months.)	Plunge frozen into boiling salted water and cook for 5–8 minutes. Serve with a sauce.

CELERY

Preparation	Blanching time	Packing	To use
Choose tender young stalks. Scrub and cut into even lengths.	Nil.	Pack in polythene bags.	Do not use raw after freezing. Reheat in the oven or in boiling salted water for 3–5 minutes.

CORN ON THE COB

Preparation	Blanching time	Packing	To use
Choose young, tender corn. Remove husk and silk and grade according to size.	Small – 4 minutes. Medium – 6 minutes. Large – 8 minutes.	Pack individually in polythene bags, or scrape off kernels, open freeze, then pack as above.	Thaw cobs before cooking, about 4 hours at room temperature. Plunge whole cob into boiling salted water for 15 minutes, or cook kernels from frozen in boiling water for about 5 minutes.

COURGETTES

Preparation	Blanching time	Packing	To use
Pick even-sized young courgettes, cut in half or into 1 cm./$\frac{1}{2}$ in. slices.	1 minute.	Open freeze, then pack in polythene bags or rigid containers. Allow 1 cm./$\frac{1}{2}$ in. headspace.	Plunge while frozen into boiling salted water for 3 minutes or thaw and sauté in butter.

LEEKS

Preparation	Blanching time	Packing	To use
Remove outer leaves. Trim ends and wash well.	Nil.	Pack in polythene bags. (Storage: 6 months.)	Plunge from frozen in boiling water for 7–10 minutes.

MARROW

Preparation	Blanching time	Packing	To use
Peel and remove the seeds. Chop into large pieces.	3 minutes.	Pack in polythene bags or rigid containers. Allow 1 cm./$\frac{1}{2}$ in. headspace. (Storage: 10 months.)	Plunge in boiling salted water for 3–5 minutes.

MIXED VEGETABLES

Preparation	Blanching time	Packing	To use
Prepare each vegetable according to kind.	Blanch according to kind.	Combine vegetables and pack in polythene bags or rigid containers, allowing 1$\frac{1}{4}$ cm./$\frac{1}{2}$ in. headspace.	Plunge in boiling salted water for 3–5 minutes, or add to stews from frozen.

MUSHROOMS

Preparation	Blanching time	Packing	To use
Choose fresh cultivated mushrooms. Wash and dry thoroughly. Leave whole if button, or slice. Open freeze buttons raw if liked and pack in polythene bags.	*Do not blanch* in water but sauté in butter allowing 90 ml./6 tablespoons of melted butter to $\frac{1}{2}$ kg./1 lb. mushrooms for 4–5 minutes.	Pack in rigid containers, with cooking liquid. Allow 1 cm./$\frac{1}{2}$ in. headspace. (Storage: raw 1 month; cooked: 3 months.)	Add while frozen to soups, sauces, stews, etc., or if packed in melted butter, reheat gently in the oven or under a grill.

Open freezing courgettes

ONIONS

Preparation	Blanching time	Packing	To use
Choose whole small onions or slice or chop larger onions. Open freeze unblanched for short storage: 3 months.	Nil.	Pack in polythene bags or rigid containers and overwrap to prevent cross-flavouring. (Storage: 6 months.)	Add while frozen to soups, sauces, casseroles and stews.

PARSNIPS

Preparation	Blanching time	Packing	To use
Choose small young parsnips. Trim and peel. Cut into strips or dice.	2 minutes.	Open freeze then pack in polythene bags.	Plunge into boiling salted water for 10 minutes.

PEAS

Preparation	Blanching time	Packing	To use
Choose young, sweet tender peas. Pod and sort carefully.	1 minute.	Open freeze, then pack in polythene bags or rigid containers. Leave 1 cm./$\frac{1}{2}$ in. headspace.	Plunge into boiling salted water for 4–7 minutes.

PEPPERS – RED OR GREEN

Preparation	Blanching time	Packing	To use
Choose firm glossy peppers. Wash, remove seeds and stem, slice or dice.	Nil.	Pack in polythene bags or rigid containers. Allow 2 cm./1 in. headspace.	Plunge frozen into boiling salted water for 5–10 minutes.

POTATOES – NEW BOILED

Preparation	Blanching time	Packing	To use
Choose small even-sized ones. Scrape or scrub the potatoes. Slightly undercook until just tender.	Nil.	Pack in polythene bags or boiling bags. (Storage: 3 months.)	Plunge into boiling salted water for 3–5 minutes, or put boiling bag in boiling water, remove from heat and stand 10 minutes.

POTATOES – CHIPPED

Preparation	Blanching time	Packing	To use
Prepare in the normal way. Deep fry in hot oil 180°C/ 350°F until just tender but not brown. Drain well and cool.	Nil.	Open freeze, then pack into polythene bags or rigid containers. (Storage: 6 months.)	Fry in shallow or deep fat – take care as spitting can occur.

POTATOES – MASHED

Preparation	Blanching time	Packing	To use
Cook and mash old potatoes in the normal way. Make into duchesse or croquette potatoes.	Nil.	Open freeze, then pack into polythene bags or rigid containers. (Storage: 3 months.)	Reheat as directed in the recipe used.

SPINACH

Preparation	Blanching time	Packing	To use
Choose young, fresh spinach, wash very thoroughly. It can be quicker to cook first, then freeze in the leaf or as a purée.	Blanch in small quantities only – 2 minutes.	Pack into polythene bags or polythene containers. Allow 1 cm./$\frac{1}{2}$ in. headspace.	Plunge frozen into boiling salted water, cook for 2–3 minutes. Drain well and toss in a little butter.

SWEDES

Preparation	Blanching time	Packing	To use
Trim, peel and dice.	3 minutes.	Pack in polythene bags or rigid containers.	Cook from frozen in boiling salted water for 8–10 minutes or add to soups, stews and casseroles.

TOMATOES

Preparation	Blanching time	Packing	To use
Choose firm tomatoes, skin and leave whole or purée.	Nil.	Pack whole skinned tomatoes in polythene bags or rigid containers. Freeze purée in rigid containers, allowing 1 cm./$\frac{1}{2}$ in. headspace.	Not suitable for eating raw as they collapse. Add to soups, stews and casseroles, or fry or grill whole or halved.

TURNIPS

Preparation	Blanching time	Packing	To use
Choose small young turnips. Trim, peel and dice, if large. Or cook and purée.	Small, whole – 4 minutes. Diced – 2 minutes.	Pack in polythene bags. Pack purée in rigid container; allow 1 cm./$\frac{1}{2}$ in. headspace.	Cook from frozen in boiling salted water for 8–10 minutes or add to soups, stews and casseroles. Reheat purée gently.

Different stages in preparing vegetables for the freezer

Storage

Once your food is in the freezer, you need to know how long it can stay there and this will, of course, vary with the type of food. Exceeding the recommended storage times will lead to loss of flavour, texture, colour and aroma. It is essential that any food to be frozen is in perfect condition, correctly prepared and packaged and kept in the freezer at a constant maximum temperature of −18°C/0°F.

Plan ahead what can best be stored before embarking on lengthy preparation and freezing. Freezer space is valuable and limited, therefore it is important to select a good variety of foods, packed in easily used quantities, which your family will really enjoy eating.

Always store food in order of freezing so that packages which have been frozen longest are used first; this ensures that the frozen food is used in rotation.

Pre-cooked foods have a shorter storage life than most other foods, so you should aim to store these within a 2 month cycle. Plan to keep cooked dishes in one section of the freezer so that the amount available can be easily seen.

RECOMMENDED MAXIMUM STORAGE LIFE AT −18°C/0°F

DAIRY PRODUCE	MONTH(S)
Butter, salted	3
Butter, unsalted	6
Lard	5
Margarine	5
Dripping (rendered down from suet)	5
Cheese, hard or blue	3
Cream – 40% butterfat and over	3
Milk homogenised	1
Eggs	6
Ice cream, commercially made	1
Ice cream, home-made	2

FISH	
White fish – cod, whiting, plaice, sole, etc.	3
Oily fish – salmon, trout, herring, mackerel, etc.	2
Crab and lobster	1
Mussels	1
Oysters and scallops	1
Raw prawns and shrimps	1
Cooked prawns and shrimps	1
Cooked fish dishes	1

MEAT
Beef (Uncooked)

Joints	8
Steaks	6
Mince	2
Sausages	2

Lamb (Uncooked)

Joints	6
Chops and cutlets	6

Pork (Uncooked)	MONTH(S)
Joints, large or small	3
Chops	3
Sausages and sausagemeat	2

Bacon (Uncooked)	
Joints, smoked	6 weeks
Joints, unsmoked	3 weeks
Vacuum-packed joints, rashers or steaks	4
Rashers, smoked	6–8 weeks
Rashers, unsmoked	3 weeks

Veal (Uncooked)	
All cuts	6

Tongue (Uncooked)	
All kinds	3

Poultry	
Chicken, unstuffed	12
Turkey	6
Duck	6
Goose	4
Giblets	2

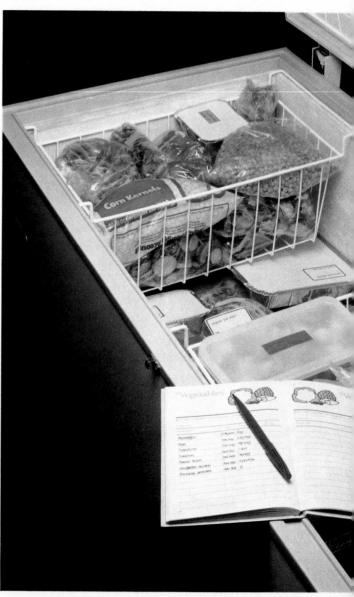

Game	MONTH(S)
Rabbit and hare	6
Venison	8
Birds – pheasant, grouse, partridge, etc.	6

Cooked meats

Bacon joints	3–4 weeks
Roast meat and poultry, whole	2
Sliced meat and poultry	1–2
Meat pies	3–4
Meat loaves, pâtés	1–3
Casseroles and stews, without bacon, ham or pork	2
Casseroles and stews including bacon, ham or pork	6 weeks
Ham, sliced or chopped	1
Tongue	1

Cured and smoked meats	1
Offal	
Raw	2
Cooked	2

Good organisation of the freezer is essential

FRUIT	MONTH(S)	
Fruit, with sugar or syrup	9–12	⎫ see
Fruit, without sugar or syrup	2–12	⎬ charts
Fruit purée	4–12	⎭
Fruit juice	6	
Fruit, dried – dates, figs	1	

VEGETABLES

Most vegetables	12
Exceptions –	
Artichokes, Jerusalem	3
Avocado, purée	2
Beetroot, sliced or small whole	6
Cabbage, braised	6
Cauliflower	6
Florence fennel	6
Leeks	6
Mushrooms, raw	1
Mushrooms, cooked	3
Onions or shallots	6
Potatoes, new, whole and boiled	3
Duchesse	3
Baked in jackets or roast	3
Croquettes	3
Chipped	6
Vegetable purées	6–12
Prepared vegetable dishes	3
Herbs	6

BREAD

Bread, baked, brown and white	6
Bread, unbaked, brown and white – unrisen	2
unbaked, brown and white – risen	3 weeks
enriched	4 weeks
Crusty bread and rolls	1 week
Breadcrumbs	3
Sandwiches	1–2
Pizzas	3
Baked yeast pastries	1
Tea breads	3
Buns	1

CAKES AND BISCUITS

Baked cakes, undecorated	4
Baked cakes, decorated	3
Unbaked cake mixtures	1
Biscuits, baked or unbaked	6
Scones, cooked	6
Cheesecakes	1
Shortbread	3

PASTRY AND PUDDINGS

Steamed puddings	3
Baked puddings	3
Mousses	3
Soufflés	3
Pies, baked	6
Pies, unbaked	3
Open flans or tarts, unbaked, unfilled	3
Open flans or tarts, baked, unfilled	6
Open flans or tarts, baked, filled	2
Pastry, shortcrust, puff and flaky	
– unbaked	3
– baked	6

MISCELLANEOUS FOODS	MONTH(S)
Pancakes, unfilled	4
Pancakes, filled	2
Pasta, cooked	1
Pasta, in composite dishes	3
Stuffing mixture	3
Soup	3
Stock	6
Sauces, white and brown	6
Sauces, tomato and apple	12
Sauces, curry and bread	3
Yoghurt, commercially frozen	1

The unfreezables
There are some foods which do not give satisfactory results when frozen.

Aspic and jelly, plain
Go gritty and runny; only freeze satisfactorily if bound or mixed with whipped cream, egg white or purée.

Bananas and avocado pears
Turn black and lose texture; will freeze satisfactorily as a purée if mixed with lemon juice (15 ml./3 tablespoons) per 600 ml./2 pints and sugar if liked.

Boiled potatoes (old)
Become discoloured and soggy unless mashed.

Carbonated drinks
There is a possibility that the low temperature could cause a minor explosion.

Celery, raw
Becomes soft on thawing, but will freeze satisfactorily for use as a cooked vegetable in soups and stews.

Cottage or cream cheeses
Only satisfactory if used in made-up dishes and then frozen.

Cream
Any cream containing less than 40% butter fat, although it may be frozen if combined with other ingredients.

Custards and custard tarts
Separate on thawing and have a poor flavour.

Eggs
In their shells will expand and break the shell. Although they may be successfully frozen if lightly stirred or separated and stored individually in ice cube trays or small containers (see page 20). Hard-boiled or Scotch eggs become tough.

Flavourings
Synthetic essences may become over-strong during storage; use natural flavourings instead, i.e. orange and lemon rind, vanilla pods.

Icings
Boiled, American frostings, royal icing and fondant will crack or crumble when thawed.

Mayonnaise
The oil will separate from the egg yolk, although it may be

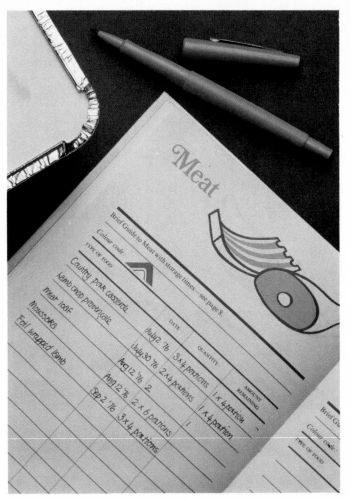

A record book is an invaluable aid and helps ensure regular rotation of frozen food

used in small quantities in the preparation of sandwich fillings or any prepared salads and fish products containing mayonnaise.

Salad vegetables
Lettuce, tomatoes, cucumber, watercress, spring onions, etc., become limp and mushy on thawing because of their high water content. No good for eating raw on thawing.

Seasonings
Herbs and spices can cause a musty flavour on storage, therefore use with discretion or add on reheating.

Soft meringue
Will become watery on thawing.

Sour cream
Separates when thawed, although it may be frozen if combined with other ingredients.

Tomatoes, raw
Collapse on thawing, although can be fried or grilled; will freeze satisfactorily as a cooked vegetable, puréed, or juice.

Yoghurt
Separates when thawed unless it is commercially frozen yoghurt, which contains a stabiliser.

40

Thawing

When frozen food is thawed the effect of raising the temperature allows the natural continued growth of micro-organisms. These will remain static while the food is defrosting and still cold, but once it is fully thawed (particularly cooked and made-up dishes), their growth is speeded up and the process of deterioration of the food resumes.

Thawing can take place in the refrigerator or at room temperature. If thawing at room temperature, the food must be placed out of any direct sunlight and the temperature of the room should not exceed 18°C/65°F.

It is not always possible to give exact thawing times because they will vary according to the packaging and the type, size, shape and texture of the food. In the recipe section you will find full instructions for thawing and heating after each recipe. However, not all foods need to be thawed completely before cooking.

Once food has been fully thawed, it should be used as soon as possible, do not leave it lying around at room temperature. Never re-freeze thawed raw food unless it can be cooked first, cooled quickly, then returned to the freezer.

Vegetables

With a few exceptions, vegetables do not need to be thawed before cooking. Many will have been blanched before freezing, so they will require less time to cook than from fresh.

Boiling All vegetables, whether fresh or frozen, retain their colour and flavour best if they are cooked in the minimum of boiling salted water. The water must be brought to rapid boiling point before adding the vegetables. If they are frozen in a solid block, choose a wide-based saucepan so that it lies flat in the base of the pan. After a few minutes, separate the vegetables with a fork to ensure even cooking.

Steaming With the exception of leaf vegetables, most can be steamed, and this may be a more satisfactory method if the vegetables are delicate. Allow them to thaw sufficiently so that they can be separated and this will aid total steam penetration.

Cooking in the oven Vegetables can be cooked very successfully in a casserole with a little water and a knob of butter. The flavour of the vegetables will be delicious and they can be served in the dish in which they were cooked.

Very good results are obtained with corn-on-the-cob if, after thawing, it is wrapped in buttered foil and cooked in the oven for 30 minutes.

Fruit

All frozen fruit should be thawed in its unopened container, particularly those fruits that tend to discolour on contact with air. For this reason thaw at one time no more than you require for immediate use.

Some fruits when fully thawed have a tendency to collapse and the natural juices will leak out, therefore soft berries such as raspberries and strawberries will require only partial thawing for eating raw so there is still some ice in them. When serving berries or soft fruit as a dessert the moment they should be removed from the freezer should be carefully judged so that the fruit remains whole but edible. Thawing slowly in the refrigerator can overcome this problem.

Fruits to be served cold should be thawed upside down in their container, in a bowl, so that all the fruit is covered with sugar or syrup.

Fruit for pies which are going to be cooked need only be thawed sufficiently to separate, so that it can be easily spread.

Fruit for stewing can be heated directly from frozen in a saucepan, but reheat gently. When cooking fruit remember to taste before adding extra sugar because it will already be fairly sweet if it has been frozen with sugar or a sugar syrup.

In emergencies both fruit and vegetables can be thawed quickly by placing the food, still wrapped, in lukewarm water or under a running tap. But there might be a loss in flavour and texture, the water could come into contact with the food, and it is difficult to judge if the food has thawed completely.

Approximate thawing times for ½ kg./1 lb. fruit packed in sugar or syrup

In the refrigerator   6–8 hours
Room temperature   2–4 hours

Meat

Raw meat is best thawed slowly in its wrapping in the refrigerator so it absorbs as much of its juices as possible. But it is a slow process; you should allow 5 hours per ½ kg./1 lb. to thaw completely. Thawing at room temperature is much faster – 2 hours per ½ kg./1 lb. – but it is not advisable for pork. All meat must remain wrapped during thawing. If this is not done the meat will drip and juice and colour will be lost.

However, with the exception of boned and rolled meat (when there is a possibility that micro-organisms may have been transferred to the inside of the meat during boning and rolling) joints can be cooked straight from frozen, providing an adequate cooking time is allowed. Cooking from frozen may, however, result in tougher meat. Frozen joints will take almost twice as long to cook as completely thawed ones so you will be using more fuel. This method requires care and accurate timing, for the meat may seem to be cooked on the outside but still be raw and cold on the inside. Use the slow-roasting method. To achieve the best results, the oven should be set to 160°C/325°F or Gas Mark 3 and the cooking time increased to approximately double the normal roasting period. A meat thermometer is an invaluable aid for cooking meat from frozen.

Approximate roasting times and temperatures when cooking from frozen

Beef Joints: 160°C/325°F or Gas Mark 3. 30 minutes to the ½ kg./1 lb. + 30 minutes over.
Lamb Joints: 160°C/325°F or Gas Mark 3. 35 minutes to the ½ kg./1 lb. + 35 minutes over.
Pork Joints: 190°C/375°F or Gas Mark 5. 40 minutes to the ½ kg./1 lb. + 40 minutes over.

Temperature readings on meat thermometer

Meat		Temperature
Beef: rare		65.5°C/150°F
	medium	71°C/160°F
	well done	77°C/170°F
Lamb		82°C/180°F
Pork		88°C/190°F

Approximate times for thawing joints of meat

In the refrigerator   5 hours per $\frac{1}{2}$ kg./1 lb.
At room temperature   2 hours per $\frac{1}{2}$ kg./1 lb.

Chops, steaks, sausages and sliced liver or kidney can all be cooked from frozen. They should be fried or grilled over a low heat until the meat has had time to thaw out, and the heat can then be increased to brown.

Minced meat and stewing steak which has been ready prepared prior to freezing, can be put from frozen straight into hot stock or fat and the pieces separated over a gentle heat; once thawed you can continue to cook in the normal way. This also applies to pot roasting, but the surfaces of the meat will need to be sealed in hot fat (be careful because it will spit) to prevent the juices being lost in cooking. If meat is to be coated with egg and breadcrumbs or fried in hot deep fat, it will need to be thawed first so that the coating will adhere and to ensure that the meat is thoroughly cooked in the centre. Once meat has thawed it must be prepared and cooked without delay.

Poultry, game birds, hare and rabbit
Raw poultry and game *must* be thawed, completely, preferably in the refrigerator, in their original wrappings. The reason for this is that the risk of contamination is higher in poultry than in other meats, and all poultry must, therefore, be cooked thoroughly so that the heat penetrates right through the bone and the body cavity, to destroy micro-organisms. Once thawed, follow the normal roasting times. Thawing can take place at room temperature providing the poultry is cooked as soon as it has thawed, and this will prove more practicable for large chickens and turkeys.

Approximate thawing times in the refrigerator for poultry and game

Birds up to 2 kg./4 lb. – 12 hours or overnight
Birds between 2–6 kg. /4–12 lb. – 24–36 hours
Birds over 6 kg./12 lb. – 36–72 hours
Rabbit and hare – 6 hours

Note: All game should be hung and prepared prior to freezing. If it is carried out after freezing and thawing it can be a very unpleasant task indeed.

Fish and shellfish
Small whole fish, fillets and steaks can all be cooked from frozen but they will take a few minutes longer than fresh or thawed fish. If fish is to be coated with egg and breadcrumbs or batter, it needs to be partially thawed first, to allow the coating to adhere. Large whole or thick pieces of fish should always be thawed in their wrappings in the refrigerator for best results. But if you are short of time, the fish can be thawed in a cool place or by placing it in cold water.

Shellfish should ideally be thawed in the refrigerator and used as soon as it has thawed.

Approximate thawing times of fish and shellfish in refrigerator

Whole fish under 2 kg./4 lb. – up to 12 hours
    or overnight
Whole fish over 2 kg./4 lb. – 24–36 hours

Steaks and fillets – 4–6 hours
Prepared and packaged lobster and crab – 6–8
    hours
Packs of seafood of $\frac{1}{2}$ kg./1 lb. – 12 hours or
    overnight

Prepared foods
Made-up dishes such as casseroles can be thawed at room temperature and then reheated in a moderately hot oven (190°C/375°F or Gas Mark 5) or cooked from frozen either in a saucepan or in the oven; but care must be taken when reheating to avoid breaking up those ingredients intended to be kept whole such as baby onions or mushrooms. The food must be thoroughly heated and served piping hot.

No cooked dish should be thawed and then re-frozen

Pâtés, meat loaves Thaw wrapped overnight in the refrigerator or for about 6 hours at room temperature.
Sauces and soups If to be served hot may be tipped frozen into a saucepan and reheated over a gentle heat, stirring continually to prevent them catching. In the event of a sauce appearing to separate, a thorough whisking during reheating is usually sufficient to restore the smooth consistency. If stored in a boiling bag, drop from frozen into a pan of boiling water and heat through.

If the soups or sauces are difficult to remove while still frozen, run cold water over the base of the container.

It is best to add milk, cream or egg yolks to soups and sauces after thawing.

Commercially frozen foods
Follow the manufacturer's instructions on the packet. Many of the prepared products such as beefburgers or fish fingers can be cooked or reheated from frozen.

Breads
Baked breads and rolls Thaw these in their wrappings at room temperature for approximately 3–6 hours. If preferred they can be thawed and reheated in a hot oven (200°C/400°F or Gas Mark 6); this is particularly suitable for crisp rolls and French bread which, after baking have the flavour and texture of freshly baked bread. But they should be eaten at once as they become stale fairly rapidly.
Sandwiches should be left wrapped and allowed to thaw at room temperature for 2–3 hours.

Scones
Thaw scones in their wrappings at room temperature for approximately 1 hour, or partially thaw and then heat in a moderate oven (180°C/350°F or Gas Mark 4), or they can be split while thawing and toasted under a hot grill.

Pancakes and drop scones
Thaw unwrapped at room temperature for approximately 20 minutes, then use as required, or wrap in foil and reheat gently in a warm oven (160°C/325°F or Gas Mark 3).
Filled pancakes: remove wrappings and lid and bake from frozen in hot oven (200°C/400°F or Gas Mark 6) for approximately 30 minutes.

Cakes
All baked cakes should be thawed in their wrappings at room temperature unless they are iced, when the wrappings should

All frozen food to be reheated should be heated right through and served piping hot

be removed before thawing so they don't spoil the appearance of the cake. Iced cakes may appear to be over-moist during thawing but they will return to their normal state.

Cakes containing fresh dairy cream are best sliced while still partially frozen and served slightly chilled.

With large cakes it is often convenient to slice the cake into portions, each one separated with a piece of waxed paper, before freezing, so you can take out slices as they are needed without having to thaw the whole cake.

Biscuits
Raw mixture frozen in a sausage-like shape can be part-thawed, sliced and baked.

Thaw cooked biscuits in their container at room temperature, but keep well wrapped to prevent them becoming soft.

Dairy products
Thaw eggs in their unopened containers under running cold water or in a refrigerator. Thawed egg yolks and whole eggs should be used immediately, but egg whites will keep for several days if they are stored in the refrigerator.

Cream, butter, margarine and cheese should ideally be thawed in the refrigerator: allow 8 hours per 150 ml./$\frac{1}{4}$ pint cream; 4 hours per 225 g./$\frac{1}{2}$ lb. butter or margarine, and for cheese, 8 hours per 225 g./$\frac{1}{2}$ lb.

Pastry
Raw pastry Allow plenty of time for the pastry to thaw and soften at room temperature, or it may crumble when rolled out. Cook in the normal way.

Baked pastry Baked pastry cases should be thawed in their wrapping at room temperature for approximately 1 hour before filling. Pastry cases which are to contain a hot filling can be filled and reheated from frozen in a low oven.

Unbaked pies Unwrap and bake from frozen in preheated oven as usual but allow 10–15 minutes longer than the normal cooking time. If the pastry starts to brown before the filling is thoroughly reheated it should be protected with foil.

Cooked pies With the exception of fruit pies which can be reheated from frozen, pies for serving hot should be thawed for 2–4 hours at room temperature, then reheated in a moderate oven (180°C/350°F or Gas Mark 4).

Baked pies which are to be served cold can be thawed in their wrappings at room temperature.

Puddings Puddings to be served cold or iced should be thawed in the refrigerator for 2–6 hours, according to type, but leave wrapped if possible. Mousses, soufflés and iced puddings which are to be unmoulded turn out more easily when still partially frozen; then they can be returned to the refrigerator to finish thawing. Iced puddings such as ice cream and water ices should be removed from the freezer and placed in the refrigerator no more than 10–30 minutes before serving.

Baked puddings should be thawed at room temperature for approximately 3–4 hours.

43

Starters

Potted shrimps

METRIC	IMPERIAL
175 g. unsalted butter	6 oz. unsalted butter
2.5 ml. ground mace	½ teaspoon ground mace
Freshly ground black pepper	Freshly ground black pepper
Pinch of cayenne pepper	Pinch of cayenne pepper
Pinch of nutmeg	Pinch of nutmeg
225 g. peeled shrimps	8 oz. peeled shrimps

Melt the butter in a saucepan, mix in the seasonings and add the shrimps. Cook gently, stirring occasionally, for 5 minutes. Remove the pan from the heat. Taste and adjust the seasoning. Spoon the shrimps and butter into small pots (yoghurt or cream cartons could be used). The butter must cover the shrimps completely.

To freeze: Cool quickly, cover, seal and freeze.

To serve: While still frozen, turn the shrimps out onto a serving dish and thaw at room temperature for 3 hours. Garnish with lemon wedges and serve with brown bread and butter.

Note: If preferred, the potted shrimps may be frozen in individual ramekin dishes and served from the ramekins. They should be unwrapped and thawed at room temperature for 4 hours.

Serves 4.

Haddock and mushroom scallops

METRIC	IMPERIAL
25 g. butter	1 oz. butter
100 g. mushrooms, washed and sliced	4 oz. mushrooms, washed and sliced
300 ml. white coating sauce	½ pint white coating sauce
2.5 ml. made English mustard	½ teaspoon made English mustard
225 g. smoked haddock, cooked, skin and bones removed and flaked	8 oz. smoked haddock, cooked, skin and bones removed and flaked
Freshly ground black pepper	Freshly ground black pepper
25 g. Cheddar cheese, grated	1 oz. Cheddar cheese, grated
15 g. fresh white breadcrumbs	½ oz. fresh white breadcrumbs

Topping	**Topping**
½ kg. potatoes, peeled and boiled	1 lb. potatoes, peeled and boiled
25 g. butter	1 oz. butter
30 ml. milk	2 tablespoons milk
Salt	Salt

Melt the butter in a saucepan, add the mushrooms and sauté for 3 minutes. Stir in the white sauce, mustard, fish and pepper to taste. Divide the mixture between 4 clean, buttered scallop shells or small buttered ovenproof or foil dishes and sprinkle with the grated cheese and breadcrumbs.

Mash the potatoes with the butter and milk until smooth, season to taste. Pipe a border of mashed potato round the edge of each shell or dish.

To freeze: Cool quickly, then open freeze. When frozen wrap in foil, seal and return to the freezer.

To serve: Thaw at room temperature for 1½ hours. Dot with 15 g./½ oz. butter and place on a baking tray in a fairly hot oven (200°C/400°F or Gas Mark 6) for 15–20 minutes or until topping is crisp and golden.

Serves 4.

Marinated herrings

METRIC	IMPERIAL
Marinade	**Marinade**
1 onion, peeled and sliced	1 onion, peeled and sliced
2 bay leaves	2 bay leaves
300 ml. dry white wine	½ pint dry white wine
100 ml. white wine vinegar	4 fl. oz. white wine vinegar
300 ml. water	½ pint water
5 ml. soft brown sugar	1 teaspoon soft brown sugar
10 ml. salt	2 teaspoons salt
6 black peppercorns	6 black peppercorns
6 fresh herrings, cleaned, scaled, heads removed and boned	6 fresh herrings, cleaned, scaled, heads removed and boned

Place all the marinade ingredients in a shallow saucepan or frying pan. Bring to the boil, then reduce heat and simmer for 15 minutes. Add the herrings, cover the pan and simmer very gently for 10 minutes. Remove the pan from the heat and allow the fish to cool in the marinade.

To freeze: Remove cold herrings from marinade and arrange in a shallow rigid container. Pour the marinade over the fish. Cover, seal and freeze.

To serve: Thaw at room temperature for 3–4 hours. Serve chilled with brown bread and butter.

Serves 4 to 6.

Potted shrimps; Marinated herrings; Haddock and mushroom scallops

46

Liver pâté

Grapefruit and grape cocktail

METRIC	IMPERIAL
3 large grapefruit	3 large grapefruit
225 g. mixed green and black grapes, halved and pips removed	8 oz. mixed green and black grapes, halved and pips removed
25 g. caster sugar	1 oz. caster sugar
45 ml. salad oil	3 tablespoons salad oil
15 ml. white wine vinegar	1 tablespoon white wine vinegar
2.5 ml. made English mustard	½ teaspoon made English mustard

Cut peel, pith and thin inner skin from grapefruit with a sharp serrated knife. Remove segments by cutting down between each membrane. Combine the grapefuit segments and grapes in a bowl and dust with caster sugar. Place in the refrigerator to chill.

Mix together the salad oil, vinegar and mustard and pour over the fruit.

To freeze: Pack into a rigid polythene container. Cover, seal and freeze.

To serve: Thaw overnight in a refrigerator or at room temperature for 4–5 hours. Stir to ensure fruit is evenly coated.

Serve chilled on a bed of green salad.

Serves 4.

Pineapple mint cocktail

METRIC	IMPERIAL
1 ripe pineapple, about 1 kg.	1 ripe pineapple, about 2 lb.
50 g. caster sugar	2 oz. caster sugar
2.5 ml. concentrated mint sauce mixed with 10 ml. wine vinegar	½ teaspoon concentrated mint sauce mixed with 2 teaspoons wine vinegar

Peel the pineapple, remove the eyes and the hard central core and cut the pineapple into bite-sized chunks. Turn into a rigid polythene container and mix in the caster sugar and mint sauce.

To freeze: Cover, seal and freeze.

To serve: Thaw overnight in a refrigerator or at room temperature for 4–5 hours. Stir to ensure fruit is evenly coated.

Divide between 4 glasses and serve chilled. Decorate with a sprig of fresh mint.

Serves 4.

Liver pâté

A quickly made pâté which requires no cooking and uses bought liver sausage. It makes an excellent spread for sandwiches.

METRIC	IMPERIAL
½ kg. soft liver sausage	1 lb. soft liver sausage
75 g. butter, softened	3 oz. butter, softened
15 ml. fresh chives, finely chopped	1 tablespoon fresh chives, finely chopped
15 ml. brandy	1 tablespoon brandy
5 ml. dried sage	1 teaspoon dried sage
Salt and freshly ground black pepper	Salt and freshly ground black pepper

Beat the liver sausage and butter together until smooth and thoroughly mixed. Stir in the chives, brandy, sage and seasoning. Taste and adjust the seasoning. Press the pâté mixture into a rigid container.

To freeze: Cover, seal and freeze.

To serve: Leave to thaw at room temperature for 3–4 hours.

Serves 4 to 6.

Grapefruit and grape cocktail; Pineapple mint cocktail; Melon and orange cocktail

Melon and orange cocktail

METRIC
1 honeydew melon, about
  1 kg.
180 ml. fresh orange juice
  or diluted orange juice
  concentrate
50 g. caster sugar
2.5 ml. ground ginger
Finely grated rind of 1
  orange

IMPERIAL
1 honeydew melon, about
  2 lb.
6 fl.oz. fresh orange juice
  or diluted orange juice
  concentrate
2 oz. caster sugar
½ teaspoon ground ginger
Finely grated rind of 1
  orange

Peel the melon, scoop out the seeds and cut the flesh into bite-sized cubes. Place in a rigid polythene container.

In a saucepan heat the orange juice and stir in the caster sugar, ginger and grated orange rind. Stir over a low heat until the sugar has dissolved. Cool and pour over the melon.
To freeze: Cover, seal and freeze.
To serve: Thaw overnight in a refrigerator or at room temperature for 5–6 hours. Stir to ensure fruit is evenly coated.

Serve the melon chilled and garnished with a little chopped stem ginger.
Serves 6.

Kipper pâté

METRIC
1 × 340 g. packet boil-in-the-bag kipper fillets
10 ml. lemon juice
Freshly ground black pepper
10 ml. horseradish sauce
225 g. unsalted butter

IMPERIAL
1 × 12 oz. packet boil-in-the-bag kipper fillets
2 teaspoons lemon juice
Freshly ground black pepper
2 teaspoons horseradish sauce
8 oz. unsalted butter

Boil the kipper fillets in the bag, as directed on the packet. Drain and reserve 60 ml./4 tablespoons of the juices. Flake the fish, removing any skin or bones and place in a food blender, add the reserved juice, lemon juice, pepper and horseradish sauce and blend until smooth.

Beat the butter until soft, stir in the kipper mixture and mix thoroughly. Taste and adjust the seasoning.

To freeze: Pack into a rigid container, cover, seal and freeze.

To serve: Thaw overnight in a refrigerator, or at room temperature for 5 hours.

Spoon into a serving dish and serve with melba toast.

Serves 6.

French country style liver pâté

METRIC
225 g. pigs' liver, ducts removed and minced
225 g. belly of pork, boned and minced
Small garlic clove, crushed
Salt and freshly ground black pepper
5 ml. dried mixed herbs
30 ml. dry white wine
4 rashers streaky bacon

IMPERIAL
8 oz. pigs' liver, ducts removed and minced
8 oz. belly of pork, boned and minced
Small garlic clove, crushed
Salt and freshly ground black pepper
1 teaspoon dried mixed herbs
2 tablespoons dry white wine
4 rashers streaky bacon

Mix together the pigs' liver and belly of pork. Stir in the garlic, seasoning to taste, herbs and wine. Mix well and turn into a 600 ml./1 pint ovenproof dish.

On a chopping board flatten and stretch the bacon rashers with the blade of a knife. Cover the pâté with the bacon then cover tightly with foil. Stand the dish in a baking tin with enough hot water to reach halfway up the side of the dish. Bake in a warm oven (160°C/325°F or Gas Mark 3) for 1–1¼ hours or until pâté has shrunk from the edges of the dish and a skewer inserted comes out clean. Pour off the excess fat.

To freeze: Cool quickly, then turn out and wrap in heavy duty foil. Place in a polythene bag, seal and freeze.

To serve: Thaw in a refrigerator overnight. Serve with hot toast or crusty French bread.

Serves 6.

Kipper pâté; French country style liver pâté

Potted ham

METRIC	IMPERIAL
75 g. butter	*3 oz. butter*
225 g. cooked ham, minced or finely chopped	*8 oz. cooked ham, minced or finely chopped*
5 ml. made English mustard	*1 teaspoon made English mustard*
Pinch of Cayenne pepper	*Pinch of Cayenne pepper*
Salt and freshly ground black pepper	*Salt and freshly ground black pepper*

Place the butter, ham and seasonings in a bowl and beat until thoroughly mixed. Taste and adjust the seasoning. Spoon the ham mixture into small dishes or one larger dish.

To freeze: Cover, seal and freeze.

To serve: Leave to thaw at room temperature for 3 hours. Serve with hot toast.

Serves 4.

Lemon and sardine pâté

METRIC	IMPERIAL
50 g. butter	*2 oz. butter*
75 g. fresh white or brown breadcrumbs	*3 oz. fresh white or brown breadcrumbs*
Grated rind and juice of ½ a lemon	*Grated rind and juice of ½ a lemon*
10 ml. finely chopped parsley	*2 teaspoons finely chopped parsley*
1 × 100 g. can sardines, boned and mashed with oil	*1 × 4 oz. can sardines, boned and mashed with oil*
Salt and freshly ground black pepper	*Salt and freshly ground black pepper*
4–6 lemon slices	*4–6 lemon slices*

Melt the butter in a saucepan, then remove from the heat and stir in the breadcrumbs, lemon juice, parsley, sardines and seasoning to taste. Beat together until smooth, taste and adjust the seasoning. Spoon the sardine mixture into 4 or 6 small dishes or 1 large dish.

Place a slice of lemon on top and chill until firm.

To freeze: Cover, seal and freeze.

To serve: Thaw at room temperature for 3 hours. Serve chilled with hot toast and lemon wedges.

Serves 4 to 6.

Potted ham; Lemon and sardine pâté

Frosted salmon mousse

METRIC
2 × 225 g. cans red salmon
30 ml. lemon juice
10 ml. tomato ketchup
15 ml. parsley, finely
 chopped
Salt and freshly ground
 black pepper
60 ml. cold water
15 ml. powdered gelatine
1 small can evaporated milk,
 chilled
2 egg whites

IMPERIAL
2 × 7½ oz. cans red salmon
2 tablespoons lemon juice
2 teaspoons tomato ketchup
1 tablespoon parsley, finely
 chopped
Salt and freshly ground
 black pepper
4 tablespoons cold water
1 tablespoon powdered
 gelatine
1 small can evaporated milk,
 chilled
2 egg whites

Remove the skin and bones from the salmon and mash the fish to a smooth paste. Stir in the lemon juice, tomato ketchup, parsley and seasoning.

Put the water in a small heatproof teacup or bowl. Sprinkle over the gelatine, stir once and leave until spongy. Place the bowl or cup in a pan of hot water and stir over a low heat until the gelatine has dissolved. Remove from the heat, strain the gelatine into the salmon mixture and mix well. Whisk the

Frosted salmon mousse; Savoury pancakes

well-chilled evaporated milk until thick and nearly doubled in volume and fold into the salmon mixture.

Place the egg whites in a clean dry bowl, whisk with a spiral or balloon whisk until standing up in peaks, then fold half of the whites into the salmon mixture with a metal spoon, lifting and folding throughout. Add the remaining whites and repeat the folding-in process, which should result in a spongy froth. Turn the mixture into a lightly oiled 1.2 l./2 pint ring mould.

To freeze: Open freeze. When frozen, cover tightly with foil or freezer wrap, place in a polythene bag, seal and return to the freezer.

To serve: Turn out the frozen mould into a serving dish and thaw at room temperature for 3–4 hours.

Fill the centre with watercress or shredded lettuce.

Serves 8.

Savoury pancakes

METRIC
100 g. plain flour
Pinch of salt
1 egg
300 ml. milk
15 ml. butter, melted
15 ml. oil

IMPERIAL
4 oz. plain flour
Pinch of salt
1 egg
½ pint milk
1 tablespoon butter, melted
1 tablespoon oil

Spread pancakes with the filling and fold or roll up.

To freeze: Pack in foil container, separating layers with foil. Cover, seal and freeze.

To serve: Place frozen pancakes on a buttered baking tray, brush with melted butter and reheat in a moderate oven (180°C/350°F or Gas Mark 4) for 35 minutes.

Makes 12 pancakes.

Note: Pancakes can be frozen unfilled if preferred. Pack in layers, interleaving each pancake with greased greaseproof paper. Wrap in foil or a polythene bag, seal and freeze. Unwrap and spread out to thaw at room temperature for 30 minutes. Reheat, covered, in a fairly hot oven (200°C/400°F or Gas Mark 6) for 10–15 minutes.

Ratatouille

Ratatouille

METRIC	IMPERIAL
60 ml. olive oil	4 tablespoons olive oil
2 medium onions, peeled and sliced	2 medium onions, peeled and sliced
1 garlic clove, crushed	1 garlic clove, crushed
2 green peppers, cored, seeded and sliced	2 green peppers, cored, seeded and sliced
2 medium aubergines, sliced	2 medium aubergines, sliced
225 g. courgettes, washed and sliced	8 oz. courgettes, washed and sliced
225 g. tomatoes, skinned, seeded and chopped	8 oz. tomatoes, skinned, seeded and chopped
1 × 396 g. can tomatoes, drained	1 × 14 oz. can tomatoes, drained
Salt and freshly ground black pepper	Salt and freshly ground black pepper
5 ml. parsley, chopped	1 teaspoon parsley, chopped
2.5 ml. dried basil	½ teaspoon dried basil
60 ml. dry white wine	4 tablespoons dry white wine

Heat the olive oil in a saucepan and add the onion and garlic. Cook gently for 5 minutes until the onion is transparent. Add the peppers and aubergines and fry for 3 minutes, stirring occasionally. Add the courgettes, tomatoes, seasoning, herbs and wine. Cover the pan and simmer for 45 minutes or until the vegetables are tender, stirring occasionally. Taste and adjust the seasoning.

To freeze: Cool quickly and pour into a foil container. Cover, seal and freeze.

To serve: *hot* – Reheat, covered, in a moderate oven, (180°C/350°F or Gas Mark 4) for 30 minutes or until heated through. Taste and adjust the seasoning.

To serve: *cold* – Allow to thaw at room temperature for 6–7 hours or overnight in a refrigerator. Taste and adjust seasoning.

Serves 4–6.

Filling

50 g. mushrooms, washed and chopped	2 oz. mushrooms, washed and chopped
25 g. butter	1 oz. butter
300 ml. béchamel sauce	½ pint béchamel sauce
15 ml. chives, chopped	1 tablespoon chives, chopped
175 g. peeled prawns	6 oz. peeled prawns
15 ml. dry sherry	1 tablespoon dry sherry
30 ml. single cream	2 tablespoons single cream
Salt and freshly ground black pepper	Salt and freshly ground black pepper

Sift flour and salt into a bowl, make a well in the centre and add the egg, then gradually beat in the milk. Stir in the melted butter and beat well until smooth. Allow the batter to stand in a cool place for 30 minutes before using.

Lightly brush the base of a 20 cm./8 in. frying pan with a little of the oil, stand the pan over a medium heat and when hot pour in enough batter to coat the base of the pan thinly and evenly. Cook until the underside is golden brown, turn and cook the other side until golden brown. Repeat the method using the rest of the batter, oiling the pan between each pancake and stacking the cooked pancakes one on top of each other.

Fry the mushrooms gently in the butter until soft. Heat the béchamel sauce gently in a saucepan. Stir in the drained mushrooms and remaining ingredients and heat without boiling. Season to taste.

Chicken and mushroom vol-au-vent

Scoop out any soft pastry from the centre of the cases.
Filling, allow to stand at room temperature for 30 minutes, then tip into a saucepan and heat very gently, stirring occasionally for 20–30 minutes or until heated through. Taste and adjust the seasoning. Divide between the pastry cases, replace the lids and serve.
Serves 4.

Chicken and mushroom vol-au-vents

METRIC	IMPERIAL
225 g. frozen puff pastry, thawed	8 oz. frozen puff pastry, thawed

Filling	**Filling**
25 g. butter	1 oz. butter
100 g. mushrooms, washed and sliced	4 oz. mushrooms, washed and sliced
175 g. cooked chicken, chopped finely	6 oz. cooked chicken, chopped finely
300 ml. béchamel sauce	$\frac{1}{2}$ pint béchamel sauce
Salt and freshly ground black pepper	Salt and freshly ground black pepper

Roll the pastry out to $\frac{1}{2}$ cm./$\frac{1}{4}$ in. thickness on a floured board. Cut the pastry into 4 circles using a 9 cm./$3\frac{1}{2}$ in. pastry cutter and place on a damp baking tray. Cut halfway through the centre of each circle with a 5 cm./2 in. pastry cutter.

Melt the butter in a saucepan, add the mushrooms and allow to cook for 3 minutes. Stir in the chicken, sauce and seasoning. Heat through gently. Taste and adjust the seasoning.
To freeze: *Pastry cases,* open freeze. When frozen, pack in a rigid container, separating the cases with foil. Cover, seal and return to the freezer.
Filling, pack into a rigid container, seal and freeze.
To serve: *Pastry cases,* unwrap, brush with beaten egg and allow to stand at room temperature for 30 minutes. Bake in the centre of a hot oven (220°C/425°F or Gas Mark 7) for 20 minutes or until well risen and crisp. Allow to cool. With a sharp knife, carefully remove the pastry lid and reserve.

Sweet corn and ham flan

METRIC	IMPERIAL
25 g. butter	1 oz. butter
1 medium onion, peeled and chopped	1 medium onion, peeled and chopped
300 ml. white coating sauce	$\frac{1}{2}$ pint white coating sauce
75 g. Cheddar cheese, grated	3 oz. Cheddar cheese, grated
175 g. frozen sweet corn kernels	6 oz. frozen sweet corn kernels
5 ml. made English mustard	1 teaspoon made English mustard
Salt and freshly ground black pepper	Salt and freshly ground black pepper
100 g. cooked ham, diced	4 oz. cooked ham, diced
20 cm. flan ring lined with shortcrust pastry, baked	8 inch flan ring lined with shortcrust pastry, baked

Melt the butter and add the onion, fry for 5 minutes and add to the sauce. Stir in 50 g./2 oz. of the cheese, the sweetcorn, mustard, seasoning and ham. Bring to the boil, remove from the heat, taste and adjust the seasoning and pour into the prepared pastry case. Sprinkle the remaining 25 g./1 oz. of cheese over the top.
To freeze: Open freeze. When frozen, remove flan from flan ring, wrap the flan, seal and return to freezer.
To serve: Return the frozen flan to the flan ring. Place on a baking tray and bake, uncovered, in a moderate oven (180°C/350°F or Gas Mark 4) for 40 minutes or until heated through, then raise the temperature to fairly hot (200°C/400°F or Gas Mark 7) for 10–15 minutes to brown the flan.
Serves 4 to 6.

Tomato and herb ring

METRIC	IMPERIAL
1 × 396 g. can and 1 × 225 g. can tomatoes	1 × 14 oz. can and 1 × 8 oz. can tomatoes
60 ml. dry white wine	4 tablespoons dry white wine
Finely grated rind and juice of $\frac{1}{2}$ a lemon	Finely grated rind and juice of $\frac{1}{2}$ a lemon
4 peppercorns	4 peppercorns
1 garlic clove, crushed	1 garlic clove, crushed
5 ml. fresh sage, finely chopped	1 teaspoon fresh sage, finely chopped
10 ml. fresh chives, finely snipped	2 teaspoons fresh chives, finely snipped
5 ml. fresh thyme, finely chopped	1 teaspoon fresh thyme, finely chopped
Salt	Salt
Pinch of sugar	Pinch of sugar
60 ml. water	4 tablespoons water
15 ml. gelatine	1 tablespoon gelatine

Place the tomatoes in a saucepan with the wine, lemon rind and juice, peppercorns and garlic. Bring to the boil and simmer for 5 minutes. Remove peppercorns and rub the mixture through a sieve. Stir in the fresh herbs, salt and the sugar.

Put the water in a small heatproof bowl or teacup. Sprinkle over the gelatine. Stir once and leave until spongy. Place the bowl or cup in a pan of hot water and stir over a low heat until the gelatine has dissolved. Remove from the heat, strain the gelatine into the tomato pulp and stir well. Taste and adjust the seasoning.

Lightly oil a 600 ml./1 pint ring mould. Pour in the tomato mixture and leave until set.

To freeze: Place in a plastic bag or cover with foil, seal and freeze.

To serve: Turn the frozen mould out onto a serving dish and thaw in a refrigerator for 6 hours.

Fill the centre with watercress and cucumber tossed in French dressing.

Serves 4 to 6.

Sweet corn and ham flan; Tomato and herb ring; Cheese and ham croquettes

Cheese and ham croquettes

METRIC	IMPERIAL
225 g. cold mashed potato	8 oz. cold mashed potato
100 g. cooked ham, cut into small cubes or minced	4 oz. cooked ham, cut into small cubes or minced
100 g. Cheddar cheese, grated	4 oz. Cheddar cheese, grated
1 egg, beaten	1 egg, beaten
5 ml. made English mustard	1 teaspoon made English mustard
Salt	Salt

Coating	**Coating**
1 egg, beaten	1 egg, beaten
30 ml. milk	2 tablespoons milk
100 g. dried white breadcrumbs	4 oz. dried white breadcrumbs

Place the mashed potato in a bowl and add the ham, cheese, beaten egg, mustard and salt to taste. Stir well to mix thoroughly. Divide the mixture into 16 equal portions, then roll into croquettes on a floured board. Beat the egg and milk together and pour into a shallow dish. Dip each croquette into the egg and milk and then roll in the breadcrumbs.

To freeze: Open freeze on a lined baking tray. When frozen, pack into a rigid container or polythene bag. Seal and return to freezer.

To serve: Thaw in a refrigerator for 2 hours. Deep fry (175°C/350°F) in a frying basket for 5 minutes or until golden. Drain on kitchen paper and serve hot with a tomato sauce.

Serves 8.

600 ml./1 pint ovenproof dish or foil container. Dot the surface with the remaining butter and cheese.

To freeze: Cover, seal and freeze.

To serve: Thaw at room temperature for 3 hours, then bake in a moderate oven (180°C/350°F or Gas Mark 4) for 45 minutes. Serve with a tomato salad or with a mornay or tomato sauce.

Serves 4 to 6.

Quiche lorraine

METRIC	IMPERIAL
Shortcrust pastry, made with 150 g. flour, 75 g. fat, etc.	Shortcrust pastry, made with 6 oz. flour, 3 oz. fat, etc.
25 g. butter	1 oz. butter
1 onion, peeled and finely chopped	1 onion, peeled and finely chopped
100 g. streaky bacon, rinded and chopped	4 oz. streaky bacon, rinded and chopped
2 large eggs	2 large eggs
50 g. Cheddar cheese, grated	2 oz. Cheddar cheese, grated
150 ml. milk	$\frac{1}{4}$ pint milk
150 ml. single cream	$\frac{1}{4}$ pint single cream
Salt and freshly ground black pepper	Salt and freshly ground black pepper

Quiche lorraine

Gnocchi

Gnocchi

METRIC	IMPERIAL
600 ml. milk	1 pint milk
Pinch of nutmeg	Pinch of nutmeg
Salt and freshly ground black pepper	Salt and freshly ground black pepper
100 g. fine semolina	4 oz. fine semolina
75 g. Cheddar cheese, finely grated	3 oz. Cheddar cheese, finely grated
50 g. butter	2 oz. butter
5 ml. made English mustard	1 teaspoon made English mustard
1 egg, beaten	1 egg, beaten

Heat the milk in a saucepan, and add the nutmeg and seasoning to taste. Sprinkle in the semolina and stir constantly until the mixture comes to the boil, reduce the heat and cook gently for 1 minute, or until the mixture thickens.

Remove the saucepan from the heat, and stir in 50 g./2 oz. of the cheese, half the butter, mustard and beaten egg. Return the saucepan to the heat and cook, stirring continuously, for 1 minute. Turn the mixture into an oiled tin 20 × 30 cm./8 × 12 in. and spread the mixture out to $\frac{1}{2}$ cm./$\frac{1}{4}$ in. thick. Cover and leave in a cool place for at least 2 hours or until set.

When firm, cut the mixture into 4 cm./1$\frac{1}{2}$ in. squares or circles and arrange the pieces overlapping in a buttered

Gazpacho

Roll out the pastry and use to line a 20 cm./8 in. flan ring set on a baking tray. Place in the refrigerator to chill for 15 minutes.

Melt the butter in a saucepan, add the onion and bacon and fry until golden brown. Cool slightly, then put into the pastry case. Beat together the eggs, cheese, milk, cream and seasoning to taste and pour into the flan case. Cook in the centre of a moderate oven (180°C/350°F or Gas Mark 4) for 35 minutes, or until the filling is set. Leave to cool.

To freeze: When cold, open freeze the flan on the baking tray. When frozen, remove the flan ring, wrap the flan, seal and return to the freezer.

To serve: Leave to thaw wrapped at room temperature for 4 hours. Unwrap, replace the flan ring and reheat on a baking tray, in a moderate oven (180°C/350°F or Gas Mark 4) for 25–30 minutes or until warmed through.

Serves 6.

Gazpacho

METRIC	IMPERIAL
½ kg. ripe tomatoes, skinned, seeded and chopped	1 lb. ripe tomatoes, skinned, seeded and chopped
1 small onion, peeled and finely grated	1 small onion, peeled and finely grated
1 garlic clove crushed with 2.5 ml. salt	1 garlic clove crushed with ½ teaspoon salt
30 ml. lemon juice	2 tablespoons lemon juice
15 ml. olive oil	1 tablespoon olive oil
1 × 400 ml. can tomato juice	1 × 15 fl.oz. can tomato juice
Freshly ground black pepper	Freshly ground black pepper

Purée the tomatoes in a food mill or blender, transfer to a bowl and add the onion and garlic. Stir in the lemon juice, olive oil, tomato juice and pepper to taste.

To freeze: Pour soup into rigid containers, in usable quantities. Cover, seal and freeze.

To serve: Thaw overnight in a refrigerator, or at room temperature for 5 hours. Beat well to produce a smooth consistency, taste and adjust the seasoning. Serve chilled with the classic accompaniments of sliced or diced cucumber, sliced green pepper, sliced tomatoes and croûtons, served separately in small dishes.

Serves 4.

Vichyssoise; Iced shrimp soup

Iced shrimp soup

METRIC
1 × 400 g. can cream of
  celery soup
1 × 454 ml. can tomato
  juice
Pinch of cayenne pepper
Juice of ½ a lemon
100 g. shrimps, peeled and
  roughly chopped
Salt and freshly ground
  black pepper

IMPERIAL
1 × 14 oz. can cream of
  celery soup
1 × 16 fl.oz. can tomato
  juice
Pinch of cayenne pepper
Juice of ½ a lemon
4 oz. shrimps, peeled and
  roughly chopped
Salt and freshly ground
  black pepper

Whisk together the celery soup, tomato juice, cayenne pepper and lemon juice. Add the shrimps and seasoning to taste.
To freeze: Pour the soup into rigid containers, in usable quantities. Cover, seal and freeze.
To serve: Allow to thaw in a refrigerator overnight. Stir in 150 ml./¼ pint single cream, taste and adjust the seasoning.

Garnish with a swirl of cream and a little chopped parsley before serving.
Serves 6.

Vichyssoise

METRIC
50 g. butter
3 medium onions, peeled and
  chopped
1 kg. potatoes, peeled and
  diced
1 kg. leeks, fresh or frozen,
  sliced
600 ml. chicken stock
Salt and freshly ground
  black pepper

IMPERIAL
2 oz. butter
3 medium onions, peeled and
  chopped
2 lb. potatoes, peeled and
  diced
2 lb. leeks, fresh or frozen,
  sliced
1 pint chicken stock
Salt and freshly ground
  black pepper

Melt the butter in a saucepan, add the onions, potatoes, and leeks and fry gently for 5 minutes. Stir in the stock and seasoning to taste and bring to the boil. Cover the pan and simmer for 40 minutes or until the vegetables are tender. Purée in a food mill or blender.
To freeze: Cool quickly and pour into rigid containers, in usable quantities. Cover, seal and freeze.
To serve: *hot* – Tip the frozen soup into a saucepan, add 300 ml./½ pint chicken stock and 600 ml./1 pint creamy milk and reheat gently. Taste and adjust the seasoning.
To serve: *cold* – Thaw overnight in the refrigerator. Stir in 300 ml./½ pint chicken stock and 600 ml./1 pint creamy milk. Taste and adjust the seasoning. Serve chilled, garnished with snipped chives.
Serves 8.

58

Cream of watercress soup

METRIC	IMPERIAL
50 g. butter	2 oz. butter
275 g. watercress, washed and roughly chopped	10 oz. watercress, washed and roughly chopped
1 medium potato, peeled and diced	1 medium potato, peeled and diced
1 medium onion, peeled and chopped	1 medium onion, peeled and chopped
400 ml. chicken stock	$\frac{3}{4}$ pint chicken stock
Salt and freshly ground black pepper	Salt and freshly ground black pepper
15 ml. cornflour	1 tablespoon cornflour
30 ml. water	2 tablespoons water

Melt the butter in a saucepan and add the watercress, potato and onion. Cover and cook gently for 3 minutes. Stir in the stock and seasoning and bring to the boil. Cover the pan and simmer for 30 minutes. Purée the vegetable mixture in a food mill or blender and return to the saucepan. Blend the cornflour with the water and add to the vegetable purée. Bring to the boil, stirring constantly, then reduce the heat and simmer for 2 minutes, stirring occasionally.

To freeze: Cool quickly and pour into rigid containers, in usable quantities. Cover, seal and freeze.

To serve: Tip the frozen soup into a saucepan, add 300 ml./$\frac{1}{2}$ pint creamy milk and reheat gently to boiling point. Blend one egg yolk with 150 ml./$\frac{1}{4}$ pint milk, stir into the soup and heat gently without boiling. Taste and adjust the seasoning. Decorate with sprigs of watercress.
Serves 4 to 6.

Cream of watercress soup

Mediterranean fish soup

Mediterranean fish soup

METRIC	IMPERIAL
50 g. butter	2 oz. butter
2 onions, peeled and sliced	2 onions, peeled and sliced
1 garlic clove, crushed	1 garlic clove, crushed
2 leeks, washed, trimmed and cut into rings	2 leeks, washed, trimmed and cut into rings
15 ml. tomato purée	1 tablespoon tomato purée
2 potatoes, peeled and sliced	2 potatoes, peeled and sliced
1 × 396 g. can tomatoes	1 × 14 oz. can tomatoes
Finely grated rind of $\frac{1}{2}$ a lemon	Finely grated rind of $\frac{1}{2}$ a lemon
600 ml. chicken stock	1 pint chicken stock
Bouquet garni	Bouquet garni
Salt and freshly ground black pepper	Salt and freshly ground black pepper
100 g. filleted haddock	4 oz. filleted haddock
100 g. filleted cod	4 oz. filleted cod
30 ml. dry white wine	2 tablespoons dry white wine
100 g. peeled shrimps or prawns	4 oz. peeled shrimps or prawns

Melt the butter in a saucepan and add the onions, garlic and leeks. Cover and cook gently for 5 minutes. Add the tomato purée, potatoes, tomatoes, lemon rind, stock, bouquet garni and seasoning. Cover the pan and simmer for 15 minutes.

Cut the haddock and cod into bite-sized pieces, removing the skin and bones and add to the saucepan with the wine. After 5 minutes add the shellfish, cover and simmer for a further 5 minutes or until fish is tender, stirring occasionally. Remove the bouquet garni.

To freeze: Cool quickly and pour into rigid containers, in usable quantities. Cover, seal and freeze.

To serve: Turn the frozen soup into a saucepan and reheat gently to boiling point. Taste and adjust the seasoning.

Serve with grated cheese and hot garlic bread.
Serves 6.

Cream of vegetable soup

METRIC
25 g. butter
1 large onion, peeled and finely chopped
600 ml. béchamel sauce
300 ml. vegetable purée, e.g., asparagus, carrot, cauliflower, onion, pea, spinach
Salt and freshly ground black pepper

IMPERIAL
1 oz. butter
1 large onion, peeled and finely chopped
1 pint béchamel sauce
½ pint vegetable purée, e.g., asparagus, carrot, cauliflower, onion, pea, spinach
Salt and freshly ground black pepper

Melt the butter in a saucepan and add the onion. Cook gently for 5 minutes. Stir in the béchamel sauce, vegetable purée and seasoning to taste and reheat to boiling point.

To freeze: Cool quickly and pour into rigid containers, in usable quantities. Cover, seal and freeze.

To serve: Tip the frozen concentrated soup into a saucepan, add 300 ml./½ pint chicken stock and heat gently, stirring occasionally, to boiling point. Reduce the heat, and stir in 30 ml./2 tablespoons single cream. Taste and adjust the seasoning.

Serves 6 to 8.

Cream of vegetable soup; Lentil and bacon broth; Country spinach soup; Corn chowder

Lentil and bacon broth

METRIC
50 g. lard
75 g. smoked bacon, rinded and chopped
225 g. onions, peeled and chopped
225 g. carrots, peeled and chopped
175 g. celery, scrubbed, trimmed and chopped
275 g. lentils, soaked overnight and drained
900 ml. chicken stock
Pinch of nutmeg
1 bay leaf
2.5 ml. dried thyme
Salt and freshly ground black pepper

IMPERIAL
2 oz. lard
3 oz. smoked bacon, rinded and chopped
8 oz. onions, peeled and chopped
8 oz. carrots, peeled and chopped
6 oz. celery, scrubbed, trimmed and chopped
10 oz. lentils, soaked overnight and drained
1½ pints chicken stock
Pinch of nutmeg
1 bay leaf
½ teaspoon dried thyme
Salt and freshly ground black pepper

Melt the lard in a saucepan, add the bacon, onion, carrot and celery and fry for 5 minutes, stirring occasionally. Add the lentils and stir in the stock, nutmeg, bay leaf, thyme and seasoning. Bring to the boil, then cover the pan and simmer for 45 minutes to 1 hour or until the lentils are soft. Remove the bay leaf and purée the soup in a food mill or blender. Taste and adjust the seasoning.

To freeze: Cool quickly and pour into rigid containers, in usable quantities. Cover, seal and freeze.

To serve: Tip the frozen soup into a saucepan, add 600 ml./1 pint chicken stock and reheat gently to boiling point, taste and adjust the seasoning.

Serve garnished with snippets of crisp bacon.

Serves 8 to 10.

Country spinach soup

METRIC	IMPERIAL
25 g. butter	1 oz. butter
1 small onion, peeled and finely chopped	1 small onion, peeled and finely chopped
15 ml. cornflour	1 tablespoon cornflour
450 ml. chicken stock	¾ pint chicken stock
Salt and freshly ground black pepper	Salt and freshly ground black pepper
Pinch of nutmeg	Pinch of nutmeg
225 g. frozen spinach	8 oz. frozen spinach

Melt the butter in a saucepan and add the onion. Cook gently for 5 minutes. Stir in the cornflour and cook, stirring constantly, for 1 minute. Gradually stir in the stock, seasoning and nutmeg and bring to the boil. Add the frozen spinach, cover and simmer for 15 minutes, stirring and turning the spinach occasionally. Purée in a food mill or blender, taste and adjust the seasoning.

To freeze: Cool quickly and pour into rigid containers, in usable quantities. Cover, seal and freeze.

To serve: Tip the frozen soup into a saucepan, add 120 ml./4 fl.oz. creamy milk and reheat gently to boiling point. Reduce the heat and stir in 30 ml./2 tablespoons double cream. Taste and adjust the seasoning.

Serve with croûtons.

Serves 4.

Corn chowder

METRIC	IMPERIAL
50 g. butter	2 oz. butter
3 onions, peeled and sliced	3 onions, peeled and sliced
3 potatoes, peeled and diced	3 potatoes, peeled and diced
450 ml. milk	¾ pint milk
1 × 350 g. can creamed sweet corn	1 × 11½ oz. can creamed sweet corn
10 ml. parsley, chopped	2 teaspoons parsley, chopped
Salt and freshly ground black pepper	Salt and freshly ground black pepper

Melt the butter in a saucepan, add the onions and potatoes and cook gently for 10 minutes, stirring occasionally. Stir in the milk, sweet corn, parsley and seasoning. Cover the pan and simmer for 20 minutes or until the vegetables are tender. Taste and adjust the seasoning.

To freeze: Cool quickly and pour into rigid containers, in usable quantities. Cover, seal and freeze.

To serve: Tip the frozen soup into a saucepan and reheat gently to boiling point. Reduce the heat and stir in 150 ml./¼ pint single cream. Taste and adjust the seasoning.

Serves 6.

Minestrone soup

METRIC

3 rashers of bacon, rinded and diced
60 ml. corn or olive oil
2 onions, peeled and chopped
2 carrots, peeled and sliced
1 small potato, peeled and diced
3 celery sticks, scrubbed, trimmed and sliced
2 leeks, washed, trimmed and sliced
225 g. tomatoes, skinned, seeded and chopped
100 g. French beans, fresh (topped and tailed) or frozen
100 g. haricot beans, soaked overnight
30 ml. tomato purée
5 ml. dried basil
10 ml. parsley, chopped
1 l. chicken stock
Salt and freshly ground black pepper
25 g. pasta, e.g., shell, mezzani, little wheels

IMPERIAL

3 rashers of bacon, rinded and diced
4 tablespoons corn or olive oil
2 onions, peeled and chopped
2 carrots, peeled and sliced
1 small potato, peeled and diced
3 celery sticks, scrubbed, trimmed and sliced
2 leeks, washed, trimmed and sliced
8 oz. tomatoes, skinned, seeded and chopped
4 oz. French beans, fresh (topped and tailed) or frozen
4 oz. haricot beans, soaked overnight
2 tablespoons tomato purée
1 teaspoon dried basil
2 teaspoons parsley, chopped
1¾ pints chicken stock
Salt and freshly ground black pepper
1 oz. pasta, e.g., shell, mezzani, little wheels

Fry the bacon in the oil until just turning colour. Add the onions, carrots, potato, celery, leeks, tomatoes and French beans (if using fresh), cover and cook gently, stirring occasionally, for 5 minutes. Add the drained haricot beans, tomato purée and herbs. Stir in the stock, add seasoning and bring to the boil. Cover the pan again and simmer for 1 hour, stirring occasionally. Add the pasta and French beans, if using frozen, 10 minutes before the end of the cooking time.

To freeze: Cool quickly and pour the soup into rigid containers, in usable quantities. Cover, seal and freeze.

To serve: Turn into a saucepan and reheat gently to boiling point, stirring and turning the block occasionally. Taste and adjust the seasoning.

Serve with crusty bread and grated Parmesan cheese.
Serves 8.

French onion soup

METRIC

75 g. butter
¾ kg. onions, peeled and sliced finely into rings
15 ml. cornflour
600 ml. beef stock
Salt and freshly ground black pepper

IMPERIAL

3 oz. butter
1½ lb. onions, peeled and sliced finely into rings
1 tablespoon cornflour
1 pint beef stock
Salt and freshly ground black pepper

Melt the butter in a heavy saucepan and add the onion rings. Cook gently for 12–15 minutes, stirring occasionally, until golden brown.

Stir in the cornflour, and after 2 minutes, gradually add the

stock, stirring continuously. Season to taste, cover the pan and simmer for 30 minutes.

To freeze: Cool quickly and pour into rigid containers, in usable quantities. Cover, seal and freeze.

To serve: Tip the frozen soup into a saucepan, add 450 ml./¾ pint beef stock and reheat gently to boiling point.

Taste and adjust the seasoning.

When serving, pour the hot soup into warmed soup bowls. Toast 6 slices of French bread then top each with a slice of Cheddar or Gruyère cheese, brown under the grill and float one slice in each bowl.
Serves 6.

Tomato soup

METRIC	IMPERIAL
50 g. butter	2 oz. butter
100 g. bacon, rinded and diced	4 oz. bacon, rinded and diced
225 g. onions, peeled and chopped	8 oz. onions, peeled and chopped
1 kg. tomatoes, skinned and roughly chopped	2 lb. tomatoes, skinned and roughly chopped
10 ml. cornflour	2 teaspoons cornflour
300 ml. chicken stock	$\frac{1}{2}$ pint chicken stock
1 bay leaf	1 bay leaf
Pinch of nutmeg	Pinch of nutmeg
2.5 ml. sugar	$\frac{1}{2}$ teaspoon sugar
Salt and freshly ground black pepper	Salt and freshly ground black pepper

Melt the butter in the saucepan, add the bacon and fry gently until just turning colour. Add the onions and tomatoes. Cover and cook gently, stirring occasionally for 5 minutes. Stir in the cornflour and gradually add the chicken stock, stirring constantly. Add the bay leaf, nutmeg, sugar and seasoning and bring to the boil. Cover the pan and simmer for 30 minutes, stirring occasionally. Remove the bay leaf and put vegetable mixture through a sieve.

To freeze: Cool quickly and pour into rigid containers, in usable quantities. Cover, seal and freeze.

To serve: Turn the frozen soup into a saucepan, add 300 ml./$\frac{1}{2}$ pint chicken stock and reheat to boiling point. Taste and adjust the seasoning. A little concentrated tomato purée may be added if the soup lacks flavour.

Serve the soup garnished with toasted cheese croûtons.
Serves 6.

Garlic bread

METRIC	IMPERIAL
1 French loaf	1 French loaf
225 g. butter, softened	8 oz. butter, softened
2 garlic cloves, crushed	2 garlic cloves, crushed
5 ml. mixed herbs	1 teaspoon mixed herbs

Make cuts approximately 2 cm./1 in. apart into but not quite through a French loaf. Cream the butter with the garlic and herbs until thoroughly mixed and spread between the slices.

To freeze: Wrap the loaf in foil and place in a polythene bag. Seal and freeze.

To serve: Remove polythene bag and place foil-wrapped frozen loaf in a moderate oven (180°C/350°F or Gas Mark 4) for 15 minutes then fold back the foil and increase the temperature to (230°C/450°F or Gas Mark 8) for a further 10 minutes or until crisp. Serve hot.

Minestrone soup; French onion soup; Tomato soup; Garlic bread

Sauces, Stuffings and Savoury Butters

Savoury butters

These are a useful 'extra' to keep in your freezer, for they can be used straight from the freezer on grilled meat, poached fish and cooked vegetables or, softened, for sandwiches, canapés and toast. Use slightly salted butter or add a little salt if using unsalted butter.

Parsley butter

Serve with grilled meats and grilled or baked white fish.

METRIC	IMPERIAL
100 g. softened butter	*4 oz. softened butter*
30 ml. parsley, finely chopped	*2 tablespoons parsley, finely chopped*
Squeeze of lemon juice	*Squeeze of lemon juice*
Freshly ground black pepper	*Freshly ground black pepper*

Beat all the ingredients together in a bowl until thoroughly mixed. Using cool, wet hands, shape the butter into a roll about 3 cm./1½ in. in diameter.
To freeze: Wrap the butter in foil or freezer paper and pack in a polythene bag. Seal and freeze.
To serve: Unwrap the frozen butter and cut into slices using a knife dipped in hot water.

Mustard butter

Serve with baked fish and with grilled gammon.

METRIC	IMPERIAL
100 g. softened butter	*4 oz. softened butter*
15 ml. French mustard	*1 tablespoon French mustard*

Beat the butter and mustard together in a bowl until thoroughly mixed. Using cool, wet hands, shape the butter into a roll about 3 cm./1½ in. in diameter.
To freeze: Wrap the butter in foil or freezer paper and pack in a polythene bag. Seal and freeze.
To serve: Unwrap the frozen butter and cut into slices using a knife dipped in hot water.

Herb butter

Serve on grilled meats and hot vegetables.

METRIC	IMPERIAL
100 g. softened butter	*4 oz. softened butter*
30 ml. mixed fresh herbs, finely chopped	*2 tablespoons mixed fresh herbs, finely chopped*
Pinch of cayenne pepper	*Pinch of cayenne pepper*

Beat all the ingredients together in a bowl until thoroughly mixed. Using cool, wet hands, shape the butter into a roll about 3 cm./1½ in. in diameter.
To freeze: Wrap the butter in foil or freezer paper and pack in a polythene bag. Seal and freeze.
To serve: Unwrap the frozen butter and cut into slices using a knife dipped in hot water.

Lemon butter

Serve with grilled or baked fish, veal and chicken.

METRIC	IMPERIAL
100 g. softened butter	*4 oz. softened butter*
10 ml. lemon rind, finely grated	*2 teaspoons lemon rind, finely grated*
10 ml. lemon juice	*2 teaspoons lemon juice*

Savoury butters

Beat all the ingredients together in a bowl until thoroughly mixed. Using cool, wet hands, shape the butter into a roll approximately 3 cm./1½ in. in diameter.
To freeze: Wrap the butter in foil or freezer paper and pack in a polythene bag. Seal and freeze.
To serve: Unwrap the frozen butter and cut into slices using a knife dipped in hot water.

Anchovy butter

Serve with poached fish.

METRIC
100 g. softened butter
10 ml. anchovy essence
10 ml. parsley, finely
   chopped

IMPERIAL
4 oz. softened butter
2 teaspoons anchovy essence
2 teaspoons parsley, finely
   chopped

Beat all the ingredients together in a bowl until thoroughly mixed. Using cool, wet hands, shape the butter into a roll about 3 cm./1½ in. in diameter.

To freeze: Wrap the butter in foil or freezer paper and pack in a polythene bag. Seal and freeze.

To serve: Unwrap the frozen butter and cut into slices using a knife dipped into hot water.

Chicken stock

METRIC	IMPERIAL
2 chicken carcasses, including giblets	2 chicken carcasses, including giblets
2 carrots, peeled and sliced	2 carrots, peeled and sliced
2 onions, peeled and sliced	2 onions, peeled and sliced
1 leek, trimmed, washed and sliced	1 leek, trimmed, washed and sliced
5 ml. salt	1 teaspoon salt
4 black peppercorns	4 black peppercorns
1 bay leaf	1 bay leaf
5 ml. dried mixed herbs	1 teaspoon dried mixed herbs
1 sprig fresh parsley	1 sprig fresh parsley

Break the carcasses into pieces and place them, with the giblets, in a large saucepan. Cover with cold water and add the remaining ingredients. Bring slowly to the boil, skimming off any scum with a spoon. Cover, reduce the heat and simmer for 1½ hours, adding more water if level drops below that of the bones. Remove from the heat, strain and allow to cool. Skim off any fat.

To freeze: Pour the stock, in usable quantities, into rigid containers. Cover, seal and freeze. Alternatively the strained stock may be reduced by boiling briskly, cooled and frozen in ice cube trays. When frozen transfer the cubes to a polythene bag, seal and return to the freezer.

To serve: Add the frozen stock to soups, casseroles, etc., or reheat in a saucepan, stirring, and use as required.

Chicken stock; Beef stock

Beef stock

METRIC	IMPERIAL
1½ kg. shin or neck of beef, or beef bones	3 lb. shin or neck of beef, or beef bones
3 carrots, peeled and sliced	3 carrots, peeled and sliced
2 onions, peeled and sliced	2 onions, peeled and sliced
1 leek, trimmed, washed and sliced	1 leek, trimmed, washed and sliced
1 celery stalk, scrubbed and sliced	1 celery stalk, scrubbed and sliced
1 bay leaf	1 bay leaf
1 sprig fresh thyme	1 sprig fresh thyme
1 sprig fresh parsley	1 sprig fresh parsley
5 ml. salt	1 teaspoon salt
6 black peppercorns	6 black peppercorns
2 cloves	2 cloves

Chop the beef bones into pieces and place them in a large saucepan. Cover with cold water and add the remaining ingredients.

Bring slowly to the boil, skimming off any scum with a spoon. Cover, reduce the heat and simmer gently for at least 2–3 hours, adding more water if level drops below that of the bones. Remove from the heat, strain and allow to cool. Skim off any fat.

To freeze: Pour the stock, in usable quantities, into rigid containers. Cover, seal and freeze. Alternatively the strained stock may be reduced by boiling briskly, cooled and frozen in ice cube trays. When frozen transfer the cubes to a polythene bag, seal and return to the freezer.

To serve: Add the frozen stock to soups, casseroles, etc., or reheat gently in a saucepan, stirring occasionally and use as required.

Béchamel sauce

METRIC	IMPERIAL
600 ml. milk	1 pint milk
1 small onion, peeled and chopped roughly	1 small onion, peeled and chopped roughly
1 carrot, peeled and sliced	1 carrot, peeled and sliced
1 small stick of celery, scrubbed, trimmed and chopped	1 small stick of celery, scrubbed, trimmed and chopped
1 bay leaf	1 bay leaf
3 peppercorns	3 peppercorns
25 g. butter	1 oz. butter
25 g. cornflour	1 oz. cornflour
Salt and freshly ground black pepper	Salt and freshly ground black pepper

Place the milk, onion, carrot, celery, bay leaf and peppercorns in a saucepan, bring to the boil and remove from the heat. Cover the pan and leave to infuse for 20 minutes, then strain.

Melt the butter in a saucepan and stir in the cornflour. Cook gently for 2 minutes, stirring constantly. Remove from the heat and gradually add the strained milk, stirring briskly until the sauce is smooth. Return to the heat, bring to the boil, then reduce the heat and simmer for 3 minutes. Add seasoning to taste.

To freeze: Cool quickly and pour into rigid containers, in usable quantities. Cover, seal and freeze.

Béchamel sauce

To serve: Tip the frozen sauce into a saucepan and reheat gently, stirring, until hot. Taste and adjust the seasoning. **Makes 600 ml./1 pint.**

Mustard sauce

To serve with herrings, white fish and salt beef.

METRIC	IMPERIAL
15 ml. dry English mustard	*1 tablespoon dry English*
5 ml. malt vinegar	*mustard*
5 ml. water	*1 teaspoon malt vinegar*
300 ml. béchamel sauce	*1 teaspoon water*
	½ pint béchamel sauce

Blend the mustard, vinegar and water to a smooth paste, stir into the basic béchamel sauce and bring to the boil, stirring constantly.
To freeze: Cool quickly and pack into rigid containers, in usable quantities. Cover, seal and freeze.
To serve: Tip the frozen sauce into a saucepan and reheat gently, stirring, until hot. Taste and adjust the seasoning.
Makes 300 ml./½ pint.

Mornay sauce

A cheese sauce to serve with vegetables, poached fish and chicken.

METRIC	IMPERIAL
50 g. Cheddar cheese, grated	*2 oz. Cheddar cheese, grated*
5 ml. made English mustard	*1 teaspoon made English*
Salt and freshly ground	*mustard*
black pepper	*Salt and freshly ground*
300 ml. béchamel sauce	*black pepper*
	½ pint béchamel sauce

Add the cheese, mustard and a little seasoning to the basic béchamel sauce and stir over a low heat until the cheese has melted.
To freeze: Cool quickly and pack into rigid containers, in usable quantities. Cover, seal and freeze.
To serve: Tip the frozen sauce into a saucepan and reheat gently, stirring until hot. Do not allow to boil. When hot, stir in 30 ml./2 tablespoons single cream. Taste and adjust seasoning.
Makes 300 ml./½ pint.

Tomato sauce

It is very useful to keep a quantity of tomato sauce in the freezer. Use it in recipes as required or serve it with pasta and dishes such as croquettes, meat loaf etc.

METRIC	IMPERIAL
60 ml. corn oil	4 tablespoons corn oil
225 g. onions, peeled and chopped	½ lb. onions, peeled and chopped
2 cloves of garlic, crushed	2 cloves of garlic, crushed
1½ kg. ripe tomatoes, skinned and chopped or 3 × 450 g. cans tomatoes, drained	3 lb. ripe tomatoes, skinned and chopped or 3 × 1 lb. cans tomatoes, drained
10 ml. sugar	2 teaspoons sugar
Salt and freshly ground black pepper	Salt and freshly ground black pepper
30 ml. tomato purée	2 tablespoons tomato purée
10 ml. dried thyme	2 teaspoons dried thyme
2 bay leaves	2 bay leaves
300 ml. beef stock or white wine	½ pint beef stock or white wine

Heat the oil in a heavy saucepan and fry the onion and garlic for 5 minutes or until transparent. Add the tomatoes and all the remaining ingredients with seasoning to taste. Bring to the boil, stir well, then cover the saucepan, reduce the heat and allow to simmer gently for 30 minutes, stirring occasionally.

Remove the bay leaves and purée the sauce in a food mill or blender. Return it to the saucepan and simmer gently, uncovered, for about 20 minutes or until reduced. Taste and adjust the seasoning.

To freeze: Cool quickly and pour into rigid containers in usable quantities. Cover, seal and freeze.

To serve: Tip the frozen sauce into a saucepan and heat very gently, stirring occasionally. Taste and adjust the seasoning.

Makes 1.2 l./2 pints.

Curry sauce

Pour over hard-boiled eggs, or add cooked meat, or vegetables and serve with rice.

METRIC	IMPERIAL
100 g. lard	4 oz. lard
2 Spanish onions, peeled and chopped	2 Spanish onions, peeled and chopped
225 g. cooking apples, peeled, cored and chopped	½ lb. cooking apples, peeled, cored and chopped
75 g. medium strength curry powder	3 oz. medium strength curry powder
50 g. cornflour	2 oz. cornflour
1 l. beef stock	1¾ pints beef stock
2 tomatoes, skinned, seeded and chopped	2 tomatoes, skinned, seeded, and chopped
Grated rind and juice of ½ lemon	Grated rind and juice of ½ lemon
10 ml. soft brown sugar	2 teaspoons soft brown sugar
30 ml. mango chutney	2 tablespoons mango chutney
Salt	Salt

Melt the lard in a saucepan, add the onion and apple and cook gently for 10 minutes or until golden brown. Stir in the curry powder and cornflour and cook, stirring for 2–3

minutes Remove from heat and gradually add the stock, stirring continuously until blended. Return to the heat, add the rest of the ingredients and bring to the boil, stirring continuously. Cover, reduce heat and simmer for 30 minutes, stirring occasionally. Taste and adjust seasoning.

For a smoother texture, rub the finished sauce through a sieve.

To freeze: Cool quickly and pour into rigid containers in

usable quantities. Cover, seal and freeze. Because of the strong flavour, it is often difficult to remove the curry smell from the container, so use containers which are expendable, such as yoghurt or cottage cheese cartons.

To serve: Tip the frozen sauce into a saucepan and reheat gently, beating well to produce a smooth sauce. Serve very hot.

Makes 1.2 l./2 pints.

Barbecue sauce

Use to brush kebabs, hamburgers, sausages or lamb cutlets during grilling or barbecuing.

METRIC	IMPERIAL
60 ml. oil	4 tablespoons oil
1 large onion, peeled and finely chopped	1 large onion, peeled and finely chopped
2 garlic cloves, crushed	2 garlic cloves, crushed
30 ml. tomato purée	2 tablespoons tomato purée
100 g. soft brown sugar	4 oz. soft brown sugar
30 ml. wine vinegar	2 tablespoons wine vinegar
5 ml. Tabasco or chilli sauce	1 teaspoon Tabasco or chilli sauce
20 ml. cornflour	4 teaspoons cornflour
300 ml. water	½ pint water
Salt	Salt

Heat the oil in a saucepan and fry the onion and garlic gently for 5 minutes or until the onion is soft. Add the tomato purée, sugar, vinegar and Tabasco or chilli sauce and stir well. Blend the cornflour to a smooth paste with a little of the water. Remove the saucepan from the heat and stir in the cornflour paste. Return to the heat, cook for 1 minute, stirring constantly, then add the remaining water and bring to the boil, stirring constantly. Add salt to taste.

To freeze: Cool quickly. Pour into small rigid containers, cover, seal and freeze.

To serve: Turn the frozen sauce into a small saucepan and heat gently, stirring, to boiling point. Taste and adjust the seasoning.

Makes 450 ml./¾ pint.

White pouring sauce

METRIC	IMPERIAL
25 g. cornflour	1 oz. cornflour
600 ml. milk	1 pint milk
15 g. butter	½ oz. butter
Salt and freshly ground black pepper	Salt and freshly ground black pepper

Blend the cornflour to a smooth paste with 30 ml./2 tablespoons of the cold milk. Heat the rest of the milk to just below boiling point and pour onto the cornflour paste, stirring constantly until blended. Rinse the saucepan and return the sauce to the pan. Bring to the boil, stirring constantly, then simmer for 2 minutes. Remove the saucepan from the heat, and stir in the butter and seasoning to taste.

To freeze: Cool quickly and pour the sauce into rigid containers, in usable quantities. Seal and freeze.

To serve: Tip the frozen sauce into a saucepan and reheat gently, stirring constantly, to boiling point. Taste and adjust the seasoning.

Makes 600 ml./1 pint.

White coating sauce

Follow the recipe and method for white pouring sauce, but increase the cornflour to a scant 50 g./2 oz.

Tomato sauce; Curry sauce; Barbecue sauce; White pouring sauce

Apple sauce; Cranberry sauce

right, Bolognese sauce (below); Italian mushroom sauce (above)

Apple sauce

For roast, grilled or fried pork, roast duck and goose.

METRIC	IMPERIAL
½ kg. cooking apples, peeled, cored and sliced	1 lb. cooking apples, peeled, cored and sliced
60 ml. water	2 fl.oz. water
25 g. butter	1 oz. butter
Salt and freshly ground black pepper, or sugar	Salt and freshly ground black pepper, or sugar

Put the apples, water and butter into a saucepan, bring to the boil, reduce the heat, cover and simmer, stirring occasionally, for about 15 minutes or until the apples are soft and fluffy. Beat with a wooden spoon until completely smooth. Season with salt and pepper, or sugar, to taste.

To freeze: Cool quickly and pack into small rigid containers. Seal and freeze.

To serve: *hot* – Melt 25 g./½ oz. butter in a saucepan, add the frozen apple sauce and reheat, stirring constantly, over a low heat.

To serve: *cold* – Thaw covered at room temperature for 4 hours.

Cranberry sauce

For poultry, duck, game, turkey and lamb.

METRIC	IMPERIAL
300 ml. water	½ pint water
100 g. granulated sugar	4 oz. granulated sugar
225 g. fresh cranberries, washed	8 oz. fresh cranberries, washed
25 g. butter, softened	1 oz. butter, softened

Put the water and sugar in a saucepan and heat gently, stirring occasionally, until the sugar dissolves. Add the cranberries and cook briskly for 2–3 minutes, or until the skins pop open. Reduce the heat and simmer uncovered, stirring occasionally for 15–20 minutes, or until soft and reduced. Remove from the heat and beat in the butter.

For a smoother sauce, rub it through a sieve.

To freeze: Cool quickly and pour into small rigid containers. Seal and freeze.

To serve: *cold* – Thaw at room temperature for 3–4 hours.

To serve: *hot* – Tip the frozen sauce into a saucepan and reheat, stirring occasionally, over a low heat.

Bolognese sauce

Serve hot over pasta, in pancakes, or use as a stuffing for peppers, marrow or cabbage.

METRIC	IMPERIAL
60 ml. corn oil	4 tablespoons corn oil
100 g. streaky bacon, rinded and chopped	4 oz. streaky bacon, rinded and chopped
1 kg. minced beef	2 lb. minced beef
3 medium onions, peeled and chopped	3 medium onions, peeled and chopped
2 cloves of garlic, crushed	2 cloves of garlic, crushed
3 sticks of celery, scrubbed, trimmed and chopped	3 sticks of celery, scrubbed, trimmed and chopped
100 g. mushrooms, washed and sliced	4 oz. mushrooms, washed and sliced
10 ml. dried mixed Italian herbs	2 teaspoons dried mixed Italian herbs
Salt and freshly ground black pepper	Salt and freshly ground black pepper
5 ml. sugar	1 teaspoon sugar
1 × 275 g. can tomato purée	1 × 10 oz. can tomato purée
450 ml. beef stock	$\frac{3}{4}$ pint beef stock
150 ml. red wine	$\frac{1}{4}$ pint red wine

Heat the oil in a large saucepan and fry the bacon until golden brown. Add the minced beef, onion and garlic and cook gently, stirring occasionally, for 10 minutes. Add the remaining ingredients with seasoning to taste and bring to the boil. Reduce the heat, cover the saucepan and simmer for 1 hour, stirring occasionally.

To freeze: Cool quickly and pour into rigid containers, in usable quantities. Cover, seal and freeze.

To serve: Tip the frozen sauce into a saucepan and stir constantly over a gentle heat until hot. Taste and adjust seasoning.

Makes 1.5 l./2$\frac{1}{2}$ pints.

Italian mushroom sauce

Serve with liver or pour over pasta and serve with grated Parmesan cheese.

METRIC	IMPERIAL
60 ml. corn or olive oil	4 tablespoons corn or olive oil
175 g. onions, peeled and sliced	6 oz. onions, peeled and sliced
1 clove of garlic, crushed	1 clove of garlic, crushed
225 g. mushrooms, washed and sliced	8 oz. mushrooms, washed and sliced
600 ml. beef stock	1 pint beef stock
10 ml. cornflour	2 teaspoons cornflour
150 ml. dry white wine	$\frac{1}{4}$ pint dry white wine
4 tomatoes, skinned, seeded and chopped	4 tomatoes, skinned, seeded and chopped
30 ml. tomato purée	2 tablespoons tomato purée
5 ml. dried oregano	1 teaspoon dried oregano
5 ml. dried marjoram	1 teaspoon dried marjoram
Salt and freshly ground black pepper	Salt and freshly ground black pepper

Heat the oil in a saucepan, add the onions and garlic and fry gently for about 5 minutes or until soft and transparent. Stir in the mushrooms and cook gently for 5 minutes. Remove from the heat and pour in the stock, the cornflour smoothly blended with the wine, tomatoes, purée, herbs and seasoning to taste. Return to the heat, bring to the boil, stirring constantly and simmer uncovered for 20 minutes, stirring occasionally. Taste and adjust the seasoning.

To freeze: Cool quickly and pour into rigid containers in usable quantities. Cover, seal and freeze.

To serve: Tip the frozen sauce into a saucepan and heat gently, stirring constantly. Add 15 ml./1 tablespoon chopped parsley, taste and adjust the seasoning.

Makes 1 l./1$\frac{3}{4}$ pints.

73

Sweet and sour lemon sauce

Serve with poached white fish, or as a hot party dip for sausages.

METRIC	IMPERIAL
50 g. butter	2 oz. butter
1 clove of garlic, crushed	1 clove of garlic, crushed
25 g. cornflour	1 oz. cornflour
30 ml. soft brown sugar	2 tablespoons soft brown sugar
Salt and freshly ground black pepper	Salt and freshly ground black pepper
1.25 ml. Tabasco sauce	$\frac{1}{4}$ teaspoon Tabasco sauce
Finely grated rind of 1 lemon	Finely grated rind of 1 lemon
120 ml. fresh lemon juice	4 fl.oz. fresh lemon juice
120 ml. chicken stock	4 fl.oz. chicken stock

Melt the butter in a saucepan, stir in the garlic and cornflour and cook for 2 minutes, stirring constantly. Remove from heat and add remaining ingredients, with seasoning to taste. Stir the liquid in gradually until smoothly blended. Return to the heat, bring to the boil stirring constantly, cover, reduce heat and simmer for 10 minutes, stirring occasionally.
To freeze: Cool quickly and pour into a rigid container. Cover, seal and freeze.
Use within 1 month.
To serve: Tip the frozen sauce into a saucepan and heat very gently, stirring constantly. Taste and adjust the seasoning.
Makes 300 ml./$\frac{1}{2}$ pint.

Piquant gherkin sauce

Serve with grilled meat or fish.

METRIC	IMPERIAL
50 g. butter	2 oz. butter
1 onion, peeled and finely chopped	1 onion, peeled and finely chopped
30 ml. cornflour	2 tablespoons cornflour
15 ml. tomato purée	1 tablespoon tomato purée
75 g. gherkins, sliced thinly	3 oz. gherkins, sliced thinly
600 ml. beef stock	1 pint brown stock
30 ml. lemon juice	2 tablespoons lemon juice
5 ml. sugar	1 teaspoon sugar
Salt and freshly ground black pepper	Salt and freshly ground black pepper

Melt the butter in a saucepan, add the onion and fry for 5 minutes or until golden brown. Stir in the cornflour and cook for 1 minute. Add the tomato purée and gherkins. Remove from heat and gradually add the stock, stirring well. Return to the heat, bring to the boil, stirring constantly and simmer gently, uncovered, for 5 minutes, stirring occasionally. Season with the lemon juice, sugar and salt and pepper to taste.
To freeze: Cool quickly and pour into rigid containers, in usable quantities. Cover, seal and freeze.
To serve: Tip the frozen sauce into a saucepan and heat very gently, stirring occasionally. Taste and adjust the seasoning.
Makes 600 ml./1 pint.

Brown sauce

METRIC	IMPERIAL
25 g. lard	1 oz. lard
10 ml. oil	2 teaspoons oil
50 g. streaky bacon, rinded and chopped	1 oz. streaky bacon, rinded and chopped
1 onion, peeled and finely chopped	1 onion, peeled and finely chopped
1 celery stalk, scrubbed, trimmed and chopped	1 celery stalk, scrubbed, trimmed and chopped
25 g. mushrooms, washed and sliced	1 oz. mushrooms, washed and sliced
1 carrot, peeled and sliced	1 carrot, peeled and sliced
15 ml. cornflour	1 tablespoon cornflour
900 ml. beef stock	1½ pints beef stock
10 ml. tomato purée	2 teaspoons tomato purée
1 bay leaf	1 bay leaf
Salt and freshly ground black pepper	Salt and freshly ground black pepper

Place the lard and oil in a saucepan, add the bacon and vegetables and fry gently, stirring occasionally, for 8–10 minutes, or until the vegetables are a rich golden brown. Add the cornflour and stir constantly until the flour turns to a light brown colour. Remove from the heat and gradually add the stock, stirring well. Return to the heat and stir constantly until the sauce comes to the boil and thickens. Add the tomato purée, bay leaf and seasoning. Cover the saucepan, and simmer gently for 30 minutes. Remove the bay leaf and rub the sauce through a sieve. Taste and adjust the seasoning.
To freeze: Cool quickly and pour into rigid containers in usable quantities. Cover, seal and freeze.
To serve: Tip the frozen sauce into a saucepan and heat gently, stirring to break up the sauce, to boiling point. Taste and adjust the seasoning.
Makes 900 ml./1½ pints.

Variations

If frozen brown sauce is used for these variations, it should be thawed first and the sauce should not be refrozen. If fresh brown sauce is made, the variations may be frozen and thawed following the instructions for basic brown sauce.

Bigarade
Traditionally for duck or goose, but this is very good poured over pork chops.

METRIC	IMPERIAL
300 ml. brown sauce	$\frac{1}{2}$ pint brown sauce
Grated rind and juice of 1 orange	Grated rind and juice of 1 orange
30 ml. red wine	2 tablespoons red wine
5 ml. redcurrant jelly	1 teaspoon redcurrant jelly
Salt and freshly ground black pepper	Salt and freshly ground black pepper

Heat the sauce to boiling point, and stir in all the ingredients, with seasoning to taste.

Mushroom sauce

For steaks, chops or beefburgers.

METRIC	IMPERIAL
50 g. butter	*2 oz. butter*
100 g. mushrooms, washed and sliced	*4 oz. mushrooms, washed and sliced*
300 ml. brown sauce	*½ pint brown sauce*
Salt and freshly ground black pepper	*Salt and freshly ground black pepper*

Melt the butter in a saucepan, add the mushrooms and fry gently for 5 minutes. Drain well with a slotted spoon and add the fried mushrooms to the brown sauce. Simmer gently for 10 minutes. Taste and adjust the seasoning.

Sweet and sour lemon sauce; Piquant gherkin sauce; Brown sauce

Sauce melba

A classic sauce to serve over peaches and ice cream or fresh strawberries. If frozen raspberries are used, they need not be thawed.

METRIC	IMPERIAL
45 ml. redcurrant jelly	3 tablespoons redcurrant jelly
175 g. frozen or fresh raspberries	6 oz. frozen or fresh raspberries
15 ml. hot water	2 tablespoons hot water
50 g. sugar	2 oz. sugar
10 ml. cornflour	2 teaspoons cornflour
15 ml. cold water	1 tablespoon cold water
Squeeze of lemon juice	Squeeze of lemon juice

Place the jelly, raspberries, hot water and sugar in a saucepan. Blend the cornflour and cold water to a smooth paste, and stir into the sauce. Bring to the boil stirring constantly and simmer for 2 minutes. Remove from the heat, allow to cool slightly and rub the sauce through a fine sieve. Add lemon juice to taste.

To freeze: Cool quickly and pour into a rigid container. Cover, seal and freeze.

To serve: Thaw at room temperature for 2–3 hours. Beat with a wooden spoon to ensure a smooth sauce.

Makes 300 ml./½ pint.

Sweet vanilla sauce

Serve hot over steamed puddings or poached fruit.

METRIC	IMPERIAL
25 g. cornflour	1 oz. cornflour
600 ml. milk	1 pint milk
30 ml. caster sugar	2 tablespoons caster sugar
5 ml. vanilla essence	1 teaspoon vanilla essence
15 g. butter	½ oz. butter

Blend the cornflour to a smooth paste with 30 ml./2 tablespoons of the milk. Heat the remaining milk until just below boiling point and pour onto the cornflour paste, stirring constantly until blended. Rinse the saucepan and return the sauce to the pan. Bring to the boil, stirring constantly, then simmer for 2 minutes. Remove from the heat and stir in the sugar, vanilla essence and butter.

To freeze: Cool quickly and pour into rigid containers, in usable quantities. Cover, seal and freeze.

To serve: Tip the frozen sauce into a saucepan and reheat gently, stirring occasionally, until hot.

Makes 600 ml./1 pint.

Brandy hard sauce

METRIC	IMPERIAL
100 g. butter	4 oz. butter
100 g. icing sugar	4 oz. icing sugar
100 g. caster sugar	4 oz. caster sugar
15 ml. milk	1 tablespoon milk
30 ml. brandy	2 tablespoons brandy
50 g. ground almonds	2 oz. ground almonds
Finely grated rind of a small orange	Finely grated rind of a small orange

In a bowl, beat the butter until soft and creamy, then gradually beat in the sugar, alternatively with a little milk and brandy. Mix until fluffy and stir in the almonds and orange rind.

To freeze: Pack into a rigid container. Cover, seal and freeze.

To serve: Thaw at room temperature for 2–3 hours. Beat to ensure a smooth sauce.

Serves 6.

Fruit sauce

A batch of fruit sauce in the freezer is invaluable for pouring over ice cream and cold sweets, for mixing with milk for milkshakes and for using in recipes instead of fruit juice.

METRIC	IMPERIAL
½ kg. raw ripe fruit, washed and prepared, e.g. cherries, black or red currants, raspberries, strawberries, gooseberries	1 lb. raw ripe fruit, washed and prepared, e.g. cherries, black or red currants, raspberries, strawberries, gooseberries
60 ml. water	4 tablespoons water
100 g. caster sugar	4 oz. caster sugar

Place the chosen fruit in a saucepan, add the water, cover and simmer gently until the fruit is soft. Sweeten with caster sugar to taste, adding extra if necessary. Pass the fruit through a fine sieve or purée in a blender, and then pass through a sieve.

To freeze: Cool quickly and pour into small rigid containers. Cover, seal and freeze.

To serve: Thaw at room temperature for 2–3 hours.

Makes 450 ml./¾ pint.

Chocolate sauce

METRIC	IMPERIAL
100 g. caster sugar	4 oz. caster sugar
100 g. soft brown sugar	4 oz. soft brown sugar
75 g. cocoa powder	3 oz. cocoa powder
5 ml. vanilla essence	1 teaspoon vanilla essence
10 ml. cornflour	2 teaspoons cornflour
300 ml. milk	½ pint milk
50 g. plain chocolate, broken into pieces	2 oz. plain chocolate, broken into pieces
25 g. butter	1 oz. butter

Place the sugars, cocoa powder and vanilla essence in a saucepan. Blend the cornflour with a little of the milk until smooth and stir into the saucepan with the remaining milk. Stir over a gentle heat until the sugar has dissolved, then increase the heat and boil briskly, without stirring, for 2 minutes. Remove from the heat, add the chocolate and butter and stir until well blended and glossy.

To freeze: Cool quickly, pour into rigid containers, in usable quantities, seal and freeze.

To serve: Tip the frozen sauce into a saucepan and reheat, stirring, until hot.

Makes 450 ml./¾ pint.

Sweet sauces

Prawn stuffing

For fish and tomatoes.

METRIC	IMPERIAL
100 g. fresh white breadcrumbs	4 oz. fresh white breadcrumbs
15 ml. parsley, finely chopped	1 tablespoon parsley, finely chopped
5 ml. finely grated lemon rind	1 teaspoon finely grated lemon rind
75 g. peeled prawns, roughly chopped	3 oz. peeled prawns, roughly chopped
25 g. butter	1 oz. butter
1 small onion, peeled and finely chopped	1 small onion, peeled and finely chopped
Salt and freshly ground black pepper	Salt and freshly ground black pepper
A little milk	A little milk

Place the breadcrumbs, parsley, lemon rind and prawns in a bowl and stir well. Melt the butter in a small saucepan, add the onion and fry for about 5 minutes or until soft and transparent. Stir the butter and onion into the breadcrumb mixture, season to taste and mix well, adding enough milk to bind the stuffing together.

To freeze: Pack the stuffing into polythene bags or foil containers, in usable quantities. Seal and freeze.

To serve: Thaw at room temperature for 3 hours. Use immediately.

Chestnut stuffing

For turkey. Canned chestnuts may be used to save time.

METRIC	IMPERIAL
½ kg. fresh chestnuts	1 lb. fresh chestnuts
300 ml. beef stock	½ pint beef stock
100 g. fresh brown breadcrumbs	4 oz. fresh brown breadcrumbs
Finely grated rind of ½ a lemon	Finely grated rind of ½ a lemon
Salt and freshly ground black pepper	Salt and freshly ground black pepper
50 g. butter	2 oz. butter
1 small onion, peeled and finely chopped	1 small onion, peeled and finely chopped
A little milk	A little milk

With a sharp knife make a slit in each chestnut and cook them in boiling water for 5 minutes. Remove from the heat, drain and peel the chestnuts. Return them to the pan, add the stock and simmer for 20–30 minutes, or until tender. Drain the chestnuts and sieve or purée in a food mill or blender. Place the puréed chestnuts, breadcrumbs, lemon rind and seasoning in a bowl and stir well.

Melt the butter in a small saucepan, add the onion, and fry gently for 5 minutes or until soft and transparent. Stir the onion into the breadcrumb mixture and mix well, adding enough milk to bind the stuffing together.

To freeze: Pack into polythene bags or foil containers in usable quantities. Seal and freeze.

To serve: Thaw at room temperature for 3 hours.

Corn and bacon stuffing

METRIC	IMPERIAL
100 g. fresh white breadcrumbs	4 oz. fresh white breadcrumbs
175 g. canned sweet corn kernels, drained	6 oz. canned sweet corn kernels, drained
15 ml. parsley, finely chopped	1 tablespoon parsley, finely chopped
10 ml. thyme	2 teaspoons thyme
Salt and freshly ground black pepper	Salt and freshly ground black pepper
50 g. lard	2 oz. lard
1 small onion, peeled and finely chopped	1 small onion, peeled and finely chopped
100 g. streaky bacon, rinded and chopped	4 oz. streaky bacon, rinded and chopped
1 egg, beaten	1 egg, beaten

Apple and prune stuffing

For pork, lamb, duck and bacon joints.

METRIC	IMPERIAL
½ kg. cooking apples, peeled, cored and chopped	1 lb. cooking apples, peeled, cored and chopped
100 g. prunes, cooked, stoned and coarsely chopped	4 oz. prunes, cooked, stoned and coarsely chopped
175 g. fresh white breadcrumbs	6 oz. fresh white breadcrumbs
25 g. toasted almonds, coarsely chopped	1 oz. toasted almonds, coarsely chopped
15 ml. onion, peeled and grated	1 tablespoon onion, peeled and grated
Salt and freshly ground black pepper	Salt and freshly ground black pepper
5 ml. dried thyme	1 teaspoon dried thyme
50 g. butter	2 oz. butter
A little milk	A little milk

Place all the ingredients, except the butter and milk, in a bowl and stir well. Melt the butter in a small saucepan, then stir it into the breadcrumb mixture. Add enough milk to bind the stuffing loosely together.

To freeze: Pack into polythene bags, or foil containers, in usable quantities. Seal and freeze.

To serve: Thaw at room temperature for 4 hours.

Sage and onion stuffing

For pork, duck and goose.

METRIC	IMPERIAL
175 g. fresh white breadcrumbs	6 oz. fresh white breadcrumbs
10 ml. sage	2 teaspoons sage
Salt and freshly ground black pepper	Salt and freshly ground black pepper
50 g. butter	2 oz. butter
½ kg. onions, peeled and finely chopped	1 lb. onions, peeled and finely chopped
1 small egg, beaten	1 small egg, beaten

Place the breadcrumbs, sage and seasoning to taste in a bowl and stir well.

Melt the butter in a saucepan, add the onions and fry gently for about 5 minutes or until soft and transparent. Stir the butter and onion into the breadcrumb mixture and mix well, adding enough egg to bind the stuffing together.

To freeze: Pack into polythene bags or foil containers, in usable quantities. Seal and freeze.

To serve: Thaw at room temperature for 3–4 hours.

Sage and onion stuffing; Chestnut stuffing; Apple and prune stuffing; Prawn stuffing; Corn and bacon stuffing

Place the breadcrumbs, sweet corn, parsley, thyme and seasoning to taste in a bowl and stir well. Melt the lard in a saucepan, add the onion and bacon, and fry until golden brown. Stir the onion and bacon into the breadcrumb mixture and mix well, adding enough egg to bind the stuffing together.

To freeze: Pack the stuffing into polythene bags or foil containers in usable quantities. Seal and freeze.

To serve: Thaw at room temperature for 3 hours.

Fish

Mushroom stuffed plaice

METRIC
25 g. butter
1 small onion, peeled and
    finely chopped
½ garlic clove, crushed
50 g. mushrooms, washed and
    finely chopped
Salt and freshly ground
    black pepper
5 ml. dried thyme
10 ml. finely chopped parsley
45 ml. fresh white
    breadcrumbs
2 whole plaice, cleaned
25 g. butter

IMPERIAL
1 oz. butter
1 small onion, peeled and
    finely chopped
½ garlic clove, crushed
2 oz. mushrooms, washed and
    finely chopped
Salt and freshly ground
    black pepper
1 teaspoon dried thyme
2 teaspoons finely chopped
    parsley
3 tablespoons fresh white
    breadcrumbs
2 whole plaice, cleaned
1 oz. butter

Melt the butter in a saucepan, add the onion and garlic and fry gently until soft and transparent. Add the mushrooms and cook for 3 minutes. Add the seasoning, herbs and breadcrumbs and mix well.

Using a very sharp knife, make an incision down the backbone of each fish, on the white side and begin to fillet each side of this cut until an oval pocket is made. Fill the pockets with the stuffing and top with the butter. Place in a buttered ovenproof dish, cover and bake in a fairly hot oven (200°C/400°F or Gas Mark 6) for 30 minutes.

To freeze: Cool quickly, cover, seal and freeze.

To serve: Unwrap and thaw for 3–4 hours at room temperature. Brush with a little melted butter and reheat, uncovered, in a fairly hot oven (200°C/400°F or Gas Mark 6) for 30 minutes or until heated through.

Serves 2.

Mushroom stuffed plaice

82

West country plaice

West country plaice

METRIC
8 small plaice fillets, skinned
1 small onion, peeled and
   finely chopped
25 g. butter
15 g. cornflour
300 ml. dry cider
15 ml. French mustard
15 ml. finely chopped parsley
Pinch of brown sugar
Salt and freshly ground
   black pepper

IMPERIAL
8 small plaice fillets, skinned
1 small onion, peeled and
   finely chopped
1 oz. butter
½ oz. cornflour
½ pint dry cider
1 tablespoon French mustard
1 tablespoon finely chopped
   parsley
Pinch of brown sugar
Salt and freshly ground
   black pepper

Roll up each fillet, arrange in a buttered shallow ovenproof dish and sprinkle over the onion.

Melt the butter in a saucepan, stir in the cornflour and cook for 1 minute, stirring constantly. Gradually stir in the cider, mustard, parsley, brown sugar and seasoning to taste. Bring to the boil, stirring constantly, then remove from the heat and pour the sauce over the plaice fillets. Bake the fish in a fairly hot oven (190°C/375°F or Gas Mark 5) for 10–15 minutes.

To freeze: Cool quickly, cover, seal and freeze.

To serve: Unwrap and thaw at room temperature for 3 hours, then cover and reheat in a fairly hot oven (190°C/375°F or Gas Mark 5) for 1 hour, or until heated through. Taste and adjust the seasoning.

Serves 4.

Sole Véronique

Sole Véronique

If preferred, plaice fillets may be used.

METRIC	IMPERIAL
4 large sole fillets, skinned	4 large sole fillets, skinned
Juice of $\frac{1}{2}$ a lemon	Juice of $\frac{1}{2}$ a lemon
1 small onion, peeled and chopped	1 small onion, peeled and chopped
Sprig of parsley	Sprig of parsley
6 peppercorns	6 peppercorns
Salt and freshly ground black pepper	Salt and freshly ground black pepper
1 wineglass of dry white wine	1 wineglass of dry white wine
25 g. butter	1 oz. butter
25 g. cornflour	1 oz. cornflour
300 ml. milk	$\frac{1}{2}$ pint milk
150 g. green grapes, skinned, halved and pips removed	6 oz. green grapes, skinned, halved and pips removed

Fold each fillet into three and place in a buttered 600 ml./1 pint ovenproof dish. Sprinkle over the lemon juice and add the onion, parsley, peppercorns and seasoning. Pour in the white wine and enough water to barely cover the fish. Cover with foil and bake in a fairly hot oven (190°C/375°F or Gas

Mark 5) for 20 minutes. Lift out the fish and set aside. Tip the fish liquor into a saucepan and boil briskly to reduce it; strain and reserve 50 ml./2 fl.oz. Return the fish to the washed, re-buttered ovenproof dish.

Melt the butter in a saucepan, add the flour and cook gently for 1 minute, stirring constantly. Gradually stir in the milk and reduced fish liquor and bring to the boil, stirring constantly until the sauce thickens and is smooth. Season with salt and pepper, fold in the grapes and pour the sauce over the fish fillets.

To freeze: Cool quickly. Cover, seal and freeze.

To serve: Thaw unwrapped at room temperature for 4 hours. Cover and place in a moderate oven (180°C/350°F or Gas Mark 4) for 40–50 minutes or until heated through.

Serves 4.

Haddock provençale

METRIC	IMPERIAL
30 ml. olive oil	2 tablespoons olive oil
2 shallots, peeled and finely chopped	2 shallots, peeled and finely chopped
1 clove of garlic, crushed	1 clove of garlic, crushed
50 g. mushrooms, washed and sliced	2 oz. mushrooms, washed and sliced
1 × 225 g. can tomatoes	1 × 8 oz. can tomatoes
120 ml. dry white wine	4 fl.oz. dry white wine
Salt and freshly ground black pepper	Salt and freshly ground black pepper
2.5 ml. dried thyme	$\frac{1}{2}$ teaspoon dried thyme
50 g. butter	2 oz. butter
4 frozen haddock portions, thawed	4 frozen haddock portions, thawed

Heat the olive oil in a saucepan and fry the shallots and garlic until transparent. Stir in the mushrooms and cook gently for 4 minutes. Add the tomatoes, wine, seasoning and thyme and bring to the boil, reduce to simmering point and cook gently stirring occasionally for 20 minutes.

Heat the butter in a large frying pan and fry the haddock for 2 minutes on either side. Pour over the sauce and simmer for 10 minutes. Taste and adjust the seasoning.

To freeze: Cool quickly and pack the fish and sauce into a foil container. Cover, seal and freeze.

To serve: Place the frozen fish, covered, in a moderate oven (180°C/350°F or Gas Mark 4) for 30 minutes. Uncover and heat for a further 30 minutes. Taste and adjust the seasoning.

Serves 4.

Mackerel in foil

METRIC
4 medium-sized mackerel
175 g. butter
1 large onion, peeled and
    finely chopped
Juice and rind of 1 lemon
Salt and freshly ground
    black pepper
10 ml. made English mustard
15 ml. parsley, finely
    chopped

IMPERIAL
4 medium-sized mackerel
6 oz. butter
1 large onion, peeled and
    finely chopped
Juice and rind of 1 lemon
Salt and freshly ground
    black pepper
2 teaspoons made English
    mustard
1 tablespoon parsley, finely
    chopped

Slit the mackerel from head to tail and clean out thoroughly.
Remove the tail, fin, eyes and gills, but leave on the heads.
Wash well and dry on absorbent paper.

Place the butter in a bowl and beat until fluffy and pale in colour. Add the onion, lemon juice and rind, seasoning and mustard, beat well and add the parsley. Divide the butter mixture equally and stuff in the cavity of each fish. Wrap each one in a piece of well-buttered foil to form parcels.

Seal the parcels, transfer to a baking tray and bake in a moderate oven (180°C/350°F or Gas Mark 4) for 20 minutes.
To freeze: Cool quickly and pack the foil parcels into a polythene bag. Seal and freeze.
To serve: Place frozen foil-wrapped fish in a moderate oven (180°C/350°F or Gas Mark 4) for 30–35 minutes or until heated through.

Serve individually in parcels or arrange on a platter and pour over the juice, garnish with lemon and parsley and set capers in position for the eyes.
Serves 4.

Haddock provençale; Mackerel in foil

Cod mornay

METRIC	IMPERIAL
15 ml. instant potato	1 tablespoon instant potato
¾ kg. cod fillets, skinned	1½ lb. cod fillets, skinned
25 g. butter	1 oz. butter
25 g. cornflour	1 oz. cornflour
300 ml. creamy milk	½ pint creamy milk
50 g. Cheddar cheese, grated	2 oz. Cheddar cheese, grated
5 ml. made English mustard	1 teaspoon made English mustard
Dash of Worcestershire sauce	Dash of Worcestershire sauce
Salt and freshly ground black pepper	Salt and freshly ground black pepper
15 ml. grated Parmesan cheese	1 tablespoon grated Parmesan cheese
15 ml. dried white breadcrumbs	1 tablespoon dried white breadcrumbs
15 g. butter, cut into pieces	½ oz. butter, cut into pieces

Lightly butter an ovenproof dish and sprinkle the base with the instant potato. Divide the cod into serving pieces and place in the ovenproof dish.

Melt the butter in a saucepan, stir in the cornflour and cook, stirring constantly, for 1 minute. Gradually stir in the milk and bring to the boil, stirring constantly, until the mixture is smooth and thick. Remove from the heat and add the Cheddar cheese, mustard, Worcestershire sauce and seasoning to taste. Pour the sauce over the fish, sprinkle with the Parmesan cheese and breadcrumbs and dot with the butter. Cook in a moderate oven (180°C/350°F or Gas Mark 4) for 20 minutes.

To freeze: Cool quickly. Wrap in foil, seal and freeze.

To serve: Heat the frozen fish, covered, in a moderate oven (180°C/350°F or Gas Mark 4) for 40 minutes or until heated through.

Serves 4.

Spicy stuffed cod steaks

METRIC	IMPERIAL
4 cod cutlets, each about 100 g.	4 cod cutlets, each about 4 oz.
Salt and freshly ground black pepper	Salt and freshly ground black pepper
25 g. butter	1 oz. butter
1 small onion, peeled and chopped	1 small onion, peeled and chopped
1 small garlic clove, crushed	1 small garlic clove, crushed
100 g. mushrooms, washed and sliced	4 oz. mushrooms, washed and sliced
25 g. fresh white breadcrumbs	1 oz. fresh white breadcrumbs
5 ml. chopped parsley	1 teaspoon chopped parsley
10 ml. lemon juice	2 teaspoons lemon juice
Pinch of cayenne pepper	Pinch of cayenne pepper

Cod mornay; Spicy stuffed cod steaks

Place each cod cutlet on a square of buttered foil and sprinkle with the salt and pepper.

Melt the butter in a saucepan, add the onion and garlic and fry over a gentle heat until pale gold in colour. Add the mushrooms and fry for 2–3 minutes. Remove from the heat and add the remaining ingredients, season with salt and pepper and use the stuffing to fill and cover 4 fish cavities. Seal the foil loosely round the cutlets, transfer them to a baking tray and bake in a moderate oven (180°C/350°F or Gas Mark 4) for 25–30 minutes.

To freeze: Cool quickly and place the foil wrapped fish in a polythene bag, seal and freeze.

To serve: Remove the polythene bag and place the foil wrapped fish on a baking tray. Reheat from frozen in a moderate oven (180°C/350°F or Gas Mark 4) for 25–30 minutes or until heated through.

Serves 4.

Baked lemon and shrimp stuffed plaice

METRIC	IMPERIAL
50 g. butter	*2 oz. butter*
1 small onion, peeled and finely chopped	*1 small onion, peeled and finely chopped*
75 g. fresh white breadcrumbs	*3 oz. fresh white breadcrumbs*
Grated rind and juice of 1 lemon	*Grated rind and juice of 1 lemon*
10 ml. parsley, finely chopped	*2 teaspoons parsley, finely chopped*
Salt and freshly ground black pepper	*Salt and freshly ground black pepper*
100 g. peeled shrimps, chopped	*4 oz. peeled shrimps, chopped*
8 small plaice fillets, skinned	*8 small plaice fillets, skinned*

Topping	**Topping**
300 ml. mornay sauce	*½ pint mornay sauce*
15 ml. grated Parmesan cheese	*1 tablespoon grated Parmesan cheese*
15 ml. fresh white breadcrumbs	*1 tablespoon fresh white breadcrumbs*

Melt the butter in a small saucepan, add the onion and fry gently for about 5 minutes or until transparent. Remove from the heat and stir in the breadcrumbs, lemon rind and juice, parsley, seasoning to taste and shrimps. Spread stuffing over the plaice fillets, roll up and arrange, join side down, in a shallow buttered ovenproof dish or foil container. Heat the mornay sauce gently and pour over the fillets. Sprinkle with the Parmesan cheese and breadcrumbs. Bake in a fairly hot oven (200°C/400°F or Gas Mark 6) for 15 minutes.

To freeze: Cool quickly and cover the dish in foil. Seal and freeze.

To serve: Thaw at room temperature for 4 hours, remove wrapping and bake in a fairly hot oven (200°C/400°F or Gas Mark 6) for 20–30 minutes or until heated through.

Serves 4.

Baked lemon and shrimp stuffed plaice

Fish cakes; Hungarian fish casserole

Fish cakes

METRIC	IMPERIAL
350 g. cooked white fish, flaked	12 oz. cooked white fish, flaked
225 g. mashed potatoes	8 oz. mashed potatoes
25 g. butter, melted	1 oz. butter, melted
10 ml. parsley, finely chopped	2 teaspoons parsley, finely chopped
Salt and freshly ground black pepper	Salt and freshly ground black pepper
1 egg, beaten	1 egg, beaten

For coating

1 egg, beaten	1 egg, beaten
75 g. dried white breadcrumbs	3 oz. dried white breadcrumbs

Place the fish, potatoes, butter, parsley, seasoning and egg in a bowl and mix gently using a fork. Chill the mixture in the refrigerator for 30 minutes. Turn the mixture out on a floured surface and roll into a long cylinder. Cut into 8 portions and shape each into flat rounds. Dip the cakes first into the beaten egg and then coat in the breadcrumbs.

To freeze: Open freeze. When frozen pack into rigid containers with foil or waxed paper between each layer. Cover, seal and freeze.

To serve: Fry the frozen fish cakes in hot shallow fat for 5 minutes on each side, or until golden brown and thawed through.

Makes 8 fish cakes.

Hungarian fish casserole

METRIC	IMPERIAL
1 kg. cod fillet, skinned and bones removed	2 lb. cod fillet, skinned and bones removed
25 g. butter	1 oz. butter
30 ml. corn oil	2 tablespoons corn oil
1 medium onion, peeled and sliced	1 medium onion, peeled and sliced
1 clove of garlic, crushed	1 clove of garlic, crushed
15 g. cornflour	½ oz. cornflour
5 ml. paprika pepper	1 teaspoon paprika pepper
1 wineglass dry white wine	1 wineglass dry white wine
15 ml. tomato purée	1 tablespoon tomato purée
3 large tomatoes, skinned, seeded and chopped	3 large tomatoes, skinned, seeded and chopped
Salt and freshly ground black pepper	Salt and freshly ground black pepper

Cut the fish into 5 cm./2 in. squares. Heat the butter and oil in a saucepan, add the onion and garlic and cook gently until the onion turns transparent. Add the cornflour and paprika and cook gently, stirring constantly for 1 minute. Gradually add the wine and bring to the boil, stirring constantly. Reduce the heat, stir in the rest of the ingredients, cover and allow to simmer for 5 minutes.

To freeze: Cool quickly and pack into rigid containers. Cover, seal and freeze.

To serve: Thaw at room temperature for 4 hours then reheat, covered, in an ovenproof container, in a fairly hot oven

(190°C/375°F or Gas Mark 5) for 25 minutes or until heated through, stirring occasionally. Taste and adjust the seasoning.

Serves 4 to 6.

Goujons

Cod may be substituted for plaice in this recipe if preferred.

METRIC	IMPERIAL
1 kg. plaice fillets, skinned	*2 lb. plaice fillets, skinned*
Flour for coating	*Flour for coating*
Salt and freshly ground	*Salt and freshly ground*
black pepper	*black pepper*
2 large eggs, beaten	*2 large eggs, beaten*
30 ml. milk	*2 tablespoons milk*
Fresh white breadcrumbs	*Fresh white breadcrumbs*
Oil for frying	*Oil for frying*

Cut the plaice fillets into strips 7 cm./3 in. long by 1 cm./½ in. wide. Toss the strips first into flour seasoned with salt and pepper, shake off the excess flour then coat in the beaten egg mixed with the milk and finally coat evenly in breadcrumbs. Chill for 30 minutes in the refrigerator.

Fry the goujons in a frying basket in hot deep fat (180°C/375°F) for 3 minutes or until golden brown and crisp. Drain on kitchen paper.

To freeze: Cool quickly, place on a baking tray and open freeze. When frozen pack in a shallow container with foil or waxed paper between each layer. Cover, seal and freeze.

To serve: Place the separated frozen goujons on a baking tray and reheat in a fairly hot oven (190°C/375°F or Gas Mark 5) for 25 minutes, or until heated through.

Serve immediately with Sauce Tartare.

Serves 6 to 8.

Goujons

Seafood casserole

METRIC	IMPERIAL
½ kg. cod, halibut or any firm white fish fillets, skinned	1 lb. cod, halibut or any firm white fish fillets, skinned
150 ml. dry white wine	¼ pint dry white wine
1 small onion, peeled and chopped	1 small onion, peeled and chopped
2 bay leaves	2 bay leaves
Sprig of parsley	Sprig of parsley
10 ml. cornflour	2 teaspoons cornflour
1 × 400 g. can lobster bisque	1 × 14 oz. can lobster bisque
Juice of ½ a lemon	Juice of ½ a lemon
Salt and freshly ground black pepper	Salt and freshly ground black pepper
225 g. peeled prawns	8 oz. peeled prawns
100 g. crab meat, frozen or canned	4 oz. crab meat, frozen or canned
100 g. jar of mussels (optional)	4 oz. jar of mussels (optional)
45 g. fresh white breadcrumbs	3 tablespoons fresh white breadcrumbs
15 g. butter	½ oz. butter

Cut the white fish into large chunks and place in a saucepan. Add the wine, onion, bay leaves and parsley, bring to the boil, then simmer gently for 5 minutes.

Lift out the fish and reserve it. Strain the fish liquor, blend the cornflour into it and return to the saucepan. Add the lobster bisque and bring to the boil, stirring constantly, then cook gently for 2 minutes. Add the lemon juice and season to taste. Place the prawns, crab, mussels and reserved white fish in an ovenproof or foil dish and pour the sauce over. Sprinkle the top with breadcrumbs and dot with butter.

To freeze: Cool quickly. Cover, seal and freeze.

To serve: Leave to thaw overnight in a refrigerator. Unwrap and reheat in a hot oven (220°C/425°F or Gas Mark 7) for 30 minutes or until the topping is brown and the casserole is heated through.

Serves 6.

Fish florentine

Cod fillets can be used if preferred.

METRIC	IMPERIAL
8 small plaice fillets, skinned	8 small plaice fillets, skinned
Juice of ½ a lemon	Juice of ½ a lemon
60 ml. water	4 tablespoons water
Salt and freshly ground black pepper	Salt and freshly ground black pepper
1 × 225 g. packet frozen leaf spinach	1 × 8 oz. packet frozen leaf spinach
25 g. butter	1 oz. butter
300 ml. white coating sauce	½ pint white coating sauce
30 ml. Parmesan cheese	2 tablespoons Parmesan cheese

Fold the fillets in half and arrange in a buttered ovenproof dish. Pour over the lemon juice, water and seasoning. Cover and bake in a fairly hot oven (190°C/375°F or Gas Mark 5) for 15 minutes or until the fish is just tender. Lift out and reserve the fish and strain off and reserve the liquor.

Cook the spinach according to the directions on the packet, season to taste and stir in the butter. Arrange the spinach in a shallow buttered ovenproof dish and place the drained fish on top.

Heat the sauce and add 30 ml./2 tablespoons of the strained fish liquor. Pour the sauce over the fish and sprinkle with the Parmesan cheese.

To freeze: Cool quickly, cover, seal and freeze.

To serve: Unwrap and thaw at room temperature for 3 hours.

Reheat uncovered in a fairly hot oven (200°C/400°F or Gas Mark 6) for 40 minutes or until heated through and the top is golden brown.
Serves 4.

Seafood casserole; Smoked haddock and tomato flan; Fish florentine

Smoked haddock and tomato flan

METRIC	IMPERIAL
Pastry	**Pastry**
100 g. plain flour	*4 oz. plain flour*
Pinch of salt	*Pinch of salt*
50 g. butter, cut into small pieces	*2 oz. butter, cut into small pieces*
15–30 ml. cold water	*1–2 tablespoons cold water*
Filling	**Filling**
25 g. butter	*1 oz. butter*
1 onion, peeled and chopped	*1 onion, peeled and chopped*
2.5 ml. dried mixed herbs	*½ teaspoon dried mixed herbs*
1 × 225 g. packet smoked haddock, cooked, skin and bones removed and flaked	*1 × 8 oz. packet smoked haddock, cooked, skin and bones removed and flaked*
2 tomatoes, skinned, seeded and chopped	*2 tomatoes, skinned, seeded and chopped*
300 ml. creamy milk or single cream	*½ pint creamy milk or single cream*
3 eggs	*3 eggs*
Salt and freshly ground black pepper	*Salt and freshly ground black pepper*
50 g. Cheddar cheese, grated	*2 oz. Cheddar cheese, grated*

Sift the flour and salt into a bowl and rub in the butter, using the fingertips, until it resembles fine crumbs. Stir in sufficient water to mix to a stiff dough. Wrap in foil and chill in the refrigerator for 30 minutes. Roll out the pastry onto a floured working surface and use to line a 20 cm./8 in. flan ring, set on a baking tray.

Melt the butter in a small saucepan, add the onion and fry until transparent. Spoon the onions into the pastry case, together with the herbs, haddock and tomatoes. Place the eggs, milk and seasoning in a bowl and beat together, then pour into the flan and sprinkle with the grated cheese. Bake the flan in a moderate oven (180°C/350°F or Gas Mark 4) for 35 minutes or until the filling is set.

To freeze: Cool quickly and open freeze. When frozen, remove the flan ring, place the flan in a polythene bag, seal and return to the freezer.

To serve: Unwrap and place the frozen flan on a baking tray in a moderate oven (180°C/350°F or Gas Mark 4) for 40–50 minutes or until heated through.
Serves 8.

fry for 5 minutes or until tender. Stir in the flour and cook for 2 minutes stirring constantly. Gradually stir in the milk and bring to the boil, stirring constantly. Remove from the heat and stir in the undrained sweet corn, fish and seasoning to taste. Add the cream and transfer the mixture to a 1.5 l./2½ pint ovenproof or foil pie dish. Allow to get cold.

Roll out the pastry on a floured surface and use to cover the pie. Seal the edges and use the trimmings to decorate the top.

To freeze: Open freeze. When frozen, place in a polythene bag, seal and return to the freezer.

To serve: Remove from the bag and thaw at room temperature for 3 hours. Brush with a little milk and bake in a hot oven (220°C/425°F or Gas Mark 7) for 20 minutes, then reduce the temperature to moderate (180°C/350°F or Gas Mark 4) for a further 15 minutes or until pastry is golden brown.

Serves 4.

Flaky fish and sweet corn parcels

Puffed topped fish pie

Puffed topped fish pie

METRIC
¾ kg. cod fillet, skinned
400 ml. milk
50 g. butter
1 small onion, peeled and
    chopped
2 sticks celery, scrubbed,
    trimmed and chopped
25 g. cornflour
1 × 300 g. can of sweet corn
Salt and freshly ground
    black pepper
30 ml. single cream
225 g. frozen puff pastry,
    thawed

IMPERIAL
1½ lb. cod fillet, skinned
¾ pint milk
2 oz. butter
1 small onion, peeled and
    chopped
2 sticks celery, scrubbed,
    trimmed and chopped
1 oz. cornflour
1 × 11 oz. can of sweet corn
Salt and freshly ground
    black pepper
2 tablespoons single cream
8 oz. frozen puff pastry,
    thawed

Place the fish in a saucepan, cover with the milk and poach for 10 minutes. Lift out the fish, remove the skin and bones and flake the flesh. Reserve the milk for the sauce.

Heat the butter in a saucepan, add the onion and celery and

Herrings in oatmeal

Flaky fish and sweet corn parcels

METRIC	IMPERIAL
225 g. frozen puff pastry, thawed	8 oz. frozen puff pastry, thawed
225 g. smoked haddock, cooked, skin and bones removed and flaked	8 oz. smoked haddock, cooked, skin and bones removed and flaked
100 g. sweet corn	4 oz. sweet corn
25 g. butter, melted	1 oz. butter, melted
5 ml. curry powder	1 teaspoon curry powder
Salt and freshly ground black pepper	Salt and freshly ground black pepper
15 ml. double cream	1 tablespoon double cream
2 tomatoes, skinned, seeded and sliced	2 tomatoes, skinned, seeded and sliced
1 egg, beaten	1 egg, beaten

Cut the pastry into two and roll out on a floured surface so that you have two 25 cm./10 in. squares.

In a bowl mix together the smoked haddock, sweet corn, butter and curry powder. Season to taste and stir in the double cream. Place equal amounts of fish on the centre of each square and cover with the tomato slices. Brush the edges with the beaten egg and fold in the corners of the pastry to overlap in the centre, giving an envelope shape. Seal securely and glaze with remaining egg.

To freeze: Open freeze, then wrap in foil or place in a polythene bag. Seal and return to freezer.

To serve: Unwrap and place the frozen parcels on a damp baking tray and bake in a very hot oven (230°C/450°F or Gas

Mark 8) for 20 minutes; when puffed reduce the heat to fairly hot (200°C/400°F or Gas Mark 6) for a further 20 minutes or until golden brown.
Each parcel will serve 2.

Herrings in oatmeal

METRIC	IMPERIAL
4 fresh herrings	4 fresh herrings
100 g. oatmeal	4 oz. oatmeal
Salt and freshly ground black pepper	Salt and freshly ground black pepper

Clean the herrings and remove the heads, tails and fins. Slit the fish along the under side and remove the roe and blood vessels. Open out each fish, place cut side down on a board and press firmly down on the backbone to flatten the fish. Turn the fish over and remove the backbone. Rinse and dry with absorbent kitchen paper.

Mix the oatmeal, salt and pepper together and use to coat the fish.

To freeze: Open freeze. When frozen, place in a rigid container with foil or waxed paper between each layer. Seal and return to the freezer.

To serve: Fry the frozen herrings in hot shallow fat for 6 minutes on each side, or until heated through. Drain on absorbent kitchen paper and serve piping hot.
Serves 4.

Fisherman's pie

METRIC
Topping
1 kg. potatoes, peeled
25 g. butter
30 ml. cream or milk

Filling
600 ml. milk
½ kg. haddock fillets
1 onion, peeled and sliced
  into rings
1 bay leaf
50 g. butter
50 g. flour
Salt and freshly ground
  black pepper
100 g. peeled shrimps
100 g. Cheddar cheese,
  grated

IMPERIAL
Topping
2 lb. potatoes, peeled
1 oz. butter
2 tablespoons cream or milk

Filling
1 pint milk
1 lb. haddock fillets
1 onion, peeled and sliced
  into rings
1 bay leaf
2 oz. butter
2 oz. flour
Salt and freshly ground
  black pepper
4 oz. peeled shrimps
4 oz. Cheddar cheese,
  grated

Cook the potatoes in boiling water, sieve while hot or mash well and beat in the butter and cream or milk.

Place the milk in a saucepan, add the haddock, onion and bay leaf and poach for 15 minutes. Strain off and reserve the liquor, discarding the flavourings. Flake the haddock, removing the skin and bones.

Melt the butter in a saucepan and stir in the flour, cook gently for 1 minute, stirring constantly. Remove from the heat and gradually add the fish liquor. Return to the heat and bring to the boil, stirring constantly until the sauce thickens and is smooth. Remove from the heat and stir in the flaked fish, seasoning to taste, shrimps and cheese. Turn into a 1.2 l./2 pint buttered pie dish and cool quickly. Place the creamed potato in a piping bag fitted with a large star nozzle and pipe over the entire surface of the fish.

To freeze: Cool completely and open freeze. When frozen, place in a polythene bag, seal and return to the freezer.

To serve: Thaw overnight in a refrigerator or for 6 hours at room temperature. Remove from the polythene bag and reheat in a fairly hot oven (200°C/400°F or Gas Mark 6) for 1 hour or until potato is brown and crisp.

Serves 4.

Crêpes à la marinière; Fisherman's pie

Crêpes à la marinière

METRIC
50 g. butter
225 g. peeled shrimps
300 ml. mornay sauce
1 × 225 g. packet frozen
    spinach, thawed
30 ml. double cream
8 pancakes, 20 cm. in
    diameter
225 g. smoked haddock,
    finely flaked
Salt and freshly ground
    black pepper

IMPERIAL
2 oz. butter
8 oz. peeled shrimps
½ pint mornay sauce
1 × 8 oz. packet frozen
    spinach, thawed
2 tablespoons double cream
8 pancakes, 8 in. in
    diameter
8 oz. smoked haddock,
    finely flaked
Salt and freshly ground
    black pepper

Melt the butter in a saucepan, add the shrimps and fry gently for 2 minutes. Add them to the mornay sauce, heat gently, taste and adjust the seasoning. Mix the spinach and cream together.

Place the first pancake on a deep ovenproof plate, cover with about ¼ each of the creamed spinach and smoked haddock, then cover with a second pancake and spread with about ⅓ of the shrimps and sauce. Season, top with a third pancake and continue the layering of pancakes and filling until both have been used up.

To freeze: Wrap the plate and pancakes, place in a polythene bag, seal and freeze.

To serve: Remove the polythene bag, loosen the foil wrapping and reheat the frozen pancakes in a hot oven (220°C/425°F or Gas Mark 7) for 50 minutes. Serve piping hot with wedges of lemon.

Serves 4.

Paella

METRIC
120 ml. olive oil
2 cloves of garlic, crushed
2 onions, peeled and chopped
1 stick of celery, scrubbed,
    trimmed and chopped
350 g. long grain rice
Pinch of saffron
6 tomatoes, skinned, seeded
    and chopped
900 ml. chicken stock
12 chicken portions
100 g. streaky bacon, rinded
    and chopped
225 g. peeled prawns
150 g. frozen peas
100 g. cooked mussels or
    cockles, shelled
Salt and freshly ground
    black pepper

IMPERIAL
4 fl.oz. olive oil
2 cloves of garlic, crushed
2 onions, peeled and chopped
1 stick of celery, scrubbed,
    trimmed and chopped
¾ lb. long grain rice
Pinch of saffron
6 tomatoes, skinned, seeded
    and chopped
1½ pints chicken stock
12 chicken portions
4 oz. streaky bacon, rinded
    and chopped
8 oz. peeled prawns
5 oz. frozen peas
4 oz. cooked mussels or
    cockles, shelled
Salt and freshly ground
    black pepper

Heat half the olive oil in a large saucepan, add the garlic and onion and fry over a brisk heat for 5 minutes or until golden brown. Add the celery, rice and saffron, reduce the heat and cook, stirring constantly for 3 minutes. Stir in the tomatoes and stock, bring to the boil, stirring constantly, then cook gently for 10 minutes, stirring occasionally.

Paella

Heat the remaining oil in another large pan, add the chicken and fry gently for 10 minutes. Add the bacon and fry until crisp. Add the fried chicken and bacon to the rice, stir in the prawns, frozen peas, mussels and seasoning to taste. Simmer gently for 10–15 minutes or until the rice has absorbed the stock but the grains are still separate. Add more stock if necessary. For freezing it is better for the paella to be slightly moist.

To freeze: Cool quickly and pack into foil or polythene containers. Seal and freeze.

To serve: Thaw for 4 hours at room temperature, then tip the paella into a greased ovenproof dish, cover with greased foil and reheat in a fairly hot oven (190°C/375°F or Gas Mark 5) for 45 minutes, or until heated through. Stir with a fork at intervals through the cooking time. Garnish with lemon wedges and whole, unshelled prawns.

Serves 8.

Sweet and sour prawns in batter

Sift the flour and salt into a bowl, gradually add the water and beat to make a smooth batter. Leave in a cool place for 15 minutes.

Heat the corn oil in a saucepan, add the onion rings and green pepper, fry briskly for 1 minute and remove from the heat. Drain the pineapple chunks and reserve 150 ml./¼ pint of pineapple juice. Put this juice in a saucepan together with the ginger, brown sugar, tomato purée and vinegar. Blend the cornflour to a smooth paste with the cold water and add to the saucepan. Bring to the boil, stirring constantly, then simmer for 2 minutes. Remove from the heat and add the pineapple chunks. Taste and add seasoning if necessary.

Toss the prawns in the flour, seasoned with salt and pepper. Holding the prawns on a fork or skewer, coat them evenly in the batter. Drop into hot oil (180°C/350°F) and fry for 2 minutes or until golden brown. Drain on absorbent kitchen paper.

To freeze: Cool quickly and pack the prawns in a rigid container with foil or waxed paper between each layer. Cover, seal and freeze. Pack the sauce separately in a rigid container, cover, seal and freeze.

To serve: Tip the frozen sauce into a saucepan and heat gently, stirring occasionally. Drop the frozen prawns into hot oil (180°C/350°F) and reheat for 3 minutes, drain on absorbent kitchen paper.

Pile into a hot serving dish and pour the sauce over.

Serve at once with boiled rice.

Serves 4.

Sweet and sour prawns in batter

METRIC	IMPERIAL
100 g. self-raising flour	4 oz. self-raising flour
Pinch of salt	Pinch of salt
150 ml. water	¼ pint water

Sweet and sour sauce	**Sweet and sour sauce**
15 ml. corn oil	1 tablespoon corn oil
1 small onion, peeled and sliced into rings	1 small onion, peeled and sliced into rings
1 green pepper, cored, seeds removed and sliced thinly	1 green pepper, cored, seeds removed and sliced thinly
1 × 350 g. can pineapple chunks	1 × 12 oz. can pineapple chunks
1 piece of stem ginger, finely chopped	1 piece of stem ginger, finely chopped
15 ml. brown sugar	1 tablespoon brown sugar
15 ml. tomato purée	1 tablespoon tomato purée
120 ml. malt vinegar	4 fl. oz. malt vinegar
15 ml. cornflour	1 tablespoon cornflour
30 ml. water	2 tablespoons water
225 g. peeled prawns	8 oz. peeled prawns
25 g. flour	1 oz. flour
Salt and freshly ground black pepper	Salt and freshly ground black pepper

Curried prawns

METRIC	IMPERIAL
50 g. butter	2 oz. butter
1 large onion, peeled and finely chopped	1 large onion, peeled and finely chopped
1 clove of garlic, crushed	1 clove of garlic, crushed
30 ml. curry powder	2 tablespoons curry powder
15 ml. cornflour	1 tablespoon cornflour
1 large pinch of ground cinnamon	1 large pinch of ground cinnamon
1 large pinch of ground ginger	1 large pinch of ground ginger
30 ml. mango chutney	2 tablespoons mango chutney
15 ml. lemon juice	1 tablespoon lemon juice
10 ml. tomato purée	2 teaspoons tomato purée
300 ml. chicken stock	½ pint chicken stock
½ kg. peeled prawns	1 lb. peeled prawns
Salt and freshly ground black pepper	Salt and freshly ground black pepper

Melt the butter in a saucepan, add the onion and garlic and fry gently for about 10 minutes or until golden in colour. Stir in the curry powder and cornflour and cook stirring constantly for 1 minute. Add the spices, chutney, lemon juice and tomato purée, remove from the heat and gradually stir in the stock. Return to the heat and slowly bring to the boil, stirring constantly. Cover the pan, reduce the heat and simmer for 1 hour, stirring occasionally. Add the prawns and heat through gently for 5 minutes, taste and adjust the seasoning.

To freeze: Cool quickly and pack into rigid containers. Cover, seal and freeze.

To serve: Turn the frozen prawns into a saucepan and reheat

Curried prawns

gently, separating with a fork after 5 minutes and stirring occasionally for about 20 minutes or until heated through.

To serve, place freshly boiled rice on a large serving dish, top with the prawns and sauce and accompany with side dishes of tomatoes, lemon wedges, chutney and sliced bananas in lemon juice.

Serves 4.

Fish steaks portugaise

METRIC	IMPERIAL
1 × 124g. can sardines, drained	1 × 4½oz. can sardines, drained
50g. soft white breadcrumbs	2oz. soft white breadcrumbs
15ml. parsley, finely chopped	1 tablespoon parsley, finely chopped
Grated rind and juice of 1 lemon	Grated rind and juice of 1 lemon
Salt and freshly ground black pepper	Salt and freshly ground black pepper
15ml. milk	1 tablespoon milk
225g. potatoes, peeled, boiled and sliced	8oz. potatoes, peeled, boiled and sliced
1 onion, peeled and sliced into rings	1 onion, peeled and sliced into rings
225g. tomatoes, skinned and cut into quarters	8oz. tomatoes, skinned and cut into quarters
Pinch of dried thyme	Pinch of dried thyme
4 cod steaks	4 cod steaks
25g. butter	1oz. butter
100ml. dry white wine	4fl.oz. dry white wine

Place the sardines in a bowl and mash finely. Stir in the breadcrumbs, parsley, lemon rind and juice, seasoning to taste and enough milk to bind the stuffing together.

Butter a foil dish and cover the base with the potatoes and onion, add the tomatoes and sprinkle with the thyme, salt and pepper. Lay the cod on the vegetables and stuff the fish cavities with the sardine mixture. Dot the fish with flakes of butter and pour over the wine. Cover the dish with foil and bake in a fairly hot oven (200°C/400°F or Gas Mark 6) for 30 minutes.

To freeze: Cool quickly. Cover, seal and freeze.

To serve: Unwrap and reheat from frozen in a moderate oven (180°C/350°F or Gas Mark 4) for 40 minutes or until heated through. Taste and adjust the seasoning.

Serves 4.

Fish steaks portugaise

Scallops au gratin

Scallops au gratin

METRIC
8 scallops

IMPERIAL
8 scallops

Court bouillon
300 ml. water
300 ml. dry white wine
*1 onion, peeled and coarsely
  chopped*
*1 carrot, peeled and coarsely
  chopped*
Piece of lemon rind
1 bay leaf
6 peppercorns
1 blade of mace

75 g. butter
*225 g. mushrooms, washed
  and sliced*
*1 small onion, peeled and
  finely chopped*
25 g. cornflour
*Juice and grated rind of ½ a
  lemon*
*Salt and freshly ground
  black pepper*
15 ml. double cream
*50 g. fresh white
  breadcrumbs*

Court bouillon
½ pint water
½ pint dry white wine
*1 onion, peeled and coarsely
  chopped*
*1 carrot, peeled and coarsely
  chopped*
Piece of lemon rind
1 bay leaf
6 peppercorns
1 blade of mace

3 oz. butter
*8 oz. mushrooms, washed
  and sliced*
*1 small onion, peeled and
  finely chopped*
1 oz. cornflour
*Juice and grated rind of ½ a
  lemon*
*Salt and freshly ground
  black pepper*
1 tablespoon double cream
*2 oz. fresh white
  breadcrumbs*

Remove the scallops from the shells and wash them in cold water. Scrub the shells, dry them and butter the insides.

Place all the ingredients for the court bouillon in a saucepan and boil briskly until the liquid is reduced by half. Reduce the heat to simmering point, add the scallops and poach them for 6–8 minutes or until tender, do not overcook or they will be tough. Remove the scallops, strain the court bouillon and reserve.

Melt the butter in a saucepan and gently fry the mushrooms and onion for 5 minutes. Stir in the cornflour and cook gently for 1 minute, stirring constantly. Remove from the heat and slowly stir in the strained court bouillon (there should be approximately 300 ml./½ pint). Return to the heat and bring to the boil, stirring constantly to make a smooth, thick sauce. Stir in the lemon juice, grated rind and seasoning to taste. Remove from the heat, add the cream and taste and adjust the seasoning. Slice the scallops and stir into the sauce. Spoon onto the buttered shells and sprinkle with the breadcrumbs.

To freeze: Open freeze the scallops. When frozen, wrap individually in foil or freezer wrap and pack together in a polythene bag. Seal and return to the freezer.

To serve: Unwrap and reheat the frozen scallops on a baking tray in a fairly hot oven (190°C/375°F or Gas Mark 5) for 25 minutes or until brown and heated through.
Serves 8.

Shrimp ramekins

METRIC
25 g. butter
100 g. peeled shrimps
300 ml. white pouring sauce
*100 g. Red Leicester cheese,
  grated*
*4 hard-boiled eggs, roughly
  chopped*
*Salt and freshly ground
  black pepper*
*Dash of Worcestershire
  sauce*

IMPERIAL
1 oz. butter
4 oz. peeled shrimps
½ pint white pouring sauce
*4 oz. Red Leicester cheese,
  grated*
*4 hard-boiled eggs, roughly
  chopped*
*Salt and freshly ground
  black pepper*
*Dash of Worcestershire
  sauce*

Melt the butter in a saucepan, add the shrimps and heat gently, stirring occasionally, for 4 minutes. Stir in the white sauce and when heated through, add 50 g./2 oz. of the grated cheese. Remove from the heat and add the hard-boiled eggs. Season to taste and add the Worcestershire sauce. Pour into 4 buttered ramekin dishes and sprinkle with the remaining grated cheese.

To freeze: Cool quickly, wrap, seal and freeze.
To serve: Unwrap and thaw for 1–2 hours at room temperature. Place under a hot grill for 10 minutes or until heated through and brown on top.
Serves 4.

Scampi provençale

METRIC	IMPERIAL
25 g. butter	1 oz. butter
1 onion, peeled and chopped	1 onion, peeled and chopped
1 clove of garlic, crushed	1 clove of garlic, crushed
100 g. mushrooms, washed and sliced	4 oz. mushrooms, washed and sliced
½ kg. tomatoes, skinned, seeded and chopped	1 lb. tomatoes, skinned, seeded and chopped
10 ml. tomato purée	2 teaspoons tomato purée
5 ml. dried mixed herbs	1 teaspoon dried mixed herbs
10 ml. cornflour	2 teaspoons cornflour
1 wineglass dry white wine	1 wineglass dry white wine
Juice of ½ lemon	Juice of ½ lemon
Salt and freshly ground black pepper	Salt and freshly ground black pepper
½ kg. peeled scampi	1 lb. peeled scampi
Seasoned flour	Seasoned flour
30 ml. corn oil	2 tablespoons corn oil

Melt the butter in a saucepan, add the onion and garlic, fry gently until soft and transparent. Stir in the mushrooms and cook for 3 minutes. Add the tomatoes, purée and herbs. Blend the cornflour with the wine and add to the saucepan together with the lemon juice. Bring to the boil, stirring constantly then cover the pan, reduce the heat and simmer gently for 25 minutes. Season to taste.

Toss the scampi in the seasoned flour and fry in the hot oil for 5 minutes, turning frequently. Pour the sauce over and simmer for a further 5 minutes.

To freeze: Cool quickly and pack into a rigid container. Cover, seal and freeze.

To serve: Thaw covered at room temperature for 2 hours. Tip into a saucepan and heat gently, stirring occasionally, for 20 minutes or until heated through. Taste and adjust the seasoning.

Serves 4 to 6.

Scampi provençale; Shrimp ramekins

Meat and Poultry

Foil wrapped
lamb.
September 197

Lamb chops provençale

Lamb chops provençale

METRIC	IMPERIAL
15 ml. olive oil	1 tablespoon olive oil
25 g. butter	1 oz. butter
½ kg. onions, peeled and sliced	1 lb. onions, peeled and sliced
1 green pepper, cored, seeded and chopped	1 green pepper, cored, seeded and chopped
1 garlic clove, crushed	1 garlic clove, crushed
1 kg. neck of lamb chops, trimmed of excess fat	2 lb. neck of lamb chops, trimmed of excess fat
300 ml. red wine	½ pint red wine
30 ml. tomato purée	2 tablespoons tomato purée
5 ml. dried thyme	1 teaspoon dried thyme
5 ml. dried marjoram	1 teaspoon dried marjoram
Salt and freshly ground black pepper	Salt and freshly ground black pepper
Pinch of sugar	Pinch of sugar

Heat the oil and butter in a large pan, add the onion, green pepper and garlic and fry gently until tender. Increase the heat and add the chops, fry until golden brown on either side. Pour in the red wine, tomato purée, thyme, marjoram, seasoning and sugar, bring to the boil then reduce the heat, cover the pan and simmer gently for 1½ hours or until chops are just tender. Stir occasionally to prevent the chops sticking. Taste and adjust the seasoning.

To freeze: Cool quickly, remove any excess fat and pack into a foil container. Cover, seal and freeze.

To serve: Reheat the frozen chops, uncovered, in a fairly hot oven (200°C/400°F or Gas Mark 6) for 45 minutes or until heated through; separate the chops after 25–30 minutes.

Serve garnished with parsley.

Serves 4.

Stuffed breast of lamb with apricots

METRIC	IMPERIAL
100 g. dried apricots, soaked overnight in cold water, drained and chopped roughly	4 oz. dried apricots, soaked overnight in cold water, drained and chopped roughly
1 onion, peeled and very finely chopped	1 onion, peeled and very finely chopped
15 ml. finely chopped parsley	1 tablespoon finely chopped parsley
5 ml. dried thyme	1 teaspoon dried thyme
Grated rind of 1 lemon	Grated rind of 1 lemon
150 g. fresh white breadcrumbs	5 oz. fresh white breadcrumbs
Salt and freshly ground black pepper	Salt and freshly ground black pepper
1 egg, beaten	1 egg, beaten
2 boned breasts of lamb	2 boned breasts of lamb
25 g. butter	1 oz. butter

Place the apricots, onion, parsley, thyme and lemon rind in a bowl, stir in the breadcrumbs and seasoning to taste. Add enough egg to bind the ingredients together.

Lay the breasts of lamb, skin sides down flat on a chopping board, season with salt and pepper and spread the stuffing evenly over each lamb breast. Roll up neatly and secure with string.

Place in a baking tin, brush with melted butter and roast in a fairly hot oven (190°C/375°F or Gas Mark 5) for 1–1½ hours.

To freeze: Cool quickly, wrap, seal and freeze.

To serve: Thaw, uncovered, at room temperature for 5 hours and reheat in a baking tin in a fairly hot oven (190°C/375°F or Gas Mark 5) for 1¼ hours. Remove string before serving.

Serves 6.

Stuffed breast of lamb with apricots

Foil-wrapped lamb

METRIC	IMPERIAL
4 lamb loin chops, trimmed of excess fat	4 lamb loin chops, trimmed of excess fat
30 ml. flour	2 tablespoons flour
Salt and freshly ground black pepper	Salt and freshly ground black pepper
50 g. butter	2 oz. butter
2 onions, peeled and cut into rings	2 onions, peeled and cut into rings
1 garlic clove, crushed	1 garlic clove, crushed
350 g. tomatoes, skinned, seeded and chopped	12 oz. tomatoes, skinned, seeded and chopped
2.5 ml. thyme	½ teaspoon thyme
10 ml. Worcestershire sauce	2 teaspoons Worcestershire sauce
10 ml. chopped parsley	2 teaspoons chopped parsley

Toss the chops in the flour seasoned with salt and pepper. Melt the butter in a frying pan and briskly fry the chops until golden brown on both sides. Remove and place each chop on a large square of heavy duty foil.

Add the onions and garlic to the pan and cook for 2 minutes. Stir in the tomatoes, thyme and Worcestershire sauce, season to taste and cook gently for 5 minutes. Remove from the heat and stir in the parsley. Taste and adjust the seasoning and divide the mixture equally between the 4 chops, spreading it over the top of them.

Fold the foil loosely, to make parcels and seal the edges securely.

To freeze: Cool quickly and place the foil parcels in a polythene bag. Seal and freeze.

To serve: Remove the polythene bag and place the frozen foil-wrapped chops on a baking tray in a fairly hot oven (190°C/375°F or Gas Mark 5) for 50 minutes to 1 hour, or until the chops are tender and heated through.
Serves 4.

Foil-wrapped lamb

Navarin of lamb printanier

Navarin of lamb printanier

METRIC	IMPERIAL
1 kg. boned shoulder of lamb, or lamb fillet, trimmed of excess fat and cut into 5 cm. cubes	2 lb. boned shoulder of lamb, or lamb fillet, trimmed of excess fat and cut into 2 in. cubes
50 g. flour	2 oz. flour
Salt and freshly ground black pepper	Salt and freshly ground black pepper
30 ml. corn oil	2 tablespoons corn oil
50 g. butter	2 oz. butter
225 g. carrots, peeled and sliced	8 oz. carrots, peeled and sliced
225 g. baby turnips, peeled	8 oz. baby turnips, peeled
225 g. button onions, peeled and left whole	8 oz. button onions, peeled and left whole
1 garlic clove, crushed	1 garlic clove, crushed
450 ml. chicken stock	¾ pint chicken stock
10 ml. tomato purée	2 teaspoons tomato purée
Very small sprig of rosemary	Very small sprig of rosemary

Toss the meat in the flour seasoned with salt and pepper, shake off the excess and reserve any flour left over. Heat the oil in a heavy pan and fry the meat briskly on all sides, then remove and reserve it. Add the butter, carrots, turnips, onions and garlic to the pan and fry until they are golden brown. Sprinkle in any left over flour and cook gently for 1 minute. Gradually stir in the stock, tomato purée, herbs and seasoning. Bring to the boil, stirring constantly until the sauce has thickened and is smooth, then return the meat to the pan. Cover, reduce the heat and simmer, stirring occasionally, for 1½ hours or until the meat is tender.

To freeze: Cool quickly and pack into a foil container. Cover, seal and freeze.

To serve: Reheat the frozen Navarin, covered, in a fairly hot oven (200°C/400°F or Gas Mark 6) for 1½ hours, or until heated through. Add 100 g./4 oz. frozen peas after 1 hour. Taste and adjust the seasoning.
Serves 4 to 6.

Soak the beans overnight, drain and put them in a large saucepan. Cover with cold water, bring to the boil then reduce to simmering point for 2 hours.

Heat the dripping or lard in a large pan and add the bacon, lamb, sausage, onions and garlic and fry briskly for 3 minutes. Stir in the tomatoes and herbs and seasoning. Pour over the stock and simmer, stirring occasionally, for 30 minutes.

Put the drained beans in a large buttered casserole and pour over the contents of the pan. (Alternatively, use 2 casseroles, dividing the contents of the pan between them.) Sprinkle with the breadcrumbs and bake uncovered in a very cool oven (140°C/275°F or Gas Mark 1) for 3 hours.

To freeze: Cool quickly, cover, seal and freeze.

To serve: Thaw overnight in a refrigerator. Reheat gently in a warm oven (160°C/325°F or Gas Mark 3) for 1½–2 hours. Taste and adjust the seasoning. Cut the sausage into slices before serving.

Serves 12.

Beef goulash

METRIC	IMPERIAL
50 g. lard	2 oz. lard
1 kg. chuck steak, trimmed of excess fat and cut into 5 cm. chunks	2 lb. chuck steak, trimmed of excess fat and cut into 2 in. chunks
350 g. onions, peeled and sliced thinly	12 oz. onions, peeled and sliced thinly
1 small green pepper, cored, seeded and diced	1 small green pepper, cored, seeded and diced
15 ml. flour	1 tablespoon flour
15 ml. paprika pepper	1 tablespoon paprika pepper
30 ml. tomato purée	2 tablespoons tomato purée
Salt and freshly ground black pepper	Salt and freshly ground black pepper
450 ml. beef stock	¾ pint beef stock

Heat the lard in a pan, add the meat and fry briskly until the meat is sealed and brown. Remove the meat and place in a casserole.

Add the onions and green pepper to the pan and fry until soft. Sprinkle in the flour and paprika pepper and cook for 1 minute. Stir in the purée and seasoning, then gradually stir in the stock and bring to the boil, stirring constantly.

Pour the sauce over the meat and cover the casserole. Cook in a warm oven (160°C/325°F or Gas Mark 3) for 2–2½ hours, or until tender.

To freeze: Cool quickly, skim off any surplus fat, cover, seal and freeze.

To serve: Reheat the frozen goulash, covered, in a moderate oven (180°C/350°F or Gas Mark 4) for 1½ hours or until heated through. Taste and adjust the seasoning. Stir in 150 ml./¼ pint soured cream and sprinkle with chopped parsley.

Serves 6.

Cassoulet

Cassoulet

METRIC	IMPERIAL
1 kg. white haricot beans	2 lb. white haricot beans
30 ml. dripping or lard	2 tablespoons dripping or lard
175 g. fat bacon, diced	6 oz. fat bacon, diced
1 kg. middle neck of lamb, trimmed of excess fat and cut into large serving pieces	2 lb. middle neck of lamb, trimmed of excess fat and cut into large serving pieces
½ kg. garlic sausage, left whole	1 lb. garlic sausage, left whole
2 large onions, peeled and cut into rings	2 large onions, peeled and cut into rings
2 garlic cloves, crushed	2 garlic cloves, crushed
225 g. tomatoes, skinned, seeded and chopped	8 oz. tomatoes, skinned, seeded and chopped
5 ml. dried thyme	1 teaspoon dried thyme
5 ml. dried marjoram	1 teaspoon dried marjoram
Salt and freshly ground black pepper	Salt and freshly ground black pepper
1 l. beef stock	1¾ pints beef stock
175 g. dried white breadcrumbs	6 oz. dried white breadcrumbs

Chilli con carne

METRIC	IMPERIAL
225 g. red kidney beans, soaked overnight	8 oz. red kidney beans, soaked overnight
60 ml. corn oil	4 tablespoons corn oil
2 onions, peeled and chopped	2 onions, peeled and chopped
2 garlic cloves, crushed	2 garlic cloves, crushed
1 kg. lean raw minced beef	2 lb. lean raw minced beef
1 green pepper, cored, seeded and chopped	1 green pepper, cored, seeded and chopped
15–30 ml. chilli powder	1–2 tablespoons chilli powder
5 ml. paprika pepper	1 teaspoon paprika pepper
5 ml. cumin	1 teaspoon cumin
15 ml. tomato purée	1 tablespoon tomato purée
15 ml. flour	1 tablespoon flour
Salt	Salt
2 × 400 g. cans tomatoes	2 × 14 oz. cans tomatoes

Drain the kidney beans and cook gently in boiling salted water for 45 minutes or until almost tender. Drain and reserve about 150 ml./¼ pint of the water.

Heat the oil in a saucepan, add the onion and garlic and fry until golden. Add the beef and green pepper and fry for 5–6 minutes stirring constantly to break up the meat. Stir in the chilli powder, paprika, cumin, tomato purée, flour and salt to taste and cook for 2 minutes. Add the undrained tomatoes and the beans, mix thoroughly and bring to the boil, then lower the heat, cover and simmer for 1½ hours, stirring occasionally, to prevent the meat sticking. If it gets rather dry, add the reserved bean water.

To freeze: Cool quickly and pack into rigid containers. Cover, seal and freeze.

To serve: Thaw overnight in the refrigerator. Turn the mixture into a heavy saucepan and cook over a low heat, stirring occasionally, for 20–30 minutes or until the meat is heated through. Taste and adjust the seasoning.

Serves 8.

Beef goulash

Chilli con carne

Dutch beef stew

METRIC	IMPERIAL
1 kg. chuck steak, trimmed of excess fat and cut into 5 cm. cubes	2 lb. chuck steak, trimmed of excess fat and cut into 2 in. cubes
30 ml. malt vinegar	2 tablespoons malt vinegar
120 ml. corn oil	4 fl.oz. corn oil
Salt and freshly ground black pepper	Salt and freshly ground black pepper
50 g. lard	2 oz. lard
3 large onions, peeled and sliced	3 large onions, peeled and sliced
25 g. flour	1 oz. flour
300 ml. brown ale	$\frac{1}{2}$ pint brown ale
150 ml. beef stock	$\frac{1}{4}$ pint beef stock
Pinch of sugar	Pinch of sugar
1 bay leaf	1 bay leaf

Place the meat in a bowl and pour over the vinegar, oil, salt and pepper. Allow the meat to marinate in the liquid for 2 hours.

Melt the lard in a heavy pan and fry the onions until lightly brown. Remove from the pan and add the meat, drained of the marinade, and fry briskly until brown and sealed. Sprinkle in the flour and cook for 1 minute, stirring constantly. Gradually stir in the ale and stock and bring to the boil, stirring constantly. Stir in the sugar and bay leaf, return the onions to the pan and season to taste.

Cover the pan, reduce the heat and simmer, stirring occasionally, for 1½–2 hours or until the meat is tender.

To freeze: Cool quickly and pour into a foil container. Cover, seal and freeze.

To serve: Reheat the frozen stew covered in a fairly hot oven (200°C/400°F or Gas Mark 6) for 1¼ hours or until hot through. Taste and adjust the seasoning.

Serves 6.

Dutch beef stew

Braised beef in burgundy

METRIC	IMPERIAL
50 g. lard	2 oz. lard
1 kg. lean stewing steak, trimmed of excess fat and cut into 5 cm. cubes	2 lb. lean stewing steak, trimmed of excess fat and cut into 2 in. cubes
100 g. streaky bacon, rinded and cut into 2½ cm. pieces	4 oz. streaky bacon, rinded and cut into 1 in. pieces
8 small onions or shallots, peeled and left whole	8 small onions or shallots, peeled and left whole
1 garlic clove, crushed	1 garlic clove, crushed
15 ml. flour	1 tablespoon flour
150 ml. beef stock or canned consommé	$\frac{1}{4}$ pint beef stock or canned consommé
150 ml. red wine	$\frac{1}{4}$ pint red wine
5 ml. dried mixed herbs	1 teaspoon dried mixed herbs
1 small bay leaf	1 small bay leaf
Salt and freshly ground black pepper	Salt and freshly ground black pepper

Melt the lard in a heavy pan, add the meat and fry briskly, a few pieces at a time, until sealed and brown. Drain and place in a casserole. Add the bacon to the pan and fry briskly, then stir in the onions or shallots and garlic and fry for 1 minute.

Sprinkle in the flour and allow to brown, stirring occasionally. Gradually add the stock and red wine, the mixed herbs and bay leaf and bring to the boil, stirring constantly. When the sauce has thickened, add seasoning to taste and pour over the meat.

Cook the casserole, covered, in a moderate oven (180°C/350°F or Gas Mark 4) for 2–2½ hours or until the meat is tender. Remove the bay leaf.

To freeze: Cool quickly, cover, seal and freeze.

To serve: Reheat the frozen beef, covered, in a moderate oven (180°C/350°F or Gas Mark 4) for 1–1½ hours or until heated through. Taste and adjust the seasoning.

Serves 6.

Beef stroganoff

METRIC	IMPERIAL
$\frac{3}{4}$ kg. fillet steak	1½ lb. fillet steak
100 g. butter	4 oz. butter
1 large onion, peeled and finely chopped	1 large onion, peeled and finely chopped
1 small garlic clove, crushed	1 small garlic clove, crushed
225 g. mushrooms, washed and sliced	8 oz. mushrooms, washed and sliced
90 ml. dry white wine	3 fl. oz. dry white wine
Salt and freshly ground black pepper	Salt and freshly ground black pepper

Cut the steak into 1 cm./½ in. thick slices and beat them out thinly between 2 sheets of greaseproof paper with a rolling pin. Cut each slice into strips 1 cm./½ in. wide and 7 cm./3 in. long.

Melt half the butter in a large frying pan, add the steak and fry briskly for 3 minutes or until browned. Remove the steak and place in a rigid container.

Add the remaining butter to the pan and fry the onion and garlic until transparent. Stir in the mushrooms and cook until tender. Stir in the wine, heat through and season to taste. Pour the sauce over the meat.

To freeze: Cool quickly, cover, seal and freeze.

To serve: Allow to stand at room temperature for 4 hours, then tip into a saucepan and reheat gently, stirring occasionally, for 20–30 minutes. Stir in 300 ml./½ pint soured cream and heat through but do not allow to boil or the sauce will curdle. Taste and adjust the seasoning. Serve with noodles or boiled rice.

Serves 4 to 5.

Braised beef in burgundy; Beef stroganoff

Steak, kidney and mushroom pie; Steak and kidney pudding

Steak, kidney and mushroom pie

METRIC
50 g. dripping or lard
2 large onions, peeled and
    sliced
1 kg. lean stewing steak,
    trimmed of excess fat and
    cut into bite-sized pieces
225 g. kidney, cores removed
    and cut into bite-sized
    pieces
50 g. flour
225 g. mushrooms, washed
    and sliced thickly
300 ml. beef stock
2.5 ml. dried marjoram
1 bay leaf
Salt and freshly ground
    black pepper
225 g. frozen puff pastry,
    thawed

IMPERIAL
2 oz. dripping or lard
2 large onions, peeled and
    sliced
2 lb. lean stewing steak,
    trimmed of excess fat and
    cut into bite-sized pieces
8 oz. kidney, cores removed
    and cut into bite-sized
    pieces
2 oz. flour
8 oz. mushrooms, washed
    and sliced thickly
10 fl.oz. beef stock
½ teaspoon dried marjoram
1 bay leaf
Salt and freshly ground
    black pepper
8 oz. frozen puff pastry,
    thawed

Melt the fat in a heavy saucepan, add the onions and fry
gently until transparent. Toss the steak and kidney in the
flour, shake off the excess and fry the meat briskly in the fat
until sealed and brown. Add the mushrooms and sprinkle in
any left over flour. Cook for 1 minute, then gradually stir in
the stock, marjoram, bay leaf and seasoning to taste. Bring to
the boil, stirring constantly, then cover, reduce heat and
simmer for 1–2 hours or until the meat is tender.

Remove the bay leaf, turn the meat into a foil or ovenproof
pie dish, put in a pie funnel and allow to cool. Roll out the
pastry on a floured surface. Dampen the edge of the pie dish
with water and cover the meat with the pastry, cutting an air
vent above the pie funnel. Press down firmly to seal the edges
and trim off any excess pastry. Use the trimmings to make
leaves to decorate the top of the pie.

To freeze: Wrap the pie in foil, seal and freeze.

To serve: Unwrap and brush the pastry with egg to glaze.
Place the pie in a hot oven (220°C/425°F or Gas Mark 7) for
30 minutes. Return the pie to the oven, reduce the heat to
moderate (180°C/350°F or Gas Mark 4) and bake for a
further 30 minutes. If the pastry is browning too much, cover
with foil.

Serves 6.

Steak and kidney pudding

METRIC	IMPERIAL
½ kg. lean stewing steak trimmed of excess fat and cut into 2 cm. cubes	1 lb. lean stewing steak trimmed of excess fat and cut into 1 in. cubes
225 g. ox kidney, cores removed and cut into cubes	8 oz. ox kidney, cores removed and cut into cubes
15 ml. flour	1 tablespoon flour
Salt and freshly ground black pepper	Salt and freshly ground black pepper
50 g. lard	2 oz. lard
1 large onion, peeled and chopped	1 large onion, peeled and chopped
150 ml. beef stock	5 fl.oz. beef stock

Suet crust pastry

225 g. self-raising flour	8 oz. self-raising flour
2.5 ml. salt	½ teaspoon salt
5 ml. baking powder	1 teaspoon baking powder
100 g. beef suet, finely shredded	4 oz. beef suet, finely shredded
Approximately 150 ml. cold water	Approximately ¼ pint cold water

Hamburgers

Toss the steak and kidney in the flour seasoned with salt and pepper. Heat the lard in a large saucepan and fry the meat briskly until brown and sealed. Add the onion and cook for 2 minutes, then gradually stir in the stock and bring to the boil, stirring constantly. Reduce the heat, cover and cook for 2–2½ hours or until the meat is tender. Allow to become cold before using.

Sift the flour, salt and baking powder into a bowl, stir in the suet, and mix to a soft pliable dough with the cold water.

Turn out onto a floured surface and knead lightly until smooth. Roll out two-thirds of the pastry and use it to line a lightly greased 1.2 l./2 pint pudding basin or foil basin. Spoon the meat into the suet-lined basin together with the gravy in which it was cooked. Moisten the edges of the suet pastry and cover with a lid rolled from the rest of the pastry. Press the edges together to seal.

To freeze: Wrap in foil, seal and freeze.

To serve: Thaw wrapped overnight in the refrigerator.

Cover with buttered foil with a pleat in the centre to allow for expansion. Secure the foil around the basin with string. Steam the pudding steadily for 2 hours, replenishing the pan with boiling water when necessary.

Serve from the basin with a napkin folded round the outside.

Serves 4.

Hamburgers

METRIC	IMPERIAL
½ kg. raw lean minced beef	1 lb. raw lean minced beef
50 g. fresh white breadcrumbs	2 oz. fresh white breadcrumbs
90 ml. milk	3 fl.oz. milk
1 small onion, peeled and finely chopped	1 small onion, peeled and finely chopped
10 ml. finely chopped parsley	2 teaspoons finely chopped parsley
2.5 ml. made English mustard	½ teaspoon made English mustard
Dash of Worcestershire sauce	Dash of Worcestershire sauce
Salt and freshly ground black pepper	Salt and freshly ground black pepper
Butter or corn oil for frying	Butter or corn oil for frying

Combine all the ingredients together, except the fat for frying, and mix thoroughly. Using floured hands, divide the mixture into 8 equal pieces and shape each into 1 cm./½ in. thick flat rounds.

To freeze: Place the hamburgers on a tray and open freeze. When frozen wrap each individually then pack together in a polythene bag. Seal and return to freezer.

To serve: Heat the butter or oil in a shallow frying pan and fry the frozen hamburgers in the hot fat for 6–8 minutes on each side. Alternatively grill under a hot grill for 8 minutes on each side.

Makes 8 hamburgers.

Mash or sieve the potatoes and beat in the butter, milk and seasoning to taste. Pipe the potato over the meat or spread it over with a fork, fluffing it up to give an attractive finish.
To freeze: Cool completely, wrap, seal and freeze.
To serve: Thaw uncovered at room temperature for 4–5 hours. Brush the topping with beaten egg and bake in a hot oven (220°C/425°F or Gas Mark 7) for 20–30 minutes, or until the topping is brown and the meat heated through.
Serves 4.

Spicy meat balls

METRIC	IMPERIAL
1 large onion, peeled and finely chopped	*1 large onion, peeled and finely chopped*
225 g. lean chuck steak, minced	*8 oz. lean chuck steak, minced*
225 g. lean pork, minced	*8 oz. lean pork, minced*
225 g. lean veal, minced	*8 oz. lean veal, minced*
or use 700 g. lean minced beef for the steak, pork and veal	*or use 1½ lb. lean minced beef for the steak, pork and veal*
100 g. fresh white breadcrumbs	*4 oz. fresh white breadcrumbs*
15 ml. chopped parsley	*1 tablespoon chopped parsley*
Salt and freshly ground black pepper	*Salt and freshly ground black pepper*
5 ml. dried mixed herbs	*1 teaspoon dried mixed herbs*
5 ml. made English mustard	*1 teaspoon made English mustard*
10 ml. Worcestershire sauce	*2 teaspoons Worcestershire sauce*
2 standard eggs, beaten	*2 standard eggs, beaten*
75 ml. corn oil	*3 fl.oz. corn oil*
600 ml. tomato sauce	*1 pint tomato sauce*

Mix the onion and meats together in a large bowl and stir in the breadcrumbs, parsley, seasoning, herbs, mustard and Worcestershire sauce. Add the beaten eggs and mix together thoroughly.

Using floured hands, divide the mixture up into 24 equal pieces and roll each into a ball.

Heat the oil in a large frying pan, add the meat balls and fry, shaking the pan frequently, until the meat balls are golden brown. Drain when cooked on absorbent kitchen paper and pack the meat balls in foil containers.

Heat the tomato sauce and pour equally over the meat balls. Place in a moderate oven (180°C/350°F or Gas Mark 4) and cook for 20 minutes.
To freeze: Cool quickly, cover, seal and freeze.
To serve: Reheat the frozen meat balls, covered, in a fairly hot oven (190°C/375°F or Gas Mark 5) for 45 minutes or until heated through. Taste and adjust the seasoning.
Makes 24 meat balls.

Shepherd's pie

Shepherd's pie

METRIC	IMPERIAL
25 g. butter	*1 oz. butter*
1 large onion, peeled and chopped	*1 large onion, peeled and chopped*
2 carrots, peeled and chopped	*2 carrots, peeled and chopped*
15 ml. flour	*1 tablespoon flour*
300 ml. beef stock	*½ pint beef stock*
15 ml. tomato purée	*1 tablespoon tomato purée*
Worcestershire sauce	*Worcestershire sauce*
2.5 ml. dried mixed herbs	*½ teaspoon dried mixed herbs*
Salt and freshly ground black pepper	*Salt and freshly ground black pepper*
½ kg. lean cold beef or lamb, coarsely minced	*1 lb. lean cold beef or lamb, coarsely minced*
½ kg. potatoes, boiled	*1 lb. potatoes, boiled*
25 g. butter	*1 oz. butter*
Top of the milk	*Top of the milk*

Melt the butter in a saucepan and fry the onion and carrots until golden brown. Stir in the flour and cook for 1 minute. Gradually stir in the stock and bring to the boil, stirring constantly. Add the tomato purée, Worcestershire sauce to taste, herbs and seasoning. Cover the pan, reduce the heat and simmer for 15 minutes. Remove from the heat and add the cold meat, mix well, taste and adjust the seasoning. Turn the minced meat into an ovenproof or foil pie dish. Allow to cool a little before topping with the potato.

Moussaka; Spicy meat balls

Moussaka

METRIC
¾ kg. aubergines, washed
    and cut into ½ cm. thick
    slices
90 ml. olive oil
25 g. butter
2 onions, peeled and sliced
1 garlic clove, crushed
½ kg. minced raw lamb or
    beef
5 ml. dried marjoram
Pinch of ground mace
Salt and freshly ground
    black pepper
15 ml. tomato purée
1 × 400 g. can tomatoes

Sauce
25 g. butter
25 g. flour
300 ml. milk
1 egg yolk
100 g. cottage cheese, sieved
A little grated nutmeg
25 g. Cheddar cheese, grated

IMPERIAL
1½ lb. aubergines, washed
    and cut into ¼ in. thick
    slices
3 fl.oz. olive oil
1 oz. butter
2 onions, peeled and sliced
1 garlic clove, crushed
1 lb. minced raw lamb or
    beef
1 teaspoon dried marjoram
Pinch of ground mace
Salt and freshly ground
    black pepper
1 tablespoon tomato purée
1 × 14 oz. can tomatoes

Sauce
1 oz. butter
1 oz. flour
½ pint milk
1 egg yolk
4 oz. cottage cheese, sieved
A little grated nutmeg
1 oz. Cheddar cheese, grated

Place the aubergine slices on a tray, sprinkle with salt and leave for 30 minutes. Drain off any liquid and dry on absorbent kitchen paper.

Heat the olive oil in a large frying pan and fry the aubergines until soft, adding more oil if necessary; remove from the pan and reserve. Add the butter to the pan and fry the onion and garlic until soft and transparent, stir in the meat, marjoram, mace and seasoning and fry briskly for 8 minutes, stirring frequently to break up the meat. Stir in the tomato purée and canned tomatoes, bring to the boil and remove from the heat.

Butter a deep casserole dish and fill it with alternative layers of the aubergines and minced meat mixture, starting and ending with a layer of aubergines.

Melt the butter in a small saucepan, stir in the flour and cook for 1 minute, stirring constantly. Remove from the heat and gradually add the milk. Return to the heat and bring to the boil, stirring constantly until the sauce is smooth and thick. Remove from the heat and stir in the egg yolk and sieved cottage cheese. Season to taste and add the nutmeg.

Pour the sauce over the casserole and sprinkle with the grated cheese.

To freeze: Cool quickly. Cover, seal and freeze.

To serve: Reheat the frozen moussaka, covered, in a fairly hot oven (200°C/400°F or Gas Mark 6) for 1 hour. Remove the foil and cook for a further 10–15 minutes to lightly brown the topping.

Serves 6.

Meat loaf; Cornish pasties

Meat loaf

METRIC	IMPERIAL
1 kg. lean raw minced beef	2 lb. lean raw minced beef
225 g. sausage meat	8 oz. sausage meat
225 g. fresh white breadcrumbs	8 oz. fresh white breadcrumbs
1 large onion, finely chopped	1 large onion, finely chopped
15 ml. Worcestershire sauce	1 tablespoon Worcestershire sauce
30 ml. tomato ketchup	2 tablespoons tomato ketchup
5 ml. dried mixed herbs	1 teaspoon dried mixed herbs
15 ml. finely chopped parsley	1 tablespoon finely chopped parsley
10 ml. made English mustard	2 teaspoons made English mustard
Salt and freshly ground black pepper	Salt and freshly ground black pepper
3 standard eggs, beaten	3 standard eggs, beaten

Place all the ingredients, except the eggs, in a large bowl and mix together thoroughly. Stir the beaten eggs into the meat mixture.

To freeze: Pack the meat mixture into 2 foil-lined 1 kg./2 lb. loaf tins, cover and freeze. When frozen, remove the loaves from the tins, wrap in foil, seal and return to the freezer.

To serve: Unwrap the frozen loaves and return to the tins. Cover and thaw overnight in the refrigerator. Heat, lightly covered, in a fairly hot oven (190°C/375°F or Gas Mark 5) for 1 hour.

Serve hot with a tomato or piquant sauce, or cold with salad.

Each loaf will serve 4 to 6.

Cornish pasties

METRIC	IMPERIAL
225 g. shortcrust pastry, thawed	8 oz. shortcrust pastry, thawed
225 g. lean beef, rump or skirt, trimmed of excess fat	8 oz. lean beef, rump or skirt, trimmed of excess fat
100 g. potatoes, peeled and diced	4 oz. potatoes, peeled and diced
1 small onion, peeled and chopped finely	1 small onion, peeled and chopped finely
50 g. swede, peeled and diced	2 oz. swede, peeled and diced
15 ml. water	1 tablespoon water
Salt and freshly ground black pepper	Salt and freshly ground black pepper
Milk to glaze	Milk to glaze

Divide the pastry into 4 equal pieces and roll each piece out on a floured surface into a 15 cm./6 in. round.

Cut the meat into thin strips ($\frac{1}{2} \times 2$ cm./$\frac{1}{4} \times 1$ in.). Mix the meat, potato, onion and swede together with the water and season with salt and pepper.

Pile a quarter of the mixture onto each pastry round, dampen the edges and draw them together to form a seam across the top. Flute the edges with the fingers.

Repeat the process with the other three pasties.

Place on a baking tray and brush with milk. Bake in a fairly hot oven (200°C/400°F or Gas Mark 6) for 15 minutes then reduce the temperature to a warm oven (160°C/325°F or Gas Mark 3) for a further 30 minutes to cook the filling. Place on a wire rack to cool.

To freeze: Wrap individually in foil and place in a polythene bag. Seal and freeze.

To serve: Remove the polythene bag and place the frozen pasties wrapped in foil on a baking tray in a moderate oven (180°C/350°F or Gas Mark 4) for 20 minutes, then unwrap and cook for a further 15–20 minutes or until brown and heated through.

Serves 4.

Sweet and sour pork spare ribs

METRIC	IMPERIAL
1 kg. pork spare ribs, American cut	2 lb. pork spare ribs, American cut
15 ml. corn oil	1 tablespoon corn oil
1 onion, peeled and chopped	1 onion, peeled and chopped
1 small carrot, peeled and cut into thin strips	1 small carrot, peeled and cut into thin strips
150 ml. pineapple juice	$\frac{1}{4}$ pint pineapple juice
90 ml. white wine vinegar	3 fl.oz. white wine vinegar
15 ml. Worcestershire sauce	1 tablespoon Worcestershire sauce
5 ml. soy sauce	1 teaspoon soy sauce
50 g. soft brown sugar	2 oz. soft brown sugar
15 ml. cornflour	1 tablespoon cornflour
60 ml. water	4 tablespoons water
Juice and grated rind of $\frac{1}{2}$ a lemon	Juice and grated rind of $\frac{1}{2}$ a lemon
Salt and freshly ground black pepper	Salt and freshly ground black pepper

Place the spare ribs in a baking tin and cook uncovered in a hot oven (220°C/425°F or Gas Mark 7) for 20 minutes. Remove the ribs, drain off any fat, wipe the tin and replace the ribs.

Heat the corn oil in a pan, add the onions and carrot and fry for 5 minutes. Pour in the pineapple juice, vinegar, Worcestershire sauce, soy sauce and brown sugar and stir until the sugar has dissolved. Lower the heat and simmer for 20 minutes, stirring occasionally. Blend the cornflour and water together until smooth and add to the sauce, off the heat, together with the lemon juice, rind and seasoning to taste. Return to the heat, bring to the boil, stirring constantly, then simmer until thick. Pour the sauce over the spare ribs, cover and cook in a moderate oven (180°C/350°F or Gas Mark 4) for 40 minutes. Baste the ribs with the sauce at 15 minute intervals.

To freeze: Cool quickly, wrap the ribs and sauce in foil and place in a polythene bag. Seal and freeze.

To serve: Unwrap and place in a baking tin. Cover and reheat in a fairly hot oven (200°C/400°F or Gas Mark 6) for 45 minutes, removing the cover for the last 15 minutes. Separate the ribs and taste and adjust the seasoning.

Serves 4.

Sweet and sour pork spare ribs

Country pork casserole

METRIC

½ kg. pork fillet or tender-
loin, trimmed of excess
fat and cut into slices
50 g. flour
Salt and freshly ground
black pepper
50 g. butter
2 onions, peeled and sliced
1 large leek, trimmed,
washed and sliced
100 g. celery, scrubbed,
trimmed and diced
1 small green pepper, seeded
cored and sliced
225 g. tomatoes, skinned,
seeded and chopped
15 ml. white wine vinegar
150 ml. tomato juice

IMPERIAL

1 lb. pork fillet or tender-
loin, trimmed of excess
fat and cut into slices
2 oz. flour
Salt and freshly ground
black pepper
2 oz. butter
2 onions, peeled and sliced
1 large leek, trimmed,
washed and sliced
4 oz. celery, scrubbed,
trimmed and diced
1 small green pepper, seeded,
cored and sliced
8 oz. tomatoes, skinned,
seeded and chopped
1 tablespoon white wine
vinegar
¼ pint tomato juice

Country pork casserole

Coat the pork slices in the flour seasoned with salt and pepper. Heat the butter and fry the pork briskly on either side until golden brown, remove and place in a casserole dish.

Add the onion, leek and celery to the pan and fry for 10 minutes, then spoon onto the pork, together with the green pepper and tomatoes. Season to taste and pour over the vinegar and tomato juice.

Cover the casserole and bake in a moderate oven (180°C/350°F or Gas Mark 4) for 40–50 minutes or until just tender.

To freeze: Cool quickly. Cover, seal and freeze.

To serve: Reheat the frozen pork, covered, in a moderate oven (180°C/350°F or Gas Mark 4) for 1–1¼ hours or until heated through. Taste and adjust the seasoning.

Serves 4.

Pork in orange sauce

METRIC

2 pieces of boned loin of
pork, each weighing about
¾ kg.
Salt and freshly ground
black pepper
2 large onions, peeled and
sliced
300 ml. orange juice, fresh
or diluted frozen
Grated rind and juice of
1 orange
30 ml. white wine vinegar
30 ml. redcurrant jelly

IMPERIAL

2 pieces of boned loin of
pork, each weighing about
1½ lb.
Salt and freshly ground
black pepper
2 large onions, peeled and
sliced
½ pint orange juice, fresh
or diluted frozen
Grated rind and juice of
1 orange
2 tablespoons white wine
vinegar
2 tablespoons redcurrant
jelly

Roll each piece of pork up neatly and secure with string. Score the skin with a sharp knife and rub salt and pepper into the surface. Place in a baking tin and roast without basting in a hot oven (220°C/425°F or Gas Mark 7) for 15 minutes, then add the onions to the fat in the tin and continue to cook for a further 20 minutes. Pour off any excess fat, pour the orange juice, rind and juice of the orange and vinegar over the meat and continue to cook in a moderate oven (180°C/350°F or Gas Mark 4) for 45 minutes. Stir in the redcurrant jelly and taste and adjust the seasoning.

To freeze: Cool quickly, place in a rigid container, cover, seal and freeze.

To serve: Return the frozen pork and sauce to a baking tin and reheat, uncovered, in a fairly hot oven (200°C/400°F or Gas Mark 6) for 1 hour or until heated through. Taste and adjust the seasoning and serve hot garnished with sliced oranges and watercress.

Each loin serves 4 to 5.

Pork in orange sauce

Pork chops in ginger beer

Pork chops in ginger beer

METRIC	IMPERIAL
25 g. butter	1 oz. butter
4 pork chops, trimmed of excess fat	4 pork chops, trimmed of excess fat
1 large onion, peeled and sliced into rings	1 large onion, peeled and sliced into rings
100 g. celery, scrubbed, trimmed and diced	4 oz. celery, scrubbed, trimmed and diced
2 carrots, peeled and thinly sliced	2 carrots, peeled and thinly sliced
25 g. flour	1 oz. flour
450 ml. ginger beer	$\frac{3}{4}$ pint ginger beer
1 beef stock cube dissolved in 60 ml. hot water	1 beef stock cube dissolved in 4 tablespoons hot water
Dash of Worcestershire sauce	Dash of Worcestershire sauce
Juice of $\frac{1}{2}$ a lemon	Juice of $\frac{1}{2}$ a lemon
225 g. tomatoes, skinned, seeded and chopped	8 oz. tomatoes, skinned, seeded and chopped
Salt and freshly ground black pepper	Salt and freshly ground black pepper

Melt the butter in a heavy pan and cook the pork chops quickly over a moderate heat until they are golden brown, remove and place in a casserole.

Add the onion, celery and carrot to the pan and fry until tender, sprinkle in the flour and cook stirring constantly for 1 minute. Gradually stir in the ginger beer and stock and bring to the boil, stirring constantly. When the sauce has thickened, stir in the Worcestershire sauce, lemon juice, tomatoes and seasoning to taste.

Pour the sauce over the chops, cover the casserole and cook in a moderate oven (180°C/350°F or Gas Mark 4) for 45 minutes or until the pork is tender.

To freeze: Cool quickly and cover, seal and freeze.

To serve: Reheat the frozen chops, covered, in a fairly hot oven (200°C/400°F or Gas Mark 6) for $1\frac{1}{4}$ hours, or until heated through. Taste and adjust the seasoning.

Serves 4.

Osso buco

bring to the boil, stirring constantly. Pour over the veal.

Cover the casserole dish and cook in a moderate oven (180°C/350°F or Gas Mark 4) for 1½ hours, or until tender.

To freeze: Cool quickly. Cover, seal and freeze.

To serve: Reheat the frozen veal, covered, in a fairly hot oven (200°C/400°F or Gas Mark 6) for 1 hour or until heated through. Taste and adjust the seasoning.

Sprinkle over the grated rind of ½ a lemon and 15ml./1 tablespoon chopped parsley and serve piping hot, with rice.

Serves 4.

Veal paupiettes

METRIC	IMPERIAL
Herb stuffing	**Herb stuffing**
50g. butter	*2oz. butter*
2 small onions, peeled and finely chopped	*2 small onions, peeled and finely chopped*
60ml. finely chopped parsley	*4 tablespoons finely chopped parsley*
5ml. dried marjoram	*1 teaspoon dried marjoram*
5ml. dried basil	*1 teaspoon dried basil*
Pinch of dried thyme	*Pinch of dried thyme*
222g. fresh white breadcrumbs	*8oz. fresh white breadcrumbs*
Salt and freshly ground black pepper	*Salt and freshly ground black pepper*
1 egg, beaten	*1 egg, beaten*
12 small veal escalopes	*12 small veal escalopes*
75g. butter	*3oz. butter*
1 large onion, peeled and sliced	*1 large onion, peeled and sliced*
100g. mushrooms, washed and sliced	*4oz. mushrooms, washed and sliced*
15ml. flour	*1 tablespoon flour*
300ml. chicken stock	*½ pint chicken stock*
120ml. dry white wine	*4fl.oz. dry white wine*
1 bay leaf	*1 bay leaf*

Melt the butter in a pan and add the onion, fry gently until tender. Remove from the heat and stir in the herbs, breadcrumbs and seasoning. Add enough egg to bind the stuffing together.

Place the veal, one slice at a time, between 2 sheets of damp greaseproof paper and beat with a rolling pin to flatten.

Spread a little of the herb stuffing on each veal slice, roll up and secure with fine string.

Heat the butter in a pan, add the veal and fry over a moderate heat until golden brown on all sides, remove and place in a casserole. Add the onions to the pan and fry until tender, then add the mushrooms and fry for 3 minutes. Sprinkle in the flour and cook for 1 minute. Gradually stir in the stock and wine, season to taste and add the bay leaf. Bring to the boil, stirring constantly, then cook until thickened and pour over the veal. Cover the casserole and cook in a warm oven (160°C/325°F or Gas Mark 3) for 1 hour or until the veal is tender. Remove the bay leaf and string.

To freeze: Cool quickly, cover, seal and freeze.

To serve: Reheat the frozen casserole, covered in a fairly hot oven (200°C/400°F or Gas Mark 6) for 1–1½ hours or until heated through. Taste and adjust the seasoning.

Serves 6.

Osso buco

METRIC	IMPERIAL
6 pieces of knuckle of veal, about 1kg. cut into 5cm. thick pieces	*6 pieces of knuckle of veal, about 2lb. cut into 2in. thick pieces*
25g. flour	*1oz. flour*
15ml. oil	*1 tablespoon oil*
50g. butter	*2oz. butter*
1 onion, peeled and chopped	*1 onion, peeled and chopped*
1 garlic clove, crushed	*1 garlic clove, crushed*
100g. carrot, peeled and cut into small cubes	*4oz. carrot, peeled and cut into small cubes*
100g. celery, scrubbed and cut into small cubes	*4oz. celery, scrubbed and cut into small cubes*
150ml. chicken stock	*¼ pint chicken stock*
150ml. dry white wine	*¼ pint dry white wine*
½kg. tomatoes, skinned, seeded and chopped	*1lb. tomatoes, skinned, seeded and chopped*
Salt and freshly ground black pepper	*Salt and freshly ground black pepper*

Coat the veal pieces with the flour, shake off the excess and reserve any left over.

Heat the oil and butter together and fry the veal briskly on all sides. When lightly brown, place the veal so that the bones stand upright in a casserole dish. Add the onion, garlic, carrot and celery to the pan and fry until golden brown. Sprinkle over any left over flour and fry for 1 minute. Gradually stir in the stock and wine, then add the tomatoes and seasoning and

Veal paupiettes; Squab pie

Squab pie

METRIC
½ kg. pork loin chops, or
  middle neck of lamb
  chops, trimmed of excess
  fat and cut into small
  cubes
1 large onion, peeled and
  sliced
½ kg. cooking apples, peeled,
  cored and sliced thickly
2.5 ml. mixed spice
10 ml. soft brown sugar
Salt and freshly ground
  black pepper
15 ml. cornflour
300 ml. beef stock
225 g. frozen shortcrust
  pastry, thawed

IMPERIAL
1 lb. pork loin chops, or
  middle neck of lamb
  chops, trimmed of excess
  fat and cut into small
  cubes
1 large onion, peeled and
  sliced
1 lb. cooking apples, peeled,
  cored and sliced thickly
½ teaspoon mixed spice
2 teaspoons soft brown
  sugar
Salt and freshly ground
  black pepper
1 tablespoon cornflour
½ pint beef stock
8 oz. frozen shortcrust
  pastry, thawed

Fill a 1 l./1¾ pint ovenproof or foil pie dish with alternate layers of meat, onion and apple, finishing with a layer of meat and sprinkling each layer with the mixed spice, brown sugar and seasoning.

Blend the cornflour until smooth with a little stock, add the remaining stock and pour over the pie. Cover with foil and bake in a moderate oven (180°C/350°F or Gas Mark 4) for 45 minutes. Allow to cool.

On a floured surface, roll out the pastry 2 cm./1 in. larger all round than the top of the pie dish and cut off a 2 cm./1 in. wide strip round the edge of the pastry. Dampen the rim of the dish with water and press the pastry strip round the rim. Dampen this strip and put on the pastry lid, press down firmly to seal the edges and trim off any surplus pastry. Knock up the edge with the back of a knife and use any pastry trimmings to decorate the top. Cut a small air vent.

To freeze: Cool quickly and pack the pie in a polythene bag, seal and freeze.

To serve: Brush the frozen pie with beaten egg, and place on a baking sheet, in a fairly hot oven (190°C/375°F or Gas Mark 5) for 1 hour or until the pastry is golden brown.

Serves 4.

117

Veal marengo

METRIC	IMPERIAL
60 ml. oil	4 tablespoons oil
25 g. butter	1 oz. butter
1 kg. veal, boned breast or knuckle, trimmed of excess fat and cut into 2 cm. cubes	2 lb. veal, boned breast or knuckle, trimmed of excess fat and cut into 1 in. cubes
2 onions, peeled and sliced	2 onions, peeled and sliced
1 garlic clove, crushed	1 garlic clove, crushed
15 ml. flour	1 tablespoon flour
300 ml. chicken stock	½ pint chicken stock
100 ml. dry white wine	4 fl.oz. dry white wine
396 g. can tomatoes, drained and tomatoes puréed	14 oz. can tomatoes, drained and tomatoes puréed
5 ml. dried marjoram	1 teaspoon dried marjoram
Salt and freshly ground black pepper	Salt and freshly ground black pepper
1 bay leaf	1 bay leaf
225 g. mushrooms, washed and thickly sliced	8 oz. mushrooms, washed and thickly sliced

Heat the oil and butter in a pan, add the veal and cook until golden brown. Add the onions and garlic, sprinkle in the flour and cook for 5 minutes, stirring occasionally. Gradually stir in the stock and wine, bring to the boil, stirring constantly, then reduce the heat and stir in the tomato purée, marjoram, seasoning, bay leaf and mushrooms. Cover and simmer gently for 1–1¼ hours or until the veal is just tender. Remove the bay leaf.

To freeze: Cool quickly and spoon into a foil container. Cover, seal and freeze.

To serve: Reheat the frozen veal, covered, in a fairly hot oven (200°C/400°F or Gas Mark 6), stirring occasionally, for 45 minutes or until hot through. Taste and adjust the seasoning.

Serves 4 to 5.

Liver hot pot

METRIC	IMPERIAL
½ kg. calves' or lambs' liver, ducts removed and thinly sliced	1 lb. calves' or lambs' liver, ducts removed and thinly sliced
25 g. flour	1 oz. flour
Salt and freshly ground black pepper	Salt and freshly ground black pepper
25 g. butter	1 oz. butter
4 rashers of streaky bacon, rinded and chopped	4 rashers of streaky bacon, rinded and chopped
2 large onions, peeled and sliced	2 large onions, peeled and sliced
300 ml. beef stock	½ pint beef stock
10 ml. tomato ketchup	2 teaspoons tomato ketchup
2.5 ml. dried mixed herbs	½ teaspoon dried mixed herbs
15 ml. finely chopped parsley	1 tablespoon finely chopped parsley

Toss the liver in the flour seasoned with salt and pepper and reserve any left over flour. Heat the butter in a pan, add the liver and fry briskly in the fat for 2 minutes, then transfer to a shallow foil container. Add the bacon and onion to the pan and fry until golden brown. Sprinkle in any left over flour and cook for 1 minute, stirring constantly. Gradually stir in the stock, ketchup and herbs and bring to the boil, stirring constantly. Remove from the heat, stir in the parsley, taste and adjust the seasoning and pour the sauce over the liver. Cover the container and bake in a moderate oven (180°C/350°F or Gas Mark 4) for 20 minutes.

To freeze: Cool quickly. Cover, seal and freeze.

To serve: Reheat, covered, in a moderate oven (180°C/350°F or Gas Mark 4) for 50 minutes or until heated through. Taste and adjust the seasoning.

Serves 4.

Braised kidneys in red wine

METRIC	IMPERIAL
75 g. butter	3 oz. butter
10 lambs' kidneys, skinned, halved and cored	10 lambs' kidneys, skinned, halved and cored
1 onion, peeled and finely chopped	1 onion, peeled and finely chopped
100 g. mushrooms, washed and thickly sliced	4 oz. mushrooms, washed and thickly sliced
50 g. flour	2 oz. flour
300 ml. beef stock	½ pint beef stock
30 ml. medium dry sherry	2 tablespoons medium dry sherry
240 ml. red wine	8 fl.oz. red wine
Salt and freshly ground black pepper	Salt and freshly ground black pepper

Melt the butter in a pan, add the kidneys and fry briskly for 5 minutes, then remove from the pan.

Add the onion to the pan and fry until transparent. Add the mushrooms and cook for 3 minutes. Sprinkle in the flour and cook stirring constantly for 1 minute. Gradually stir in the stock, sherry and red wine and bring to the boil, stirring constantly. Add the kidneys, season to taste, reduce the heat and simmer for 10 minutes.

To freeze: Cool quickly and pour into a foil container. Cover, seal and freeze.

To serve: Reheat the frozen kidneys, covered, in a fairly hot oven (200°C/400°F or Gas Mark 6) for 40 minutes or until heated through. Taste and adjust the seasoning.

Serves 4 to 5.

Oxtail casserole

METRIC	IMPERIAL
1 good-sized oxtail, trimmed of excess fat and cut into serving pieces	1 good-sized oxtail, trimmed of excess fat and cut into serving pieces
50 g. flour	2 oz. flour
Salt and freshly ground black pepper	Salt and freshly ground black pepper
50 g. lard or dripping	2 oz. lard or dripping
2 onions, peeled and sliced	2 onions, peeled and sliced
2 carrots, peeled and sliced	2 carrots, peeled and sliced
2 sticks of celery, scrubbed, and diced	2 sticks of celery, scrubbed, and diced
450 ml. brown stock	¾ pint beef stock
5 ml. dried mixed herbs	1 teaspoon dried mixed herbs
1 bay leaf	1 bay leaf
Juice of ½ a lemon	Juice of ½ a lemon

Toss the oxtail pieces in the flour seasoned with salt and pepper and reserve any flour left over. Heat the lard or dripping in a large saucepan and fry the oxtail in the hot fat until golden brown. Remove and place it in a casserole. Add the onions, carrots and celery to the pan and cook for 2 minutes, sprinkle in any left over flour and stir constantly until the flour browns. Gradually stir in the stock, herbs, bay leaf and lemon juice and bring to the boil, stirring constantly. Season to taste and pour over the oxtail. Cover the casserole and cook in a fairly hot oven (190°C/375°F or Gas Mark 5) for 30 minutes, then reduce the heat to cool (150°C/300°F or Gas Mark 2) for a further 2 hours or until the oxtail is very tender.

To freeze: Cool quickly, remove any excess fat, cover, seal and freeze.

To serve: Thaw, covered, overnight in the refrigerator. Reheat, covered, in a warm oven (160°C/325°F or Gas Mark 3) for 1 hour or until heated through. Taste and adjust the seasoning.

Serves 4.

Rabbit chasseur

METRIC	IMPERIAL
1 tender rabbit, cut into serving pieces	1 tender rabbit, cut into serving pieces
½ lemon	½ lemon
25 g. flour	1 oz. flour
50 g. butter	2 oz. butter
15 ml. corn or olive oil	1 tablespoon corn or olive oil
1 onion, peeled and chopped	1 onion, peeled and chopped
2 carrots, peeled and sliced	2 carrots, peeled and sliced
100 g. button mushrooms, washed and left whole	4 oz. button mushrooms, washed and left whole
240 ml. dry white wine	8 fl.oz. dry white wine
240 ml. chicken stock	8 fl.oz. chicken stock
10 ml. tomato purée	2 teaspoons tomato purée
5 ml. dried thyme	1 teaspoon dried thyme
1 bay leaf	1 bay leaf
Salt and freshly ground black pepper	Salt and freshly ground black pepper

Leave the rabbit overnight in a bowl, covered with cold water with the half lemon. Drain, rinse under cold water and dry on absorbent kitchen paper. Toss the rabbit pieces in the flour.

Heat the butter and oil together in a large pan, add the rabbit and cook briskly until golden brown. Remove the rabbit and reserve. Add the onion, carrots and mushrooms and cook for 2 minutes over a moderate heat. Sprinkle in the flour and cook stirring constantly until the flour starts to brown. Gradually stir in the wine, stock and tomato purée, bring to the boil, stirring constantly, add the thyme, bay leaf and season to taste. Return the rabbit to the pan, cover, reduce the heat and simmer for 40–50 minutes or until rabbit is tender. Skim off any excess fat.

To freeze: Cool quickly, pack into a foil container, cover, seal and freeze.

To serve: Thaw, covered, overnight in the refrigerator. Reheat, covered, in a fairly hot oven (190°C/375°F or Gas Mark 5) for 1¼ hours or until heated through. Taste and adjust the seasoning.

Serves 4.

Rabbit chasseur

Coq au vin

Normandy chicken

Heat the oil and butter in a large pan, add the bacon, onions, garlic and mushrooms and fry briskly for 2 to 3 minutes until lightly brown. Remove from the pan and place in a casserole dish. Add the chicken to the pan and fry until golden brown. Pour in the brandy, remove the pan from the heat and flame the chicken, by igniting the brandy with a match; shake the pan to encourage the flaming. Remove the chicken and place in the casserole. Return the pan to the heat, sprinkle in the flour and cook, stirring constantly for 1 minute. Gradually stir in the red wine and stock and bring to the boil, stirring constantly. Add the bay leaf, herbs, sugar and seasoning and pour over the chicken.

Cover the casserole and cook in a moderate oven (180°C/350°F or Gas Mark 4) for 1 hour or until just tender.
To freeze: Cool quickly. Cover, seal and freeze.
To serve: Thaw, covered, overnight in the refrigerator. Reheat, covered, in a fairly hot oven (200°C/400°F or Gas Mark 6) for 1 hour, or until heated through. Taste and adjust the seasoning.
Serves 6.

Normandy chicken

METRIC	IMPERIAL
15 ml. corn oil	1 tablespoon corn oil
100 g. butter	4 oz. butter
1 chicken, about 1½ kg. in weight, cut into portions	1 chicken, about 3 lb in weight, cut into portions
1 small onion, peeled and sliced	1 small onion, peeled and sliced
25 g. flour	1 oz. flour
450 ml. dry cider	¾ pint dry cider
100 ml. chicken stock	4 fl.oz. chicken stock
5 ml. dried mixed herbs	1 teaspoon dried mixed herbs
Salt and freshly ground black pepper	Salt and freshly ground black pepper
1 kg. cooking apples, peeled, cored and sliced thickly	2 lb. cooking apples, peeled, cored and sliced thickly
30 ml. Calvados (optional)	2 tablespoons Calvados (optional)

Heat the oil and half the butter in a frying pan, add the chicken portions and fry on either side until golden brown, remove and place in a casserole. Add the onion to the pan and fry until tender. Sprinkle in the flour and cook, stirring constantly, until light brown. Gradually stir in the cider, stock and herbs and bring to the boil, stirring constantly. Cook until thickened, season to taste and pour over the chicken.

Cover the casserole and cook in a moderate oven (180°C/350°F or Gas Mark 4) for 1 hour or until just tender.

Meanwhile, melt the remaining butter in a pan, add the apples and cook for 2 minutes, stirring occasionally. Add the Calvados, if used, and spoon on top of the chicken.
To freeze: Cool quickly. Cover, seal and freeze.
To serve: Reheat the frozen chicken, covered, in a fairly hot oven (200°C/400°F or Gas Mark 6) for 1 hour, or until heated through. Taste and adjust the seasoning.
Serves 6.

Coq au vin

METRIC	IMPERIAL
15 ml. corn oil	1 tablespoon corn oil
50 g. butter	2 oz. butter
100 g. streaky bacon, rinded and chopped	4 oz. streaky bacon, rinded and chopped
175 g. button onions or shallots, peeled and left whole	6 oz. button onions or shallots, peeled and left whole
1 garlic clove, crushed	1 garlic clove, crushed
225 g. mushrooms, washed and sliced	8 oz. mushrooms, washed and sliced
6 chicken portions	6 chicken portions
50 ml. brandy	4 tablespoons brandy
45 ml. flour	3 tablespoons flour
300 ml. red wine	½ pint red wine
150 ml. beef stock	¼ pint beef stock
1 small bay leaf	1 small bay leaf
2.5 ml. dried thyme	½ teaspoon dried thyme
1 sprig parsley	1 sprig parsley
Pinch of sugar	Pinch of sugar
Salt and freshly ground black pepper	Salt and freshly ground black pepper

Chicken with peaches à l'indienne

METRIC	IMPERIAL
50 g. butter	2 oz. butter
15 ml. corn oil	1 tablespoon corn oil
4 chicken portions	4 chicken portions
2 onions, peeled and sliced	2 onions, peeled and sliced
1 garlic clove, crushed	1 garlic clove, crushed
25 g. flour	1 oz. flour
15 ml. curry powder	1 tablespoon curry powder
2.5 ml. ground ginger	½ teaspoon ground ginger
2.5 ml. ground cinnamon	½ teaspoon ground cinnamon
300 ml. chicken stock	½ pint chicken stock
Salt	Salt
15 ml. mango chutney	1 tablespoon mango chutney
2 fresh peaches, skinned and stoned, or 4 canned peach halves, drained	2 fresh peaches, skinned and stoned, or 4 canned peach halves, drained
Juice of ½ a lemon	Juice of ½ a lemon

Heat the butter and oil in a large pan, add the chicken joints and fry until crisp and golden on both sides. Remove from the pan and reserve.

Add the onions and garlic to the pan and fry until tender. Sprinkle in the flour, curry powder, ginger and cinnamon and cook for 1 minute stirring constantly. Gradually stir in the chicken stock and bring to the boil, stirring constantly. When the sauce has thickened, season with salt to taste and add the mango chutney. Return the chicken portions to the curry sauce, cover the pan, reduce the heat and simmer for 45 minutes or until the chicken is tender. Add the peaches and lemon juice.

To freeze: Cool quickly, cover, seal and freeze.

To serve: Thaw, covered, overnight in the refrigerator. Reheat, covered in a fairly hot oven (200°C/400°F or Gas Mark 6) for 1 hour or until heated through. Taste and adjust the seasoning.

Serve with boiled rice and side dishes of lemon wedges, sliced cucumber in plain yoghurt and fried poppodums.

Serves 4.

Chicken breasts à la Kiev

METRIC	IMPERIAL
8 large chicken breasts on the bone	8 large chicken breasts on the bone
225 g. butter, softened	8 oz. butter, softened
1 garlic clove, crushed	1 garlic clove, crushed
Salt and freshly ground black pepper	Salt and freshly ground black pepper
15 ml. chopped parsley	1 tablespoon chopped parsley

Coating

30 ml. flour	2 tablespoons flour
2 eggs, beaten	2 eggs, beaten
225 g. dried white breadcrumbs	8 oz. dried white breadcrumbs

Remove the skin from the chicken breasts and cut away the flesh entirely from the breast bone, taking care to keep the flesh in one whole piece. Place between 2 sheets of damp greaseproof paper and beat with a rolling pin to flatten the meat to approximately ½ cm./¼ in. thick.

Beat the butter, garlic, seasoning and parsley together until thoroughly blended. Form into 8 cylindrical shapes, wrap in foil and chill until firm.

Place the chicken, skinned side down, on a board and put one piece of butter onto each breast. Fold one end of the meat over the butter, then fold the sides inwards to the centre and roll up to enclose the butter completely. Coat well in the flour seasoned with salt and pepper, then dip in the egg and coat thoroughly in the breadcrumbs. They must be well coated or the butter will leak out during frying.

To freeze: Open freeze. When frozen, wrap, seal and return to the freezer.

To serve: Thaw for 4 hours in the refrigerator, then cook, a few at a time, in hot deep fat (160°C/325°F) for 10 minutes or until crisp and brown. Drain on absorbent kitchen paper and keep warm while completing the frying.
Serves 8.

Chicken with peaches à l'indienne; Chicken breasts à la Kiev; Chicken pie

Chicken pie

METRIC	IMPERIAL
1 chicken, about 1½ kg. in weight	*1 chicken, about 3 lb. in weight*

Court bouillon

2 carrots, peeled and roughly chopped	*2 carrots, peeled and roughly chopped*
1 onion, peeled and sliced	*1 onion, peeled and sliced*
1 celery stalk, scrubbed and chopped	*1 celery stalk, scrubbed and chopped*
1 bay leaf	*1 bay leaf*
6 peppercorns	*6 peppercorns*
50 g. butter	*2 oz. butter*
1 small onion, peeled and finely chopped	*1 small onion, peeled and finely chopped*
2 carrots, peeled and sliced	*2 carrots, peeled and sliced*
100 g. mushrooms, washed and sliced	*4 oz. mushrooms, washed and sliced*
5 ml. dried mixed herbs	*1 teaspoon dried mixed herbs*
50 g. flour	*2 oz. flour*
150 ml. creamy milk	*¼ pint creamy milk*
Salt and freshly ground black pepper	*Salt and freshly ground black pepper*
Shake of celery salt (optional)	*Shake of celery salt (optional)*
350 g. frozen shortcrust pastry, thawed	*12 oz. frozen shortcrust pastry, thawed*

Place the chicken in a large heavy saucepan, add the court bouillon ingredients and enough cold water just to cover the chicken. Bring to the boil then reduce the heat and cover the pan. Simmer gently for 2 hours or until tender.

Drain the chicken, strain the liquor and reserve it. Remove all the meat from the chicken, discard the skin and bones and cut the meat into bite-sized pieces.

Melt the butter in a pan, add the onion and carrots and fry for 10 minutes. Add the mushrooms and herbs and cook for 2 minutes. Sprinkle in the flour and cook for 1 minute without browning. Gradually stir in 300 ml./½ pint of the reserved court bouillon and the milk, bring to the boil, stirring constantly, then remove from the heat, season to taste and add the celery salt. Fold in the chicken meat, add more stock if necessary and transfer to a 1.2 l./2 pint ovenproof or foil pie dish.

Roll out the pastry on a floured surface, dampen the edge of the pie dish with water and cover the filling with the pastry. Press down firmly to seal and trim the edges with a sharp knife. Use any pastry trimmings to make leaves to decorate the top. Cut an air vent in the pastry, to allow the steam to escape.

To freeze: Cool quickly and pack into a polythene bag, seal and freeze.

To serve: Remove the polythene bag. Brush the pastry with egg and bake from frozen in a fairly hot oven (190°C/375°F or Gas Mark 5) for 1¼ hours. If the pastry becomes too brown, cover the top with foil.
Serves 6.

Chicken casserole

METRIC
50 g. butter
15 ml. oil
6 chicken portions
2 medium-sized onions,
   peeled and sliced
100 g. mushrooms, washed
   and sliced
4 carrots, peeled and finely
   chopped
1 green pepper, cored,
   seeded and sliced
Salt and freshly ground
   black pepper
5 ml. dried mixed herbs
25 g. cornflour
150 ml. dry white wine
60 ml. chicken stock or water
396 g. can tomatoes

IMPERIAL
2 oz. butter
1 tablespoon oil
6 chicken portions
2 medium-sized onions,
   peeled and sliced
4 oz. mushrooms, washed
   and sliced
4 carrots, peeled and finely
   chopped
1 green pepper, cored,
   seeded and sliced
Salt and freshly ground
   black pepper
1 teaspoon dried mixed herbs
1 oz. cornflour
$\frac{1}{4}$ pint dry white wine
4 tablespoons chicken stock
   or water
14 oz. can tomatoes

Melt the butter with the oil in a frying pan, add the chicken portions and fry them on both sides until golden brown. Transfer the chicken to a heavy casserole.

Add the vegetables to the frying pan and fry for 3 minutes, stirring occasionally. Sprinkle the seasoning, herbs and cornflour over the vegetables and cook for 1 minute, stirring constantly. Stir in the wine, stock or water and tomatoes and bring to the boil, stirring constantly. Pour over the chicken portions.

Cover the casserole and cook in a fairly hot oven (190°C/375°F or Gas Mark 5) for 45–50 minutes or until the chicken and vegetables are tender.
To freeze: Cool quickly, cover, seal and freeze.
To serve: Thaw, covered, overnight in the refrigerator. Reheat, covered, in a fairly hot oven (200°C/400°F or Gas Mark 6) for 1 hour or until heated through. Taste and adjust the seasoning.
Serves 6.

Turkey à la king

METRIC
50 g. butter
1 small onion, peeled and
   finely chopped
1 small green pepper,
   cored, seeded and diced
225 g. button mushrooms,
   washed and left whole
30 ml. cornflour
300 ml. creamy milk
300 ml. chicken stock
$\frac{1}{2}$ kg. cooked turkey, diced
Pinch dried thyme
15 ml. dry sherry
Salt and white pepper

IMPERIAL
2 oz. butter
1 small onion, peeled and
   finely chopped
1 small green pepper,
   cored, seeded and diced
8 oz. button mushrooms,
   washed and left whole
2 tablespoons cornflour
$\frac{1}{2}$ pint creamy milk
$\frac{1}{2}$ pint chicken stock
1 lb. cooked turkey, diced
Pinch dried thyme
1 tablespoon dry sherry
Salt and white pepper

Melt the butter in a pan, add the onion and green pepper and

Chicken casserole

Turkey à la king

Duck with orange

fry gently until tender. Add the mushrooms and fry for 3 minutes. Sprinkle in the cornflour and cook for 1 minute stirring constantly. Stir in the milk and stock and bring to the boil, stirring constantly. Add the turkey, herbs, sherry and season to taste and simmer for 5 minutes.

To freeze: Cool quickly, pour into rigid containers, cover, seal and freeze.

To serve: Thaw, uncovered, for 4 hours at room temperature. Turn into a saucepan and reheat, stirring occasionally, for 30 minutes, or until heated through. Taste and adjust the seasoning.

Serves 6 to 8.

Duck with orange

METRIC	IMPERIAL
1 duck, about 2 kg. in weight	*1 duck, about 4 lb. in weight*
1 onion, peeled	*1 onion, peeled*
Salt and freshly ground black pepper	*Salt and freshly ground black pepper*
Coarsely grated rind and juice of 2 oranges	*Coarsely grated rind and juice of 2 oranges*
Coarsely grated rind and juice of 1 lemon	*Coarsely grated rind and juice of 1 lemon*
15 ml. flour	*1 tablespoon flour*
30 ml. red wine	*2 tablespoons red wine*
240 ml. chicken stock	*8 fl. oz. chicken stock*
15 ml. redcurrant jelly	*1 tablespoon redcurrant jelly*

Sprinkle the duck inside and out with salt and pepper and insert the onion into the body cavity. Prick the skin all over

with a fork and stand the duck on a grid or rack in a roasting tin. Bake in the centre of a moderate oven (180°C/350°F or Gas Mark 4) for 25 minutes per ½ kg./1 lb. Do not baste or cover. When cooked, discard the onion, cut the duck into 4 to 6 portions and place in a large foil container. Drain and reserve 15 ml./1 tablespoon of the juices.

Blanch the orange and lemon rind in boiling water for 2 minutes and drain.

Melt the reserved 15 ml./1 tablespoon of the duck fat in a saucepan, stir in the flour and cook for 1 minute, stirring constantly. Add the blanched rind, the juice of the oranges and lemon and gradually stir in the wine, stock and jelly. Bring slowly to the boil, stirring constantly, season to taste and cook, stirring constantly until the sauce is smooth and thick. Pour over the duck.

To freeze: Cool quickly, cover, seal and freeze.

To serve: Thaw, covered, overnight in the refrigerator. Reheat, covered, in a fairly hot oven (200°C/400°F or Gas Mark 6) for 30–35 minutes or until heated through. Taste and adjust the seasoning.

Serves 4.

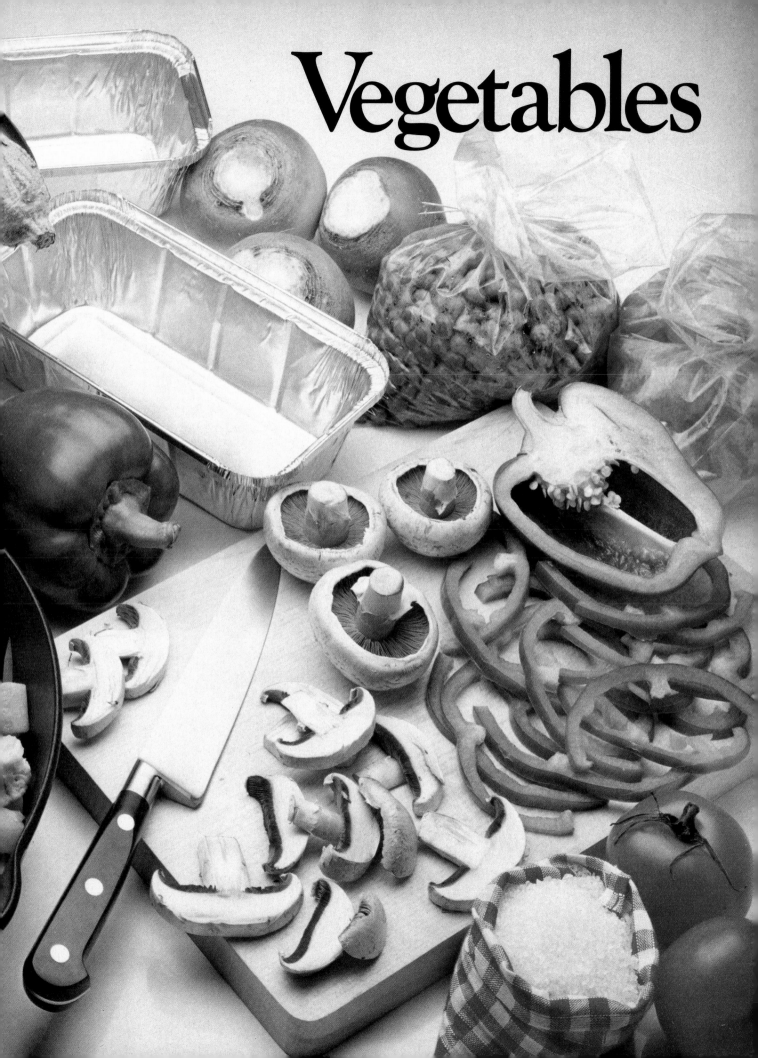

Vegetables

Chinese braised vegetables

Stuffed aubergines

Chinese braised vegetables

METRIC	IMPERIAL
30 ml. corn oil	2 tablespoons corn oil
3 sticks of celery, washed, trimmed and diced	3 sticks of celery, washed, trimmed and diced
2 large carrots, peeled and cut into very fine strips	2 large carrots, peeled and cut into very fine strips
1 green pepper, seeded and cut into very fine strips	1 green pepper, seeded and cut into very fine strips
1 small onion, peeled and cut into fine rings	1 small onion, peeled and cut into fine rings
1 small cauliflower, washed and broken into very small sprigs	1 small cauliflower, washed and broken into very small sprigs
½ cucumber, peeled and diced	½ cucumber, peeled and diced
6 canned waterchestnuts, sliced	6 canned waterchestnuts, sliced
100 g. mushrooms, washed and sliced	4 oz. mushrooms, washed and sliced
100 ml. water	4 fl.oz. water
Salt	Salt
5 ml. brown sugar	1 teaspoon brown sugar
10 ml. soy sauce	2 teaspoons soy sauce

Heat the oil in a large saucepan, and add the celery and carrots, fry for 3 minutes. Stir in the remaining vegetables and cook, stirring constantly, for 2 minutes. Add the water, salt to taste, brown sugar and soy sauce, and cook briskly, stirring occasionally, for 6–8 minutes, until cooked but still crisp. Taste and adjust the seasoning.

To freeze: Cool quickly and pack into rigid containers. Cover, seal and freeze.

To serve: Thaw for 4–5 hours at room temperature, then place in a moderate oven (180°C/350°F or Gas Mark 4) for 30 minutes.

Serves 4.

Stuffed aubergines

METRIC	IMPERIAL
4 aubergines, medium-sized	4 aubergines, medium-sized
60 ml. corn oil	4 tablespoons corn oil
1 Spanish onion, peeled and chopped finely	1 Spanish onion, peeled and chopped finely
1 clove of garlic, crushed	1 clove of garlic, crushed
175 g. mushrooms, washed and sliced	6 oz. mushrooms, washed and sliced
5 ml. dried mixed herbs	1 teaspoon dried mixed herbs
Salt and freshly ground black pepper	Salt and freshly ground black pepper
100 g. fresh white breadcrumbs	4 oz. fresh white breadcrumbs
1 egg, beaten	1 egg, beaten

Cut the aubergines in half lengthways and scoop out most of the flesh with a metal spoon, being careful not to split the skin. Chop the flesh finely.

Heat the oil in a saucepan and fry the onion and garlic for 5 minutes. Stir in the mushrooms and aubergine, add the herbs and seasoning to taste. Continue to cook the mixture for 15–20 minutes or until soft, then remove from the heat and stir in 75 g./3 oz. of the breadcrumbs, and enough egg to bind the mixture together.

Spoon the mixture into the aubergine cases and sprinkle with the remaining breadcrumbs. Place the stuffed aubergines into an ovenproof dish and pour in enough water to cover the base of the dish. Cover and bake in a moderate oven (180°C/350°F or Gas Mark 4) for 35 minutes.

To freeze: Cool quickly and wrap individually in foil or cover the dish. Seal and freeze.

To serve: Place the frozen covered aubergines in a moderate oven (180°C/350°F or Gas Mark 4) for 40 minutes. 15 minutes before the end of cooking, remove the covering, to brown the breadcrumbs.

Serves 8.

Harvard beetroot

METRIC	IMPERIAL
50 g. soft brown sugar	2 oz. soft brown sugar
Salt and freshly ground black pepper	Salt and freshly ground black pepper
15 ml. cornflour	1 tablespoon cornflour
100 ml. wine vinegar	4 fl.oz. wine vinegar
30 ml. cold water	2 tablespoons cold water
½ kg. cooked beetroot, skinned and sliced	1 lb. cooked beetroot, skinned and sliced

Place the sugar, seasoning to taste and cornflour into a saucepan and slowly stir in the vinegar and water. Bring the sauce to the boil, stirring constantly and when it thickens, simmer gently for 5 minutes. Add the beetroot, cover and continue to cook for 10 minutes.

To freeze: Cool quickly and pack into rigid containers. Cover, seal and freeze.

To serve: Tip the frozen beetroot into a large saucepan, add 30 ml./2 tablespoons water, cover and heat through gently, stirring occasionally, for 40 minutes. After 20 minutes, separate the beetroot slices gently. Serve piping hot with a knob of butter.

Serves 4.

Harvard beetroot

Braised chicory

METRIC	IMPERIAL
8 large heads of chicory, washed and bases trimmed and cored	8 large heads of chicory, washed and bases trimmed and cored
50 g. butter	2 oz. butter
Pinch of nutmeg	Pinch of nutmeg
Salt and freshly ground black pepper	Salt and freshly ground black pepper
Juice of ½ a lemon or orange	Juice of ½ a lemon or orange
100 ml. chicken stock	4 fl.oz. chicken stock

Blanch the chicory in boiling salted water for 4 minutes. Drain well and place in a buttered casserole or shallow baking dish. Dot the surface with the butter, and sprinkle with nutmeg, seasoning to taste and lemon or orange juice. Pour over the stock, cover the dish and bake in a warm oven (160°C/325°F or Gas Mark 3) for 1 hour, or until the chicory is tender.

To freeze: Cool quickly and pack in a single layer in a large foil dish. Cover, seal and freeze.

To serve: Thaw overnight in the refrigerator. Reheat, covered, in a fairly hot oven (200°C/400°F, Gas Mark 6) for ½ hour.

Serves 8.

Braised chicory

129

Stuffed cabbage leaves; Cabbage au gratin; Austrian red cabbage

Stuffed cabbage leaves

METRIC
*12 medium-sized cabbage
  leaves*
25 g. lard
*1 onion, peeled and chopped
  finely*
1 clove of garlic, crushed
½ kg. lean minced beef
15 ml. tomato purée
10 ml. Worcestershire sauce
*Salt and freshly ground
  black pepper*
5 ml. dried mixed herbs
*25 g. long grain rice, boiled
  and drained*
100 ml. chicken stock

IMPERIAL
*12 medium-sized cabbage
  leaves*
1 oz. lard
*1 onion, peeled and chopped
  finely*
1 clove of garlic, crushed
1 lb. lean minced beef
1 tablespoon tomato purée
*2 teaspoons Worcestershire
  sauce*
*Salt and freshly ground
  black pepper*
1 teaspoon mixed herbs
*1 oz. long grain rice, boiled
  and drained*
4 fl.oz. chicken stock

Blanch the cabbage leaves for 1 minute in boiling salted water, then plunge into cold water. Drain well, and remove any coarse stem.

Heat the lard in a saucepan, add the onions and garlic and fry over a gentle heat for about 5 minutes or until soft. Stir in the minced beef and fry for a further 5 minutes. Add the tomato purée, Worcestershire sauce, herbs and seasoning to taste. Remove from the heat and stir in the rice.

Divide the stuffing evenly between the cabbage leaves, then fold carefully to make a square parcel. Place in a buttered foil container and pour over the stock. Cover and bake in a moderate oven (180°C/350°F or Gas Mark 4) for about 30 minutes.

To freeze: Cool quickly, cover, seal and freeze.

To serve: Thaw overnight in the refrigerator, then place, covered, in a hot oven (200°C/400°F or Gas Mark 6) for 25–30 minutes or until heated through.

Serve with tomato sauce (see page 71).

Serves 6.

Cabbage au gratin

METRIC	IMPERIAL
¾ kg. white winter cabbage, trimmed and washed	1½ lb. white winter cabbage, trimmed and washed
300 ml. béchamel sauce	½ pint béchamel sauce
60 ml. double cream	4 tablespoons double cream
Salt and freshly ground black pepper	Salt and freshly ground black pepper
5 ml. dry mustard	1 teaspoon dry mustard
50 g. Cheddar cheese, grated	2 oz. Cheddar cheese, grated
25 g. fresh white breadcrumbs	1 oz. fresh white breadcrumbs
25 g. butter	1 oz. butter

Shred the cabbage in ½ cm./¼ in. slices, and cook in boiling salted water for 5 minutes. Drain well.

Heat the béchamel sauce gently in a saucepan, and stir in the cream, seasoning and mustard. Add the cabbage and heat through gently, stirring well, taste and adjust the seasoning. Remove from the heat and stir in the cheese.

Turn the cabbage into a foil container, sprinkle with the breadcrumbs and dot with butter.

To freeze: Cool quickly, cover, seal and freeze.

To serve: Place the covered foil container in a hot oven (220°C/425°F or Gas Mark 7) for 1 hour or until heated through; remove covering 10 minutes before the end of cooking to brown the top.

Serves 4 to 6.

Austrian red cabbage

METRIC	IMPERIAL
50 g. butter or lard	2 oz. butter or lard
1 large onion, peeled and sliced	1 large onion, peeled and sliced
1 clove of garlic, crushed	1 clove of garlic, crushed
1 kg. red cabbage, shredded ½ cm. thick	2 lb. red cabbage, shredded ¼ in. thick
2 large cooking apples, peeled, cored and sliced	2 large cooking apples, peeled, cored and sliced
2 cloves or 5 ml. caraway seeds	2 cloves or 1 teaspoon caraway seeds
60 ml. wine vinegar	4 tablespoons wine vinegar
60 ml. water	4 tablespoons water
15 ml. sugar	1 tablespoon sugar
Salt and freshly ground black pepper	Salt and freshly ground black pepper

Melt the butter or lard in a large saucepan, and fry the onion and garlic for 5 minutes. Stir in the cabbage and apples and simmer for 10 minutes, stirring occasionally. Add all the other ingredients, with seasoning to taste and bring to the boil, cover and simmer for 30 minutes until all the liquid has been absorbed and the cabbage is tender.

To freeze: Cool quickly and pack the cabbage into a rigid container. Cover, seal and freeze.

To serve: Uncover and thaw the red cabbage at room temperature for 4–5 hours. Place in a large saucepan, cover and reheat gently, stirring occasionally, for 30–40 minutes or until heated through.

Serves 6 to 8.

Leeks and ham

METRIC	IMPERIAL
8 large leeks, trimmed, split and washed	8 large leeks, trimmed, split and washed
8 thin slices of cooked ham	8 thin slices of cooked ham
600 ml. mornay sauce	1 pint mornay sauce

Topping	**Topping**
30 ml. Cheddar cheese, grated	2 tablespoons Cheddar cheese, grated
30 ml. fresh white breadcrumbs	2 tablespoons fresh white breadcrumbs

Cook the leeks in a large pan of boiling salted water for 20 minutes. Drain well.

Wrap the slices of ham round the leeks and place in a greased foil dish, pour over the mornay sauce, and sprinkle with the cheese and breadcrumbs.

To freeze: Cool quickly, cover, seal and freeze.

To serve: Allow to thaw at room temperature for 4–5 hours, and reheat in a fairly hot oven (190°C/375°F or Gas Mark 5) for 45 minutes or until crisp and brown.

Serves 4.

Leeks and ham

Marrow provençale

METRIC	IMPERIAL
60 ml. olive oil	4 tablespoons olive oil
2 large onions, peeled and chopped finely	2 large onions, peeled and chopped finely
1 clove of garlic, crushed	1 clove of garlic, crushed
1 medium-sized marrow, peeled, seeded and cut into cubes	1 medium-sized marrow, peeled, seeded and cut into cubes
6 large tomatoes, skinned and chopped	6 large tomatoes, skinned and chopped
30 ml. tomato purée	2 tablespoons tomato purée
10 ml. dried mixed herbs	2 teaspoons dried mixed herbs
Salt and freshly ground black pepper	Salt and freshly ground black pepper

Heat the oil in a saucepan, add the onions and garlic and cook gently for 5 minutes or until they are transparent. Add the marrow and fry gently for 5 minutes. Stir in all the other ingredients with seasoning to taste and simmer, stirring occasionally, for 30 minutes, or until the vegetables are tender. Taste and adjust the seasoning.
To freeze: Cool quickly and pack into a rigid container. Cover, seal and freeze.
To serve: Uncover and thaw at room temperature for 4–5 hours. Place in a large saucepan, cover and reheat gently, stirring occasionally for 30 minutes or until heated through.
Serves 4 to 6.

Marrow provençale

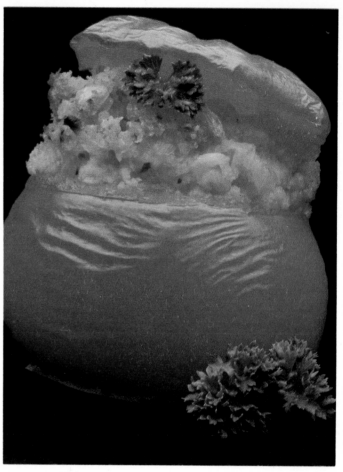

Bacon stuffed tomatoes

Bacon stuffed tomatoes

METRIC	IMPERIAL
6 large, even-sized tomatoes	6 large, even-sized tomatoes
25 g. butter	1 oz. butter
100 g. bacon, rinded and chopped	4 oz. bacon, rinded and chopped
1 small onion, peeled and finely chopped	1 small onion, peeled and finely chopped
5 ml. dried mixed herbs	1 teaspoon dried mixed herbs
25 g. fresh white breadcrumbs	1 oz. fresh white breadcrumbs
Salt and freshly ground black pepper	Salt and freshly ground black pepper

Cut the top off each tomato and scoop out the seeds and core with a teaspoon.

Melt the butter in a saucepan, add the bacon and onion, and fry briskly for 2–3 minutes. Remove from the heat and stir in the other ingredients with seasoning to taste. Fill the tomatoes with this mixture, and replace the tops.
To freeze: Arrange in foil trays, cover, seal and freeze.
To serve: Uncover and thaw at room temperature for 1 hour, then place in a fairly hot oven (190°C/375°F or Gas Mark 5) for 20–25 minutes, or until heated through.
Serves 6.

Courgettes milano

METRIC	IMPERIAL
30 ml. olive oil	2 tablespoons olive oil
½ kg. courgettes, washed, topped and tailed and cut into 1 cm. slices	1 lb. courgettes, washed, topped and tailed and cut into ½ in. slices
6 spring onions, washed, topped and tailed and roughly chopped	6 spring onions, washed, topped and tailed and roughly chopped
1 clove of garlic, crushed	1 clove of garlic, crushed
2.5 ml. dried basil	½ teaspoon dried basil
Pinch of paprika pepper	Pinch of paprika pepper
4 tomatoes, skinned, seeded and chopped	4 tomatoes, skinned, seeded and chopped
15 ml. tomato purée	1 tablespoon tomato purée
1 bay leaf	1 bay leaf
30 ml. white wine	2 tablespoons white wine
Salt and freshly ground black pepper	Salt and freshly ground black pepper

Heat the oil in a saucepan, add the courgettes, spring onions and garlic and cook for 3 minutes. Stir in the remaining ingredients with seasoning to taste. Bring to the boil, then cover and reduce the heat to simmer for 15 minutes.

To freeze: Cool quickly and pack into rigid containers. Cover, seal and freeze.

To serve: *cold* – uncover and thaw at room temperature for 5–6 hours.

To serve: *hot* – tip the frozen mixture into a large saucepan and heat through gently, covered, stirring occasionally to separate the pieces of courgettes, for 30–40 minutes or until heated through.

Serves 4.

Cauliflower au gratin

METRIC	IMPERIAL
1 medium-sized cauliflower, washed and coarse stalk removed	1 medium-sized cauliflower, washed and coarse stalk removed
300 ml. white coating sauce	½ pint white coating sauce
30 ml. single cream	2 tablespoons single cream
100 g. Cheddar cheese, grated	4 oz. Cheddar cheese, grated
Salt and freshly ground black pepper	Salt and freshly ground black pepper
50 g. Parmesan cheese, grated	2 oz. Parmesan cheese, grated
30 ml. fresh white breadcrumbs	2 tablespoons fresh white breadcrumbs

Cook the cauliflower in boiling salted water for 10 minutes, until tender, but still firm. Drain well.

In a saucepan, gently heat the white sauce, and when hot add the cream, Cheddar cheese and salt and pepper to taste.

Turn the cauliflower into a foil container, pour over the sauce and sprinkle with the Parmesan cheese and bread-crumbs.

To freeze: Cool quickly, cover, seal and freeze.

To serve: Place the frozen cauliflower in a warm oven (160°C/325°F or Gas Mark 3) for 45–50 minutes, or until thawed through. Remove the cover and increase the heat to a fairly hot oven (200°C/400°F or Gas Mark 6) for 10–15 minutes, until golden brown.

Serves 4.

Courgettes milano; Cauliflower au gratin

Stuffed green peppers

METRIC	IMPERIAL
100 g. long grain rice	4 oz. long grain rice
25 g. butter	1 oz. butter
100 g. bacon, rinded and chopped	4 oz. bacon, rinded and chopped
3 large tomatoes, skinned and chopped	3 large tomatoes, skinned and chopped
5 ml. dried thyme	1 teaspoon dried thyme
1 clove of garlic, crushed	1 clove of garlic, crushed
Salt and freshly ground black pepper	Salt and freshly ground black pepper
4 green peppers, medium-sized	4 green peppers, medium-sized
50 g. Cheddar cheese, grated	2 oz. Cheddar cheese, grated

Cook the rice in boiling salted water until just tender, drain, rinse in running cold water and drain well.

Melt the butter in a saucepan, add the bacon and fry until crisp. Stir the bacon, tomatoes, thyme, garlic and seasoning to taste into the rice.

Cut the peppers in half lengthways, remove the seeds and membrane from the inside of the pepper, blanch for 3 minutes and drain. Place in a shallow foil container, fill the pepper cavities with the rice mixture, and sprinkle with the grated cheese.

To freeze: Cool quickly, cover, seal and freeze.

To serve: Loosen foil covering and place peppers in a hot oven (220°C/425°F, Gas Mark 7) for 1 hour. Uncover and cook for further 20 minutes to brown.

Serves 8 for an hors d'œuvre or 4 for a supper dish.

Onions à la grecque

METRIC	IMPERIAL
½ kg. pickling onions or shallots, peeled	1 lb. pickling onions or shallots, peeled
100 ml. beef stock	4 fl.oz. beef stock
100 ml. white wine	4 fl.oz. white wine
Juice of ½ a lemon	Juice of ½ a lemon
30 ml. tomato purée	2 tablespoons tomato purée
15 ml. olive oil	1 tablespoon olive oil
5 ml. sugar	1 teaspoon sugar
50 g. sultanas (optional)	2 oz. sultanas (optional)
Salt and freshly ground black pepper	Salt and freshly ground black pepper

Put all the ingredients, with seasoning to taste, in a saucepan, and bring to the boil. Reduce the heat and simmer for 30 minutes or until the onions are tender.

Remove the onions from the sauce and place in a rigid container. Return the sauce to the heat and boil for 8 minutes or until reduced and fairly thick; pour over the onions.

To freeze: Cool quickly, cover, seal and freeze.

To serve: *hot* – tip the frozen onions and sauce into a large saucepan, cover and heat through very gently for 20–30 minutes, stirring occasionally. Serve sprinkled with parsley.

To serve: *cold* – allow to thaw at room temperature for 2–3 hours.

Serves 4.

Crispy onion rings

METRIC	IMPERIAL
Batter	**Batter**
100 g. plain flour	4 oz. plain flour
30 ml. corn oil	2 tablespoons corn oil
150 ml. milk	¼ pint milk
5 ml. dried mixed herbs	1 teaspoon dried mixed herbs
Salt and freshly ground black pepper	Salt and freshly ground black pepper
1 egg white	1 egg white
4 large onions, peeled and sliced into thick rings	4 large onions, peeled and sliced into thick rings
30 ml. plain flour	2 tablespoons plain flour
Deep fat for frying	Deep fat for frying

Sift the flour into a bowl, and stir in the oil, gradually add the milk and beat to make a smooth batter. Add the herbs and seasoning to taste. Whisk the egg white until stiff and fold into the batter.

Separate the onion slices into rings and toss them in the plain flour. Using a fork, dip into the batter, shake lightly to remove excess batter and drop a few at a time into the hot fat (180°C/350°F). Fry for approximately 20 seconds or until golden brown and crisp. Drain on absorbent kitchen paper and continue frying remaining rings in the same way.

To freeze: Cool quickly and open freeze. When solid, pack into rigid containers or a polythene bag. Seal and freeze. *Store for up to 2 months.*

To serve: Place the frozen rings onto a baking tray and place in a fairly hot oven (200°C/400°F or Gas Mark 6) for 15 minutes or until heated through and crisp.

Serves 6.

Onions in white sauce

METRIC	IMPERIAL
½ kg. pickling onions, peeled	1 lb. pickling onions, peeled
25 g. butter	1 oz. butter
25 g. cornflour	1 oz. cornflour
300 ml. milk	½ pint milk
100 ml. chicken stock	4 fl.oz. chicken stock
Pinch of nutmeg	Pinch of nutmeg
Salt and freshly ground black pepper	Salt and freshly ground black pepper

Place the onions in a saucepan, and cover with cold water. Bring to the boil and reduce to simmer for 30 minutes, or until the onions are just tender. Remove from the heat and drain well.

Melt the butter in a saucepan, stir in the cornflour and allow to cook for 1 minute. Remove from the heat and gradually add the milk and stock, stirring constantly. Return to the heat, bring slowly to the boil stirring constantly and cook for 1–2 minutes until the sauce is smooth and has thickened. Add the drained onions, nutmeg and seasoning to taste.

To freeze: Cool quickly and pack in a rigid container. Cover, seal and freeze.

To serve: Place the frozen onions and sauce in a large saucepan, cover and heat gently, stirring occasionally for 20–30 minutes. Garnish with lightly fried breadcrumbs.

Serves 4.

Potato croquettes

METRIC	IMPERIAL
1 kg. potatoes, peeled and halved	*2 lb. potatoes, peeled and halved*
50 g. butter	*2 oz. butter*
1 egg, beaten	*1 egg, beaten*
15 ml. milk	*1 tablespoon milk*
Salt and freshly ground black pepper	*Salt and freshly ground black pepper*

Coating	**Coating**
2 eggs, beaten	*2 eggs, beaten*
50 g. fresh white breadcrumbs	*2 oz. fresh white breadcrumbs*
Deep fat for frying	*Deep fat for frying*

Cook the potatoes in boiling salted water for 15–20 minutes or until tender. Drain well and mash with the butter. Beat in the egg, milk and seasoning to taste. Allow the mixture to become cold before shaping.

Divide the mixture into 16, and form into croquettes by rolling with floured hands. Dip the croquettes into the egg and roll in the breadcrumbs. Chill, then fry the croquettes in hot deep fat (180°C/350°F) for 4–5 minutes or until golden brown. Drain well on absorbent kitchen paper.

To freeze: Cool quickly and open freeze. When solid pack into rigid containers or a polythene bag. Seal and freeze.

To serve: Place the frozen croquettes on a baking tray, and heat through in a hot oven (200°C/400°F or Gas Mark 6) for 20 minutes or until heated through and crisp.

Serves 8.

Duchesse potatoes

METRIC	IMPERIAL
1 kg. old potatoes, peeled and halved	*2 lb. old potatoes, peeled and halved*
50 g. butter	*2 oz. butter*
2 eggs, beaten	*2 eggs, beaten*
Pinch of nutmeg	*Pinch of nutmeg*
Salt and freshly ground black pepper	*Salt and freshly ground black pepper*
Beaten egg for glazing	*Beaten egg for glazing*

Cook the potatoes in boiling salted water for 15–20 minutes or until tender, drain well and sieve them while still hot. Return to the pan and dry them over a gentle heat, stirring continually for 3 minutes. Remove from the heat and add the butter, beaten eggs, nutmeg and seasoning to taste. Add a little milk if mixture is too thick to pipe.

Place the potato into a piping bag, fitted with a large rosette nozzle and pipe 16 rosettes onto a greased baking tray. Brush carefully with beaten egg, and bake in a fairly hot oven (200°C/400°F or Gas Mark 6) for 15 minutes or until light brown.

To freeze: Cool quickly on a wire rack and open freeze. When solid pack into rigid containers or a polythene bag. Seal and freeze.

To serve: Place the frozen potatoes onto a greased baking tray and bake in a hot oven (220°C/425°F or Gas Mark 7) for 20–25 minutes or until the potatoes are heated through.

Serves 8.

French fried potatoes

METRIC	IMPERIAL
1 kg. potatoes, peeled	*2 lb. potatoes, peeled*
Deep fat for frying	*Deep fat for frying*

Cut the potatoes into small strips (approximately $\frac{1}{2} \times 5$ cm./2 $\times \frac{1}{4}$ in.) and blanch for 2 minutes in boiling water, drain and dry well on absorbent kitchen paper.

Heat the fat to 180°C/350°F and add the potatoes in batches. Fry for approximately 5 minutes or until golden brown.

Drain very thoroughly on absorbent kitchen paper.

To freeze: Cool quickly and open freeze. When solid pack into rigid containers or a polythene bag. Seal and freeze.

Store for up to 3 weeks.

To serve: Spread the frozen potatoes on a baking tray and bake in a fairly hot oven (200°C/400°F or Gas Mark 6) for 20 minutes or until brown and crisp. Sprinkle with salt and serve.

Serves 6 to 8.

Baked potatoes with cheese and bacon

METRIC	IMPERIAL
4 large old potatoes (each approximately 175 g.), scrubbed and wiped dry	*4 large old potatoes (each approximately 6 oz.), scrubbed and wiped dry*
15 ml. corn oil	*1 tablespoon corn oil*
50 g. butter	*2 oz. butter*
30 ml. Cheddar cheese, grated	*2 tablespoons Cheddar cheese, grated*
10 ml. parsley, finely chopped	*2 teaspoons parsley, finely chopped*
4 rashers of bacon, rinded and finely chopped	*4 rashers of bacon, rinded and finely chopped*
15 g. butter	*½ oz. butter*
Salt and freshly ground black pepper	*Salt and freshly ground black pepper*

Place the potatoes on a baking tray, and prick with a fork. Rub the skins with a little corn oil and bake in a fairly hot oven (200°C/400°F or Gas Mark 6) for 1½ hours or until cooked.

Cut off the tops of the potatoes lengthways and scoop out the centre. Mash the potato in a bowl with the 50 g./2 oz. of butter, cheese and parsley.

Fry the bacon in the remaining butter until golden brown and stir into the mashed potato, season to taste, and return the mixture to the potato cases.

To freeze: Cool quickly, wrap individually in foil and pack into polythene bags. Seal and freeze.

To serve: Unwrap and bake the frozen potatoes on a baking tray in a fairly hot oven (190°C/375°F or Gas Mark 5) for 40 minutes, or until heated through.

Serves 4.

French fried potatoes; Baked potatoes with cheese and bacon; Potato croquettes; Duchesse potatoes

Christmas Brussels sprouts

METRIC
¼ kg. dried chestnuts,
   soaked overnight and
   chopped coarsely
½ kg. frozen Brussels
   sprouts
25 g. butter
1 small onion, peeled and
   chopped finely
Pinch of ground cloves
Salt and freshly ground
   black pepper

IMPERIAL
½ lb. dried chestnuts,
   soaked overnight and
   chopped coarsely
1 lb. frozen Brussels
   sprouts
1 oz. butter
1 small onion, peeled and
   chopped finely
Pinch of ground cloves
Salt and freshly ground
   black pepper

Place the chestnuts in boiling salted water and cook gently for 20–30 minutes or until just tender.

Place the Brussels sprouts in boiling salted water and cook for 5 minutes or until tender. Drain and keep hot in a serving dish.

Melt the butter in a saucepan and add the onion and chestnuts, fry gently for 5 minutes, stir in the cloves and seasoning to taste, and spoon over the Brussels sprouts.
Serves 4 to 6.

Carrots à la Vichy

METRIC
1 kg. frozen baby carrots
300 ml. chicken stock
25 g. caster sugar
75 g. butter
Salt and freshly ground
   black pepper

IMPERIAL
2 lb. frozen baby carrots
½ pint chicken stock
1 oz. caster sugar
3 oz. butter
Salt and freshly ground
   black pepper

Put the frozen carrots in a saucepan, and add the other ingredients with seasoning to taste. Simmer for about 30 minutes or until the stock has been absorbed, and the carrots are cooked. Shake the pan frequently to prevent the carrots sticking.
Serves 6 to 8.

Cauliflower à la polonaise

METRIC	IMPERIAL
½ kg. frozen cauliflower flowerets	1 lb. frozen cauliflower flowerets
50 g. butter	2 oz. butter
45 ml. dry white breadcrumbs	3 tablespoons dry white breadcrumbs
1 hard-boiled egg, finely chopped	1 hard-boiled egg, finely chopped
15 ml. Parmesan cheese, grated	1 tablespoon Parmesan cheese, grated
Salt and freshly ground black pepper	Salt and freshly ground black pepper
15 ml. parsley, finely chopped	1 tablespoon parsley, finely chopped

Cook the cauliflower in boiling salted water for 10 minutes or until just tender. Drain well, place in a serving dish and keep hot.

Heat the butter in a saucepan until it is foaming, add the breadcrumbs, and stir over a medium heat until they are crisp and golden brown. Remove from the heat and add the egg and cheese. Season with salt and pepper, and spoon the crumbs over the cauliflower. Sprinkle with chopped parsley and serve at once.
Serves 4.

Chantilly carrots with peas

METRIC	IMPERIAL
½ kg. frozen carrots	1 lb. frozen carrots
100 g. packet frozen peas	4 oz. packet frozen peas
25 g. butter	1 oz. butter
60 ml. double cream	4 tablespoons double cream
15 ml. lemon juice	1 tablespoon lemon juice
Salt and freshly ground black pepper	Salt and freshly ground black pepper
Knob of butter	Knob of butter

Cook the frozen carrots in boiling salted water until just tender, and drain well.

Melt the butter in a saucepan, add the carrots and fry shaking occasionally, over medium heat for about 10 minutes or until the carrots absorb the butter and turn golden brown. Add the cream, lemon juice and seasoning to taste. Cover and keep warm.

Meanwhile cook the peas, drain and toss in the knob of butter.

Arrange the carrots around the sides of a serving dish and pile the peas into the centre.
Serves 4.

Cauliflower amandine

METRIC	IMPERIAL
½ kg. frozen cauliflower flowerets	1 lb. frozen cauliflower flowerets
50 g. almonds, blanched and slivered	2 oz. almonds, blanched and slivered
75 g. butter	3 oz. butter
Salt and freshly ground black pepper	Salt and freshly ground black pepper

Cook the cauliflower in boiling salted water for about 10 minutes or until just tender. Drain and keep hot in a serving dish.

Toast the almonds under the grill until golden brown. Melt the butter in a saucepan and add the almonds and seasoning to taste. Pour the sauce over the hot cauliflower and serve.
Serves 4.

Chantilly carrots with peas; Cauliflower amandine; Christmas Brussels sprouts; Carrots à la Vichy; Cauliflower à la polonaise

Desserts

Apple pie

Apple pie

METRIC
Shortcrust pastry
225 g. plain flour
Pinch of salt
*100 g. butter or margarine,
 cut into small pieces*
30–45 ml. cold water

Filling
*½ kg. cooking apples, peeled,
 cored and sliced thinly*
100 g. caster sugar
*Grated rind of ½ a lemon
 (optional)*

Milk for brushing
Caster sugar

IMPERIAL
Shortcrust pastry
8 oz. plain flour
Pinch of salt
*4 oz. butter or margarine,
 cut into small pieces*
2–3 tablespoons cold water

Filling
*1 lb. cooking apples, peeled,
 cored and sliced thinly*
4 oz. caster sugar
*Grated rind of ½ a lemon
 (optional)*

Milk for brushing
Caster sugar

Sift the flour and salt into a bowl, add the butter or margarine and rub in using the fingertips until the mixture resembles fine breadcrumbs. Add enough cold water to mix to a stiff dough with a palette knife. Draw the pastry together with the fingers and knead lightly on a floured surface for 1 minute, until smooth. Wrap in foil and chill in the refrigerator for 30 minutes.

Divide the pastry into two and roll out one-half on a floured surface. Use it to line a 20 cm./8 in. ovenproof plate. Pile the apples onto the pastry, sprinkle with the sugar and lemon rind if used and dampen the edge with a little cold water. Roll out the remaining pastry and use it to cover the pie. Seal the edges well and trim off any pastry with a sharp knife. Brush with milk and make a slit in the top of the pie to allow the steam to escape. Place the pie plate on a baking tray and bake in a hot oven (220°C/425°F or Gas Mark 7) for 20 minutes then reduce the heat to moderate (180°C/350°F or Gas Mark 4) for a further 35 minutes or until the pastry is brown. Remove from the oven and sprinkle with caster sugar.
To freeze: Cool completely and wrap in foil or place in a polythene bag. Seal and freeze.
To serve: Place the frozen pie in a hot oven (220°C/425°F or Gas Mark 7) for 20 minutes, then reduce the heat to moderate (180°C/350°F or Gas Mark 4) for a further 20 minutes. Serve warm with cream or custard.
Note: The pie may also be frozen uncooked. Wrap and freeze as for the cooked pie. Bake the frozen uncovered pie in a hot oven (220°C/425°F or Gas Mark 7) for 30 minutes, then turn the oven down to fairly hot (190°C/375°F or Gas Mark 5) for a further 40 minutes or until the pastry is brown.
Serves 4 to 6.

Apple and rhubarb crumble

METRIC
*225 g. cooking apples,
 peeled, cored and thinly
 sliced*
*225 g. rhubarb, washed,
 trimmed and cut into small
 pieces*
100–150 g. caster sugar
Grated rind of 1 orange

Crumble topping
175 g. plain flour
75 g. butter
75 g. caster sugar

IMPERIAL
*8 oz. cooking apples,
 peeled, cored and thinly
 sliced*
*8 oz. rhubarb, washed,
 trimmed and cut into small
 pieces*
4–5 oz. caster sugar
Grated rind of 1 orange

Crumble topping
6 oz. plain flour
3 oz. butter
3 oz. caster sugar

Place the fruit in a 900 ml./1½ pint pie dish, layering with the sugar to taste and the orange rind. Sift the flour into a bowl, rub in the butter until the mixture resembles fine breadcrumbs and stir in the sugar. Sprinkle the crumble evenly over the fruit, smooth the surface and press down lightly.
To freeze: Cover the dish with foil, place in a polythene bag, seal and freeze.
To serve: Place the uncovered frozen crumble in a hot oven (220°C/425°F or Gas Mark 7) for 20 minutes, then reduce the heat to fairly hot (190°C/375°F or Gas Mark 5) for a further 45 minutes or until heated through.
Serves 4.

Apple and rhubarb crumble; French apple tart

French apple tart

METRIC

Sweet flan pastry
150 g. plain flour
Pinch of salt
75 g. butter, cut into small
pieces
15 ml. caster sugar
10 ml. ground almonds
1 egg yolk
30–45 ml. cold water

Filling
450 g. cooking apples,
cooked unsweetened and
puréed
2 cooking apples, peeled,
cored and thinly sliced
50 g. sugar
Grated rind of ½ a lemon

Glaze
15 ml. apricot jam, sieved
10 ml. water
5 ml. lemon juice

IMPERIAL

Sweet flan pastry
5 oz. plain flour
Pinch of salt
2½ oz. butter, cut into small
pieces
1 tablespoon caster sugar
2 teaspoons ground almonds
1 egg yolk
2–3 tablespoons cold water

Filling
1 lb. cooking apples,
cooked unsweetened and
puréed
2 cooking apples, peeled,
cored and thinly sliced
2 oz. sugar
Grated rind of ½ a lemon

Glaze
1 tablespoon apricot jam,
sieved
2 teaspoons water
1 teaspoon lemon juice

Sift the flour and salt into a bowl, add the butter and using the fingertips, rub the fat and flour together until it resembles fine breadcrumbs; add the sugar and almonds. Stir in the egg and enough cold water to mix to a stiff dough with a palette knife. Turn out onto a floured surface and knead lightly for 1 minute, until smooth. Wrap in foil and chill in the refrigerator for 30 minutes.

Roll out the pastry on a floured surface and use to line a 20 cm./8 in. flan ring, set on a baking tray. Add the sugar and lemon rind to the apple purée and spoon into the flan case. Arrange the sliced apples neatly over the surface. Bake in a fairly hot oven (200°C/400°F or Gas Mark 6) for 25–30 minutes or until the pastry is cooked and the apples golden brown.

Put the jam, water and lemon juice in a saucepan and heat, stirring occasionally, until syrupy, then brush or spoon the glaze over the tart. If preferred, the tart may be glazed after freezing.

To freeze: Cool quickly and open freeze. When frozen, remove from the flan ring, wrap in foil, seal and return to the freezer.

To serve: Place the frozen wrapped tart in a hot oven (220°C/425°F or Gas Mark 7) for 20–30 minutes, removing the wrapping after 5 minutes. Cover the surface with foil if the pastry edges start to brown.

Serves 4 to 6.

Crêpes suzette

METRIC
Pancake batter
100 g. plain flour
Pinch of salt
2 eggs
300 ml. milk
10 ml. corn oil
Oil and butter for frying

Sauce
100 g. butter
100 g. caster sugar
Grated rind of 1 orange
Juice of 2 oranges
Juice of ½ a lemon
30 ml. brandy
15 ml. orange curaçao

IMPERIAL
Pancake batter
4 oz. plain flour
Pinch of salt
2 eggs
½ pint milk
2 teaspoons corn oil
Oil and butter for frying

Sauce
4 oz. butter
4 oz. caster sugar
Grated rind of 1 orange
Juice of 2 oranges
Juice of ½ a lemon
2 tablespoons brandy
1 tablespoon orange curaçao

Sift the flour and salt into a bowl, make a well in the centre, add the eggs, and gradually beat in half the milk. Mix until smooth, add the rest of the milk and the oil and beat until smooth. Allow to stand in a cool place for 30 minutes.

Melt a little oil and butter in a 15 cm./6 in. frying pan or omelette pan and when hot pour off any excess fat and pour in about 30 ml./2 tablespoons of batter, swirl round the pan until the base is evenly covered. Cook until the underside is golden brown, then turn and brown the other side. Repeat the process until all the mixture has been used, lightly greasing the pan between each addition and stacking the pancakes one on top of each other.

For the sauce, place the butter, sugar, rind and orange and lemon juice in a large frying pan and stir over a low heat until the butter has melted, and the sugar has dissolved. Increase the heat and simmer for 5 minutes, then add the brandy and curaçao. Fold the pancakes in half, then half again, to form a triangular shape and place in the sauce, spooning it over the pancakes so they are coated; remove from the heat.

To freeze: Arrange the pancakes overlapping in a large buttered ovenproof dish and pour over any remaining sauce. Cool quickly, cover with foil, seal and freeze.

To serve: Place the unwrapped frozen pancakes in a moderate oven (180°C/350°F or Gas Mark 4) for 15–20 minutes, or until heated through. After heating, the pancakes may be placed in a chafing dish, 30 ml./2 tablespoons warm brandy poured over and set alight.

Makes 12 pancakes.

Crêpes suzette

Chocolate sponge pudding

METRIC
100 g. butter
100 g. caster sugar
2 large eggs, beaten
75 g. self-raising flour
Pinch of salt
15 g. cornflour
15 g. cocoa powder
50 g. plain chocolate, melted with 15 ml. warm milk

IMPERIAL
4 oz. butter
4 oz. caster sugar
2 large eggs, beaten
3 oz. self-raising flour
Pinch of salt
½ oz. cornflour
½ oz. cocoa powder
2 oz. plain chocolate, melted with 1 tablespoon warm milk

Cream the butter and sugar together until fluffy and pale in colour. Add the eggs, a little at a time. Sift the flour, salt, cornflour and cocoa powder and fold into the creamed mixture. Add the melted chocolate and milk mixture and stir to make a soft mixture that will fall easily from a spoon.

Grease a 900 ml./1½ pint foil pudding basin and spoon in the mixture. Cover with buttered heavy duty foil with a pleat in the centre to allow for expansion. Secure the foil around the rim of the basin with string. Stand the basin in a saucepan with boiling water one third up the sides of the basin and steam for 1½–2 hours.

To freeze: Cool quickly, place in a plastic bag, seal and freeze.

To serve: Thaw at room temperature for 4 hours. Reheat by steaming for 45 minutes as above.

Serve with hot chocolate sauce.

Serves 4.

Chocolate sponge pudding; Normandy pear pie

Normandy pear pie

METRIC
Pastry
175 g. self-raising flour
Pinch of salt
100 g. butter, cut into small
    pieces
50 g. walnuts, chopped very
    finely
50 g. caster sugar
1 egg yolk, beaten
15–30 ml. cold water

Filling
15 ml. fine semolina
1 kg. ripe eating pears,
    peeled, quartered and
    cored
25 g. soft brown sugar
5 ml. ground cinnamon

IMPERIAL
Pastry
6 oz. self-raising flour
Pinch of salt
4 oz. butter, cut into small
    pieces
2 oz. walnuts, chopped very
    finely
2 oz. caster sugar
1 egg yolk, beaten
1–2 tablespoons cold water

Filling
1 tablespoon fine semolina
2 lb. ripe eating pears,
    peeled, quartered and
    cored
1 oz. soft brown sugar
1 teaspoon ground cinnamon

Sift the flour and salt into a bowl and rub in the fat with the fingertips until the mixture resembles fine breadcrumbs. Stir in the walnuts and caster sugar. Add the egg yolk and sufficient cold water to mix to a stiff dough. Turn onto a floured surface and knead lightly for 1 minute. Wrap in foil and chill in the refrigerator for 30 minutes.

Roll out half the pastry onto a floured surface and use it to line a 20 cm./8 in. ovenproof plate. Sprinkle the base with the semolina, arrange the pears on top and sprinkle with the sugar and cinnamon. Roll out the remaining pastry and use to top the pie. Seal the edges and make a small slit in the top of the pie.

To freeze: Cover with foil or place in a polythene bag. Seal and freeze.

To serve: Unwrap and place in a fairly hot oven (200°C/400°F or Gas Mark 6) for 30 minutes, then reduce the heat to moderate (180°C/350°F or Gas Mark 4) for a further 15 minutes. If the pie is browning too quickly, cover with foil. Serve warm, dusted with icing sugar.

Serves 4 to 6.

Treacle tart

METRIC
Shortcrust pastry
175 g. flour
Pinch of salt
75 g. butter
15–30 ml. cold water

IMPERIAL
Shortcrust pastry
6 oz. flour
Pinch of salt
3 oz. butter
1–2 tablespoons cold water

Filling
225 g. golden syrup
50 g. fresh white
  breadcrumbs
Grated rind of 1 lemon
Juice of ½ lemon

Filling
8 oz. golden syrup
2 oz. fresh white
  breadcrumbs
Grated rind of 1 lemon
Juice of ½ lemon

Sift the flour and salt into a bowl and rub in the butter until the mixture resembles fine breadcrumbs. Add enough cold water to mix to a stiff dough. Draw the pastry together with the fingers and knead lightly on a floured surface for 1 minute, until smooth. Wrap in foil and chill in the refrigerator for 30 minutes. Roll out the pastry on a floured surface and use to line a 20 cm./8 in. shallow ovenproof plate. Trim the edges and reserve the pastry trimmings.

Put the syrup, breadcrumbs and lemon rind and juice in a saucepan, heat gently until just melted and pour into the pastry case. Decorate the top with a lattice work of pastry strips, cut from the trimmings.

Bake in a moderate oven (180°C/350°F or Gas Mark 4) for 30 minutes, or until the pastry is lightly browned.

To freeze: Cool quickly and open freeze. When frozen, cover with foil or place in a polythene bag, seal and return to the freezer.

To serve: Unwrap and thaw for 3 hours at room temperature. Serve cold or reheat in a moderate oven (180°C/350°F or Gas Mark 4) for 10 minutes.

Serves 4 to 6.

Treacle tart

Syrup and orange pudding

Syrup and Orange Pudding

METRIC
100 g. butter
100 g. caster sugar
2 large eggs, beaten
Grated rind of 1 small orange
100 g. self-raising flour
Pinch of salt
15 ml. fresh orange juice
30 ml. golden syrup

IMPERIAL
4 oz. butter
4 oz. caster sugar
2 large eggs, beaten
Grated rind of 1 small orange
4 oz. self-raising flour
Pinch of salt
1 tablespoon fresh orange juice
2 tablespoons golden syrup

Cream the butter and sugar together until fluffy and pale in colour. Add the eggs a little at a time and the orange rind. Sift the flour with the salt and fold into the creamed mixture, adding the orange juice to make a soft mixture that will fall easily from a spoon.

Grease a 900 ml./1½ pint foil pudding basin, place the golden syrup in the bottom of the dish and spoon in the sponge mixture. Cover with buttered heavy duty foil with a pleat in the centre to allow for expansion. Secure the foil around the rim of the basin with string. Stand the basin in a saucepan with boiling water one third up the sides of the basin and steam for 1½–2 hours.

To freeze: Cool quickly, place in a plastic bag, seal and freeze.

To serve: Thaw at room temperature for 4 hours. Reheat by steaming for 45 minutes as above.

Serves 4.

Cherub peaches

METRIC	IMPERIAL
50 g. butter	2 oz. butter
100 g. soft brown sugar	4 oz. soft brown sugar
120 ml. sweet white wine	4 fl.oz. sweet white wine
1 cinnamon stick	1 cinnamon stick
4 peaches, skinned, halved and stoned	4 peaches, skinned, halved and stoned
15 ml. cornflour	1 tablespoon cornflour
60 ml. water	4 tablespoons water
15 ml. brandy	1 tablespoon brandy

Place the butter, sugar, wine and cinnamon in a large saucepan and stir over a low heat until the sugar dissolves. Bring slowly to simmering point and add the peaches. Simmer for 5 minutes. Lift out the fruit and place in a rigid container. Discard the cinnamon stick.

Blend the cornflour and water together until smooth, add to the sauce and bring to the boil, stirring constantly until the sauce thickens. Cook, stirring constantly, for a further 2 minutes then remove from the heat and stir in the brandy. Pour over the fruit.

To freeze: Cool quickly, cover, seal and freeze.
To serve: Tip the contents into a saucepan and heat very gently until warmed through. Serve with single cream.
Serves 4.

Granny's mixed fruit pudding

METRIC	IMPERIAL
100 g. plain flour	4 oz. plain flour
Pinch of salt	Pinch of salt
5 ml. baking powder	1 teaspoon baking powder
2.5 ml. mixed spice	½ teaspoon mixed spice
2.5 ml. ground cinnamon	½ teaspoon ground cinnamon
100 g. soft brown sugar	4 oz. soft brown sugar
100 g. fresh white breadcrumbs	4 oz. fresh white breadcrumbs
75 g. shredded suet	3 oz. shredded suet
225 g. mixed dried fruit	8 oz. mixed dried fruit
Grated rind of 1 orange	Grated rind of 1 orange
2 standard eggs, beaten	2 standard eggs, beaten
15 ml. orange marmalade, softened	1 tablespoon orange marmalade, softened
90–120 ml. milk	3–4 fl.oz. milk

Sift the flour, salt, baking powder, mixed spice and cinnamon into a bowl and stir in the sugar, breadcrumbs, suet, dried fruit and orange rind. Add the beaten eggs, marmalade and enough milk to give a soft consistency.

Spoon into a 1 l./1¾ pint buttered foil basin. Cover with buttered heavy duty foil with a pleat in the centre to allow for expansion. Secure the foil round the rim of the basin with string. Stand the basin in a saucepan with boiling water one third up the sides of the basin and boil for 2½ hours.

To freeze: Cool quickly, wrap, seal and freeze.
To serve: Thaw at room temperature for 4 hours and reheat by steaming for 1 hour or until heated through.
Serves 4 to 6.

Cherub peaches; Granny's mixed fruit pudding

Mince pies

METRIC	IMPERIAL
225 g. plain flour	*8 oz. plain flour*
1.25 ml. salt	*¼ teaspoon salt*
150 g. butter, cut into small pieces	*5 oz. butter, cut into small pieces*
15 g. caster sugar	*½ oz. caster sugar*
15 g. ground almonds	*½ oz. ground almonds*
15–30 ml. cold water	*1–2 tablespoons cold water*
350 g. mincemeat	*12 oz. mincemeat*

Sift the flour and salt into a bowl, add the butter, and rub in with the fingertips, until the mixture looks like fine breadcrumbs. Stir in the sugar and almonds. Add 15 ml./1 tablespoon water and, using a knife, mix to a stiff crumbly dough, adding more water if necessary. Draw the dough together with the fingertips, and turn out onto a floured working surface. Knead lightly for 1 minute, then wrap in foil and chill in the refrigerator for 30 minutes.

Roll out the pastry thinly and cut 12 circles using a 7½ cm./3 in. plain cutter and 12 circles using a 6½ cm./2½ in. cutter. Use the larger circles to line deep patty tins and divide the mincemeat equally between them. Dampen the edges of the pastry and top with the remaining circles, sealing well.

To freeze: Open freeze. When frozen, remove the mince pies from the patty tins and place in a polythene or rigid container. Seal and return to the freezer.

To serve: Return the frozen mince pies to the patty tins, brush them with beaten egg, sprinkle with a little caster sugar and place them in a fairly hot oven (200°C/400°F or Gas Mark 6) for 20 minutes or until brown.

Serve warm with cream or brandy hard sauce.

Note: The mince pies can be frozen cooked if preferred, but they will need 10–15 minutes in a hot oven before serving.

Makes 12.

Mince pies; Iced Christmas pudding

Iced Christmas pudding

METRIC	IMPERIAL
15 ml. glacé cherries, roughly chopped	1 tablespoon glacé cherries, roughly chopped
15 ml. sultanas, roughly chopped	1 tablespoon sultanas, roughly chopped
30 ml. glacé pineapple, roughly chopped	2 tablespoons glacé pineapple, roughly chopped
15 ml. currants	1 tablespoon currants
30 ml. brandy or kirsch	2 tablespoons brandy or kirsch
600 ml. vanilla ice cream	1 pint vanilla ice cream

Place the fruits in a bowl, add the brandy or kirsch and allow to marinate for 2 hours. Place the ice cream in a bowl and beat, to soften. Add the marinated fruits and marinade and mix well. Turn the mixture into a 900 ml./1½ pint foil basin.
To freeze: Wrap, seal and freeze.
To serve: Unwrap, unmould, place on a serving dish and thaw at room temperature for 15 minutes. Cover the pudding completely with rosettes of whipped cream and decorate with small pieces of glacé cherries and angelica.
Serves 4 to 6.

Walnut and brown sugar flan

Walnut and brown sugar flan

METRIC	IMPERIAL
Pastry	**Pastry**
225 g. plain flour	8 oz. plain flour
2.5 ml. salt	½ teaspoon salt
50 g. butter, cut into small pieces	2 oz. butter, cut into small pieces
50 g. margarine, cut into small pieces	2 oz. margarine, cut into small pieces
15–30 ml. cold water	1–2 tablespoons cold water
Filling	**Filling**
100 g. butter	4 oz. butter
100 g. soft brown sugar	4 oz. soft brown sugar
1 large egg, beaten	1 large egg, beaten
50 g. walnuts, finely chopped	2 oz. walnuts, finely chopped
100 g. self-raising flour sifted with 2.5 ml. cinnamon	4 oz. self-raising flour sifted with ½ teaspoon cinnamon
15 ml. milk	1 tablespoon milk
15 ml. sultanas (optional)	1 tablespoon sultanas (optional)

Sift the flour and salt into a bowl, add the butter and margarine and rub in using the fingertips until the mixture resembles fine breadcrumbs. Stir in enough cold water to mix to a firm dough. Knead lightly on a floured surface for 1 minute. Wrap in foil and chill in the refrigerator for 30 minutes. Roll out on a floured surface and use to line a 20 cm./8 in. flan ring placed on a baking tray.

For the filling, place the butter and sugar in a bowl and beat until the mixture is light and fluffy. Beat in the egg and walnuts and fold in the sifted flour and cinnamon alternately with the milk. Stir in the sultanas if using and turn the mixture into the flan case. Smooth the top with a knife and bake in a hot oven (220°C/425°F or Gas Mark 7) for 15 minutes, then reduce the temperature to warm (160°C/325°F or Gas Mark 3) for a further 25 minutes or until browned. Remove from the oven and allow to cool.
To freeze: When cold, remove carefully from the flan ring, wrap in foil, seal and freeze.
To serve: Thaw wrapped for 2–3 hours at room temperature. The flan may either be warmed in the oven or served cold. If serving cold, blend 90 ml./3 tablespoons sieved icing sugar with 10 ml./2 teaspoons lemon juice. Stir well and pour over the flan, decorate with walnut halves.
Serves 6.

Rum baba

METRIC	IMPERIAL
15 g. fresh yeast	*½ oz. fresh yeast*
125 ml. lukewarm milk	*4 fl.oz. lukewarm milk*
225 g. plain flour	*8 oz. plain flour*
1.25 ml. salt	*¼ teaspoon salt*
25 g. sugar	*1 oz. sugar*
4 eggs	*4 eggs*
100 g. butter, melted	*4 oz. butter, melted*
50 g. raisins	*2 oz. raisins*
25 g. currants	*1 oz. currants*

Syrup

100 g. sugar	*4 oz. sugar*
120 ml. water	*4 fl.oz. water*
60 ml. rum	*4 tablespoons rum*

Blend the yeast with the warm milk. Sift the flour and salt into a basin, make a well in the centre, add the yeasted milk and sprinkle in the sugar. Cover and leave in a warm place for 20 minutes or until frothy.

Beat the eggs and add to the yeast dough together with the butter, raisins and currants. Beat well for 5 minutes, until smooth. Half fill 12 small greased baba moulds or a savarin mould with the mixture. Cover with a greased polythene bag and allow the mixture to rise in a warm room, for 30 minutes or until double in bulk.

Bake in a fairly hot oven (200°C/400°F or Gas Mark 6) for 20–25 minutes for small moulds or 40 minutes to 1 hour for a large savarin mould. Turn out and cool on a wire rack.

Place the sugar and water in a small saucepan and stir over a low heat until the sugar has dissolved. Increase the heat and boil rapidly, without stirring, for 6 minutes. Remove from the heat, add the rum and pour over the warm babas.

To freeze: When cold, wrap in foil or place in a polythene bag. Seal and freeze.

To serve: Unwrap, unmould and thaw for 3 hours at room temperature.

Serves 12.

Iced gâteau

METRIC	IMPERIAL
100 g. butter	*4 oz. butter*
150 g. caster sugar	*5 oz. caster sugar*
4 eggs, separated	*4 eggs, separated*
Grated rind and juice of 1 lemon	*Grated rind and juice of 1 lemon*
32 sponge fingers	*32 sponge fingers*
2 oranges, peel, pith and outer membrane removed and cut into segments	*2 oranges, peel, pith and outer membrane removed and cut into segments*

Place the butter and sugar in a bowl and beat until pale and fluffy. Add the egg yolks, one at a time, beating well between each addition and stir in the lemon juice and rind. Place the

egg whites in a clean dry bowl and whisk until stiff. Gently fold the egg whites into the lemon mixture.

Use a strip of doubled foil to line the base of a 1 kg./2 lb. loaf tin, leaving the foil sticking up at either end of the tin. Line the sides with sponge fingers. Spoon in a layer of the lemon mixture and top with half the orange segments. Repeat the layers finishing with the remaining sponge fingers, cut to size. Press down gently with the palm of your hand, cover and chill in the refrigerator for 4 hours. Using scissors, trim the sponge fingers level with the tin.

To freeze: Open freeze. When frozen, dip the tin quickly in hot water and lift out the gateau using the foil strip. Wrap the gateau in foil, seal and return to the freezer.

To serve: Thaw unwrapped at room temperature for 20 minutes. Decorate with 150 ml./¼ pint whipped cream and toasted almonds.

Serves 6.

Chestnut vacherin

METRIC
Meringue
6 egg whites
350 g. caster sugar

Filling
300 ml. double cream
15 ml. milk
250 g. can sweetened
*   chestnut purée*

IMPERIAL
Meringue
6 egg whites
12 oz. caster sugar

Filling
½ pint double cream
1 tablespoon milk
9 oz. can sweetened
*   chestnut purée*

Line 3 baking trays with greased greaseproof paper and mark a 23 cm./9 in. circle on each.

Place the egg whites in a clean dry bowl and whisk until stiff and standing in peaks. Whisk in half the sugar, whisk again for 1 minute then, using a metal spoon, fold in the remaining sugar. Spoon equal amounts of meringue on each baking tray, and spread evenly over the circle using a palette knife. Dry the meringue in the oven at the lowest setting for about 4 hours or until crisp. Remove from the oven and allow to cool. To prevent cracking, lift from the baking tray and gently peel away the greaseproof.

Whisk the cream and milk together until the mixture holds its shape and fold into the chestnut purée. Sandwich the 3 layers together with the chestnut filling.

To freeze: Open freeze. When frozen, place in a rigid container or polythene bag. Seal and return to the freezer, store very carefully as the meringue remains fragile.

To serve: Unwrap, place on a serving dish and thaw for 3 hours at room temperature. Decorate the top with grated chocolate.

Serves 8.

Rum baba; Iced gâteau; Chestnut vacherin

Rich lemon cheesecake

Melt the butter gently in a saucepan, remove from the heat and add the crushed biscuits and brown sugar. Mix well and turn the crumbs into an 18 cm./7 in. flan ring, set on a baking tray. Press the crumbs around the sides and base of the flan ring. Chill in the refrigerator for 20 minutes.

Place the cheese, sugar, lemon rind and juice in a bowl and beat until smooth. Place the water in a small bowl, sprinkle on the gelatine, stir once and leave until spongy. Place the bowl in a pan of hot water and stir until dissolved then strain it into the cheese mixture and stir well. Whip the double cream until just stiff and fold into the cheese mixture. Turn the mixture into the flan ring.

To freeze: Open freeze. When solid, remove the flan ring and wrap the flan in foil. Seal and return to the freezer.

To serve: Unwrap, place on a serving dish and thaw in the refrigerator overnight or at room temperature for 4–5 hours. Decorate with grated chocolate.

Serves 6.

Raspberry layer gâteau

METRIC	IMPERIAL
Sponge bases	**Sponge bases**
4 standard eggs, beaten	*4 standard eggs, beaten*
100 g. caster sugar	*4 oz. caster sugar*
5 ml. vanilla essence	*1 teaspoon vanilla essence*
100 g. plain flour, sifted	*4 oz. plain flour, sifted*
Syrup	**Syrup**
30 ml. sugar	*2 tablespoons sugar*
30 ml. water	*2 tablespoons water*
15 ml. sherry	*1 tablespoon sherry*

Grease three 20 cm./8 in. sandwich tins and line the bases with greased greaseproof paper.

Place the eggs, sugar and vanilla essence in a bowl standing over a pan of hot water, and whisk until the mixture is thick and pale in colour. Remove from the heat and continue to whisk until the mixture is cool. Sift half the flour into the egg mixture and gently but quickly fold in, using a large metal spoon. Repeat the process with the remaining flour. Divide the mixture equally between the 3 tins and bake in a fairly hot oven (190°C/375°F or Gas Mark 5) for 15 minutes or until cakes spring back when lightly pressed. Allow to stand in the tin for 5 minutes, then turn out onto a wire rack to cool and remove the greaseproof paper.

Place the sugar and water in a saucepan and stir over a low heat until the sugar dissolves. Increase the heat and boil for 2 minutes, without stirring. Remove from the heat and add the sherry. Moisten the sponge layers with the syrup.

To freeze: Wrap the sponges in a polythene bag, with freezer wrap or waxed paper between each layer. Seal and freeze.

To serve: Unwrapped thaw at room temperature for 2 hours. Whip 300 ml./½ pint whipping cream with 10 ml./2 teaspoons caster sugar and sandwich the 3 layers together with the cream, arranging raspberries (from a 225 g./8 oz. packet frozen raspberries) over the cream. Dust with icing sugar and stand at room temperature for 30 minutes before serving.

Serves 6.

Rich lemon cheesecake

METRIC	IMPERIAL
Biscuit crust	**Biscuit crust**
50 g. butter	*2 oz. butter*
100 g. chocolate digestive biscuits, crushed finely	*4 oz. chocolate digestive biscuits, crushed finely*
25 g. soft brown sugar	*1 oz. soft brown sugar*
Filling	**Filling**
350 g. full fat cream cheese, softened	*12 oz. full fat cream cheese, softened*
75 g. caster sugar	*3 oz. caster sugar*
Grated rind of 1 lemon	*Grated rind of 1 lemon*
Juice of 2 lemons	*Juice of 2 lemons*
30 ml. cold water	*2 tablespoons cold water*
15 g. gelatine	*½ oz. gelatine*
150 ml. double cream	*¼ pint double cream*

Apricot torte

METRIC
3 eggs, separated
100 g. caster sugar
2.5 ml. ground cinnamon
50 g. fine semolina
25 g. ground almonds

IMPERIAL
3 eggs, separated
4 oz. caster sugar
½ teaspoon ground cinnamon
2 oz. fine semolina
1 oz. ground almonds

Grease a 20 cm./8 in. sandwich tin and line with greased greaseproof paper. Place the egg yolks and sugar in a bowl standing over a saucepan of simmering water and whisk until the mixture is thick and pale. Remove from the heat and continue to whisk until the mixture cools. With a metal spoon gently fold in the cinnamon, semolina and almonds.

Place the egg whites in a clean, dry bowl and whisk until stiff, then fold into the egg mixture. Turn the mixture into the prepared tin and bake in a moderate oven (180°C/350°F or Gas Mark 4) for 25–30 minutes or until the cake springs back when lightly pressed. Turn out onto a wire rack to cool and remove the greaseproof paper.

To freeze: When cold, wrap in foil or place in a polythene bag. Seal and freeze.
To serve: Unwrap and thaw for 2 hours at room temperature. Split the cake in half and spread with 150 ml./¼ pint whipped cream and the contents of a 400 g./14 oz. can of apricot pie filling. Sandwich together and decorate the top with a further 150 ml./¼ pint whipped cream.
Serves 6.

Raspberry layer gâteau   Apricot torte

153

Chocolate profiteroles

Oranges in caramel sauce

Chocolate profiteroles

METRIC	IMPERIAL
150 g. plain flour	*5 oz. plain flour*
1.25 ml. salt	*¼ teaspoon salt*
300 ml. water	*½ pint water*
100 g. butter	*4 oz. butter*
4 standard eggs, well beaten	*4 standard eggs, well beaten*

Sift the flour and salt together. Place the water and butter in a saucepan and heat gently until the butter melts, then increase the heat and bring to the boil. Remove the pan from the heat and quickly pour in all the flour. Beat well for about 30 seconds or until the paste is smooth and leaves the sides of the pan clean. Do not overbeat. Cool slightly and add the eggs gradually, beating well until the mixture is smooth and glossy. Cover the pan and leave until cold.

Place the mixture in a piping bag fitted with a plain 1 cm./½ in. nozzle. Pipe 36 equal amounts of choux pastry in ball shapes, well apart on greased baking trays. Bake in a fairly hot oven (200°C/400°F or Gas Mark 6) for 10 minutes, then reduce the temperature to moderate (180°C/350°F or Gas Mark 4) for a further 20 minutes, or until crisp, golden and puffed. Remove from the oven, make a small slit in each bun to release the steam and return to the oven for a further 5 minutes to dry out. Cool on a wire tray.

To freeze: Pack in polythene bags, seal and freeze.

To serve: Thaw wrapped for 1–1½ hours at room temperature. Remove from the bag and place on a baking tray in a moderate oven (180°C/350°F or Gas Mark 4) for 5 minutes. Cool, and fill the whipped cream. Pile in a pyramid shape in a serving dish and pour over warm chocolate sauce (see page 77).

Makes 36.

Oranges in caramel sauce

METRIC	IMPERIAL
6 oranges	*6 oranges*
175 g. granulated sugar	*6 oz. granulated sugar*
180 ml. water	*6 fl. oz. water*
30 ml. brandy or kirsch	*2 tablespoons brandy or kirsch*

Using a serrated knife, cut the rind, pith and outer membrane from the oranges. Leave whole or cut into slices and place in a rigid container.

Place the sugar and water in a small heavy saucepan and stir over a gentle heat until the sugar has dissolved. Increase the heat and boil rapidly, without stirring, until the sauce turns a rich caramel colour (take care not to burn it), remove from the heat and add the brandy. Pour over the oranges.

To freeze: Cool quickly, cover, seal and freeze.

To serve: Thaw covered in the refrigerator for 4–6 hours.

Serves 4 to 6.

Honey lemon cream pie

METRIC	IMPERIAL
50 g. butter	2 oz. butter
100 g. digestive biscuits, crushed finely	4 oz. digestive biscuits, crushed finely
25 g. soft brown sugar	1 oz. soft brown sugar
Small can evaporated milk, chilled	Small can evaporated milk, chilled
Finely grated rind and juice of 1 large lemon	Finely grated rind and juice of 1 large lemon
15 ml. clear honey	1 tablespoon clear honey
30 ml. water	2 tablespoons water
15 g. gelatine	$\frac{1}{2}$ oz. gelatine

Gently melt the butter in a saucepan, remove from the heat and stir in the biscuit crumbs and brown sugar. Press around the base of an 18 cm./7 in. loose bottomed cake tin. Place in the refrigerator to chill for 30 minutes.

Pour the evaporated milk into a large bowl, and whisk until very thick and creamy. Add the rind and juice of the lemon and the honey and whisk well. Place the water in a small bowl, sprinkle on the gelatine, stir once and leave until spongy, then place the bowl in a pan of hot water and stir until dissolved. Strain into the honey lemon mixture, whisk well and pour into the biscuit crust, smoothing the surface with a knife.

To freeze: Open freeze. When frozen, remove the pie from the cake tin, wrap in foil, seal and return to the freezer.

To serve: Unwrap and thaw for $1\frac{1}{2}$–2 hours at room temperature. Decorate with grated chocolate.

Serves 4.

Honey lemon cream pie

Charlotte russe

METRIC	IMPERIAL
½ packet lemon or orange jelly	½ packet lemon or orange jelly
Glacé cherries and angelica	Glacé cherries and angelica
28 sponge fingers	28 sponge fingers
150 ml. double cream	¼ pint double cream
600 ml. cold custard of good pouring consistency	1 pint cold custard of good pouring consistency
30 ml. orange curaçao	2 tablespoons orange curaçao
Juice of 1 orange	Juice of 1 orange
Finely grated rind of 2 oranges	Finely grated rind of 2 oranges
60 ml. water	4 tablespoons water
15 g. gelatine	½ oz. gelatine

Make up the jelly as directed on the packet and pour a thin layer of it into the bottom of a 600 ml./1 pint mould or deep cake tin. Leave to set. Decorate the jelly layer with small pieces of cherry and angelica and spoon over a little more jelly to secure the decoration.

Measure the sponge fingers against the side of the mould and trim if necessary. Dip the sides of the fingers in the reserved liquid jelly and arrange the fingers closely together, sugar side outwards, around the sides of the mould.

Whip the cream until it just holds its shape. Mix together the custard, cream, curaçao, orange juice and rind. Place the water in a small basin, sprinkle on the gelatine, stir once and leave until spongy. Place the basin in a pan of hot water and stir until dissolved. Strain into the custard mixture and stir well. Leave the mixture in a cool place, stirring occasionally and, when just beginning to set, pour into the mould.

To freeze: Cover, seal and freeze.
To serve: Unwrap, unmould, place on a serving dish and thaw for 3–4 hours at room temperature.
Serves 8.

Strawberry soufflé

METRIC	IMPERIAL
45 ml. water	3 tablespoons water
15 ml. gelatine	1 tablespoon gelatine
150 ml. strawberry purée, made from fresh, frozen or canned fruit	¼ pint strawberry purée, made from fresh, frozen or canned fruit
10 ml. lemon juice	2 teaspoons lemon juice
50 g. icing sugar, sifted	2 oz. icing sugar, sifted
150 ml. double cream	¼ pint double cream
3 egg whites	3 egg whites

Firmly tie a double band of oiled foil or greaseproof paper round a 15 cm./6 in. soufflé dish so that the band stands 5 cm./2 in. above the rim.

Place the water in a small bowl, sprinkle in the gelatine, stir once and leave until spongy. Place the bowl in a pan of hot water and stir until dissolved. Strain the gelatine into the fruit purée and add the lemon juice and sugar. Taste and add more sugar if necessary. Leave the purée in a cool place, stirring occasionally, until it is just beginning to set. Whip the cream until it is just standing in peaks. Place the egg whites in a clean dry bowl and whisk until stiff. Gently fold the cream and then the egg whites into the purée. Pour into the prepared dish.

To freeze: Open freeze. When frozen wrap carefully in a polythene bag, seal and return to the freezer.
To serve: Unwrap, remove the band and thaw in the refrigerator for 4–5 hours. Serve chilled, decorated with whipped cream and strawberries.
Serves 4 to 5.

Milanese soufflé

METRIC	IMPERIAL
4 eggs, separated	4 eggs, separated
100 g. caster sugar	4 oz. caster sugar
Finely grated rind of 2 lemons	Finely grated rind of 2 lemons
Juice of 3 lemons	Juice of 3 lemons
30 ml. water	2 tablespoons water
15 g. gelatine	½ oz. gelatine
150 ml. double cream	¼ pint double cream

Firmly tie a double band of oiled foil or greaseproof paper round a 13 cm./5 in. soufflé dish, so that the band stands 5 cm./2 in. above the rim.

Place the egg yolks, sugar, lemon rind and juice into a bowl and set over a pan of simmering water. Whisk until thick, creamy and pale yellow in colour then remove from the saucepan. Place the water in a small bowl, sprinkle the gelatine over, stir once and leave until spongy. Place the bowl in a pan of hot water and stir until dissolved. Strain into the lemon mixture and stir well.

Whip the cream until it is just standing in peaks. Whisk the egg whites until stiff, and with a metal spoon fold the cream and then the egg whites into the lemon mixture. Pour immediately into the prepared dish.

To freeze: Open freeze. When frozen, place in a polythene bag, seal and return to the freezer.
To serve: Unwrap and thaw in the refrigerator for 5 hours. Remove the foil band from the soufflé dish carefully, and decorate the sides with finely chopped walnuts or almonds. Top with swirls of cream and serve chilled.
Serves 6 to 8.

Gooseberry fool

Frozen gooseberry purée can be used in this recipe; you will need 450 ml./¾ pint thick purée, partially thawed.

METRIC	IMPERIAL
½ kg. gooseberries, topped and tailed	1 lb. gooseberries, topped and tailed
60 ml. water	4 tablespoons water
Finely grated rind of ½ an orange	Finely grated rind of ½ an orange
Caster sugar to taste	Caster sugar to taste
300 ml. whipping cream	½ pint whipping cream

Place the gooseberries in a saucepan with the water, cover and cook until tender. Pass the fruit and juice through a sieve. Stir the orange rind and sugar to taste into the purée. Whip the cream until it is just standing in peaks and fold into the purée.

To freeze: Pour into 4–6 dishes, cover, seal and freeze.
To serve: Thaw covered in the refrigerator for 4 hours or at room temperature for 2 hours. Serve chilled.
Serves 4 to 6.

Charlotte russe; Strawberry soufflé; Milanese soufflé; Gooseberry fool

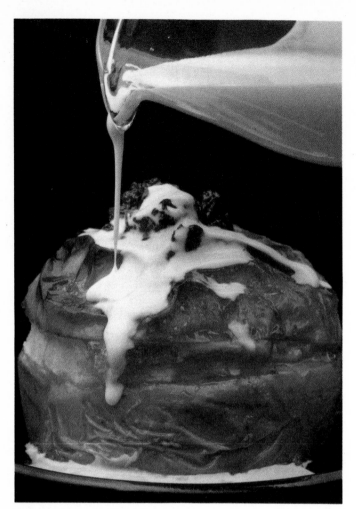

Baked cinnamon and raisin apples

Baked cinnamon and raisin apples

METRIC	IMPERIAL
4 large cooking apples	4 large cooking apples
75 g. soft brown sugar	3 oz. soft brown sugar
5 ml. ground cinnamon	1 teaspoon ground cinnamon
15 ml. mincemeat	1 tablespoon mincemeat
30 ml. raisins	2 tablespoons raisins
120 ml. cider	4 fl.oz. cider
25 g. butter	1 oz. butter

Wash the apples and, using a knife or corer, hollow out the centres and remove the cores. Score a line round each apple, about halfway down from the top. Place the apples in a shallow baking dish. Mix the sugar, cinnamon, mincemeat and raisins together and use to fill the centres of each apple, packing down firmly. Pour the cider round the apples and top each apple with a little butter. Bake in a moderate oven (180°C/350°F or Gas Mark 4), basting frequently to prevent burning, for 45 minutes to 1 hour, or until tender.
To freeze: Pack the apples and juice into a rigid container. Cover, seal and freeze.
To serve: Thaw covered in the refrigerator for 5–6 hours or at room temperature for 3 hours.
  Serve cold, or heat through in a moderate oven for 25 minutes.
Serves 4.

Summer pudding

Frozen fruit can be used in this recipe, allow it to thaw first.

METRIC	IMPERIAL
150 g. sugar	5 oz. sugar
60 ml. water	4 tablespoons water
225 g. blackcurrants, washed and stalks removed	8 oz. blackcurrants, washed and stalks removed
225 g. ripe red plums, washed, halved and stones removed	8 oz. ripe red plums, washed, halved and stones removed
225 g. raspberries, washed and hulled	8 oz. raspberries, washed and hulled
225 g. strawberries, washed and hulled	8 oz. strawberries, washed and hulled
8–10 slices of white bread, crusts removed	8–10 slices of white bread, crusts removed

Put the sugar and water in a saucepan and heat gently, stirring, until sugar has dissolved. Add the blackcurrants and plums, cover and cook gently until tender. Add the raspberries and strawberries and cook for 2 minutes. Remove from the heat, and allow to cool.
  Cut the bread into fingers and line the base and sides of a 1 l./1¾ pint basin, reserving enough for the lid. Pour in the stewed fruit and top with the reserved bread. Cover with a plate or saucer small enough to fit inside the basin. Put a weight on top so that the fruit is firmly pressed down and

Summer pudding

Rich chocolate mousse

leave in a cool place for 4–5 hours.
To freeze: Remove the weight and plate. Place the basin in a polythene bag or wrap in foil. Seal and freeze.
To serve: Thaw overnight in a refrigerator. Turn out and serve chilled with double cream.
Serves 8.

Rich chocolate mousse

METRIC	IMPERIAL
225 g. plain chocolate, broken into pieces	8 oz. plain chocolate, broken into pieces
4 eggs, separated	4 eggs, separated
15 ml. rum	1 tablespoon rum
15 g. butter	½ oz. butter

Melt the chocolate in a double boiler or in a basin over hot water. When melted, stir in the egg yolks, one at a time, the rum and the butter. Whisk the egg whites in a clean dry bowl until stiff and fold them into the chocolate mixture until thoroughly mixed.
To freeze: Spoon into 4 small dishes, cover, seal and freeze.
To serve: Thaw in the refrigerator for 2–3 hours and serve chilled, decorated with whipped cream.
Serves 4.

Fruit salad

METRIC	IMPERIAL
225 g. caster sugar	½ lb. caster sugar
600 ml. water	1 pint water
Juice and pared rind of 1 lemon	Juice and pared rind of 1 lemon
225 g. eating apples, peeled, cored and sliced	½ lb. eating apples, peeled, cored and sliced
4 oranges, peel, pith and outer membrane removed and cut into segments	4 oranges, peel, pith and outer membrane removed and cut into segments
100 g. grapes, peeled, halved and pips removed	4 oz. grapes, peeled, halved and pips removed
225 g. cherries, stones removed	½ lb. cherries, stones removed
1 pineapple, peeled, cored and cut into chunks	1 pineapple, peeled, cored and cut into chunks
1 small melon, peeled, seeds removed and cut into chunks	1 small melon, peeled, seeds removed and cut into chunks

Place the sugar, water, lemon juice and peel in a saucepan, stir over a low heat until the sugar has dissolved then increase the heat and boil without stirring for 1 minute. Remove from the heat, discard the lemon rind and chill the syrup.

Place the prepared fruit in a rigid container and pour over the chilled syrup.
To freeze: Cover, seal and freeze.
To serve: Thaw, covered, overnight in the refrigerator.
Serves 8 to 10.

Fruit salad

Pears in red wine

Baked Alaska

Pears in red wine

METRIC	IMPERIAL
150 ml. water	¼ pint water
150 ml. red wine	¼ pint red wine
175 g. sugar	6 oz. sugar
Strip of lemon rind	Strip of lemon rind
Cinnamon stick	Cinnamon stick
6 eating pears, peeled and	6 eating pears, peeled and
left whole with stalks on	left whole with stalks on

Place the water, wine, sugar, lemon rind and cinnamon stick in a saucepan, and stir over a gentle heat until the sugar has dissolved. Bring to the boil and boil briskly without stirring for 3 minutes.

Add the pears to the syrup, and poach for 20–30 minutes or until just tender.

Remove the pears and place in a polythene container.

Remove the lemon rind and cinnamon stick and boil the syrup briskly, uncovered, until reduced by about half. Pour over the pears.

To freeze: Cool quickly. Cover, seal and freeze.

To serve: Thaw overnight in the refrigerator or at room temperature, uncovered, for 5 hours. Serve chilled, garnished with flaked toasted almonds and serve with whipped cream.

Serves 6.

Baked Alaska

METRIC	IMPERIAL
100 g. trifle sponges	4 oz. trifle sponges
30 ml. sweet sherry	2 tablespoons sweet sherry
3 egg whites	3 egg whites
150 g. caster sugar	6 oz. caster sugar
600 ml. vanilla ice cream	1 pint vanilla ice cream

Halve the trifle sponges and use them to line a shallow foil dish. Moisten with the sherry. Whisk the egg whites in a clean dry bowl until they are stiff. Whisk in half the sugar and continue to whisk for 1 minute. Fold in the remaining sugar.

Pile the ice cream onto the sponge cakes, leaving a 1 cm./½ in. margin round the edge. Swirl the meringue completely over the ice cream and cake, so that everything, including the margin, is thickly covered in meringue.

To freeze: Open freeze immediately. When frozen, wrap lightly, seal and return to the freezer. The meringue always remains slightly soft.

To serve: Unwrap and place immediately in a hot oven (220°C/425°F or Gas Mark 7) for 4–5 minutes or until brown and crisp. Serve immediately.

Serves 6.

Snow queen

Bombe tortoni

Snow queen

METRIC
300 ml. double cream
30 ml. brandy
15 ml. caster sugar
100 g. meringue, roughly
  broken

IMPERIAL
½ pint double cream
2 tablespoons brandy
1 tablespoon caster sugar
4 oz. meringue, roughly
  broken

Whisk the cream until stiff and stir in the brandy and caster sugar. Fold in the roughly broken meringue. Taste and add more sugar if necessary. Pour the mixture into a lightly oiled 600 ml./1 pint pudding basin or bombe mould.
To freeze: Cover, seal and freeze.
To serve: Unwrap, unmould, place on a serving dish and thaw for 15 minutes in the refrigerator. Decorate with raspberries or serve with sauce melba.
Serves 4.

Bombe tortoni

METRIC
300 ml. double cream
150 ml. single cream
75 g. icing sugar, sifted
2.5 ml. vanilla essence
2 egg whites
100 g. crushed macaroons
30 ml. sweet sherry

IMPERIAL
½ pint double cream
¼ pint single cream
3 oz. icing sugar, sifted
½ teaspoon vanilla essence
2 egg whites
4 oz. crushed macaroons
2 tablespoons sweet sherry

Pour the double and single cream into a bowl and whip until thick. Stir in half the icing sugar and the vanilla essence. Whisk the egg whites until stiff and fold in the remaining icing sugar. Fold the whisked egg whites into the cream mixture. Stir in the macaroons and sherry. Taste and add more icing sugar if necessary.
  Spoon into 2 lightly oiled 600 ml./1 pint bombe moulds, or foil-lined pudding basins.
To freeze: Cover, seal and freeze.
To serve: Unwrap, unmould and place the frozen bombe on a serving dish and thaw for 2½ hours in a refrigerator. Serve while still slightly hard, decorated with strawberries.
Each bombe serves 6.

Grapefruit sorbet

METRIC	IMPERIAL
100 g. caster sugar	4 oz. caster sugar
240 ml. water	8 fl.oz. water
1 × 175 ml. can frozen concentrated grapefruit juice	1 × 6¼ fl.oz. can frozen concentrated grapefruit juice
Grated rind and juice of 1 grapefruit	Grated rind and juice of 1 grapefruit
2 egg whites	2 egg whites

Place the sugar and water in a saucepan. Stir over a low heat until the sugar has dissolved. Increase the heat and boil for 1 minute without stirring, then remove from the heat and allow to get cold. Add the concentrated juice and the rind and juice of the grapefruit to the syrup, pour into an ice tray or shallow rigid container. Place in the freezer for 1 hour or until the sorbet is just beginning to reach a mushy stage. Turn the mixture into a bowl and beat until smooth. Whisk the egg whites until stiff, and fold into the sorbet. Return to the tray or container.
To freeze: Cover, seal and return to the freezer.
To serve: Thaw covered in the refrigerator for 10 minutes.
Serves 6.

Orange and lemon ice cream

METRIC	IMPERIAL
6 egg yolks	6 egg yolks
225 g. caster sugar	8 oz. caster sugar
Finely grated rind and juice of 2 small oranges	Finely grated rind and juice of 2 small oranges
Finely grated rind and juice of 1 lemon	Finely grated rind and juice of 1 lemon
300 ml. double cream	½ pint double cream

Place the egg yolks and sugar in a bowl and whisk until they are thick and creamy. Gradually whisk in the rind and juice of the oranges and lemon. Whisk the double cream until it just holds its shape and fold into the egg yolk mixture. Turn into a 1.2 l./2 pint foil basin.
To freeze: Cover, seal and freeze.
To serve: Turn out the ice cream and thaw at room temperature for 5–10 minutes before serving. Decorate with piped whipped cream and crystallised orange and lemon slices.
Serves 8.

Raspberry sorbet

This may also be made with blackcurrants.

METRIC	IMPERIAL
½ kg. raspberries, frozen with sugar	1 lb. raspberries, frozen with sugar
100 g. sugar	4 oz. sugar
300 ml. water	½ pint water
2 egg whites	2 egg whites

Thaw the raspberries at room temperature for 3–4 hours. When soft, pass them through a sieve. Put the sugar and water in a saucepan and stir over a gentle heat until the sugar has dissolved. Increase the heat and boil briskly, without stirring, for 8 minutes or until a syrup has formed. Allow to cool.

Stir the syrup into the raspberry purée and pour into an ice tray or shallow rigid container. Place in the freezer for 1 hour or until it is just becoming mushy. Remove from the freezer, turn into a bowl and beat until smooth. Whisk the egg whites until stiff and fold into the raspberry mixture. Return to the container.
To freeze: Cover, seal and return to the freezer.
To serve: Thaw, covered, in the refrigerator for 10–15 minutes.
Serves 6.

French custard ice cream

METRIC	IMPERIAL
300 ml. single cream	½ pint single cream
3 eggs, beaten	3 eggs, beaten
100 g. caster sugar	4 oz. caster sugar
10 ml. vanilla essence	2 teaspoons vanilla essence
100 ml. double cream	4 fl.oz. double cream

Place the single cream, beaten eggs and sugar into a double boiler or a bowl standing over a saucepan of simmering water. Using a wooden spoon, stir constantly until the custard becomes thick enough to coat thinly the back of the spoon. Do not allow the custard to boil or you will curdle the mixture. Remove from the heat and stir in the vanilla essence. Cover the pan and place in cold water to cool quickly. When cold, pour into an ice tray or shallow rigid container and place in the freezer for 30 minutes or until the ice cream is just beginning to freeze around the edge of the tray. Remove from the freezer, tip the mixture into a bowl and beat until smooth. Lightly whip the double cream, fold it into the mixture and return to the container.
To freeze: Cover the container, seal and return to the freezer.
To serve: Remove from the freezer and place in the refrigerator 30 minutes before serving.
Serves 4 to 6.

French custard ice cream

Orange and lemon ice cream; Raspberry sorbet; Grapefruit sorbet

Rum and raisin ice cream

METRIC
75 g. sugar
100 ml. water
3 egg yolks
5 ml. vanilla essence
450 ml. double cream
100 g. raisins marinated for
    4 hours in 30 ml. rum

IMPERIAL
3 oz. sugar
4 fl.oz. water
3 egg yolks
1 teaspoon vanilla essence
¾ pint double cream
4 oz. raisins marinated for
    4 hours in 2 tablespoons
    rum

Put the sugar and water in a small saucepan and stir occasionally over a low heat until the sugar has dissolved. Increase the heat and boil rapidly for 5 minutes.

Meanwhile place the egg yolks and vanilla essence in a bowl and whip until light and creamy, beating constantly. Slowly pour the hot syrup onto the egg yolk mixture. Allow to cool and then add the marinated raisins. Whip the cream until just stiff and fold into the egg yolk and raisin mixture. Pour into an ice tray or shallow rigid container and place in the freezer. Remove ice cream after 1 hour, turn into a bowl and beat well. Return to freezer and remove after a further hour for another beating.

To freeze: Wrap, seal and return to the freezer.
To serve: Allow to stand at room temperature for 10 minutes before serving.
Serves 6.

Chocolate ice cream

METRIC
300 ml. double cream
30 ml. milk
50 g. icing sugar, sifted
2.5 ml. vanilla essence
30 ml. cocoa powder
60 ml. boiling water

IMPERIAL
½ pint double cream
2 tablespoons milk
2 oz. icing sugar, sifted
½ teaspoon vanilla essence
2 tablespoons cocoa powder
4 tablespoons boiling water

Put the cream and milk in a bowl and whisk until just stiff. Stir in the icing sugar and vanilla essence. Pour the mixture into an ice tray or shallow rigid container and freeze for 30 minutes or until the ice cream begins to set around the edge of the tray. Blend the cocoa and hot water together to a smooth paste. Remove the ice cream and spoon into a bowl. Add the cocoa paste, beat the mixture until smooth and return to the container.

To freeze: Cover, seal and freeze.
To serve: Thaw, covered, in the refrigerator for 30 minutes.
Serves 4.

Rum and raisin ice cream; Chocolate ice cream; Dairy vanilla ice cream; Brown bread ice cream

Dairy vanilla ice cream

METRIC	IMPERIAL
4 egg yolks	*4 egg yolks*
100 g. caster sugar	*4 oz. caster sugar*
Pinch of salt	*Pinch of salt*
450 ml. single cream	*¾ pint single cream*
5 ml. vanilla essence	*1 teaspoon vanilla essence*

Place the egg yolks, sugar and salt in a bowl and whisk until light and creamy. Heat the cream in a double boiler until just hot but not boiling and pour over the egg mixture, beating well to produce a thin custard. Strain the mixture into a double boiler and cook until the mixture coats the back of a spoon, stirring constantly. Remove from the heat and stir in the vanilla essence. Allow to cool.

Pour the mixture into an ice tray or shallow rigid container and freeze for 1 hour or until the ice cream starts to freeze around the edge. Remove from the freezer, tip the ice cream into a bowl and beat until smooth and creamy.

To freeze: Return to the container, wrap, seal and return to the freezer.

To serve: Thaw for 10 minutes in the refrigerator.

Serves 4.

Brown bread ice cream

METRIC	IMPERIAL
100 g. wholemeal bread, crusts removed	*4 oz. wholemeal bread, crusts removed*
450 ml. double cream	*¾ pint double cream*
100 g. icing sugar, sifted	*4 oz. icing sugar, sifted*
2.5 ml. vanilla essence	*½ teaspoon vanilla essence*
50 g. granulated sugar	*2 oz. granulated sugar*
50 ml. water	*2 fl.oz. water*

Place the sliced bread in a slow oven (140°C/275°F or Gas Mark 1) for 1 hour or until crisp and dry. Blend in a liquidiser to fine crumbs. Whisk the cream until just standing in soft peaks, be careful not to overwhisk, and stir in the icing sugar and vanilla essence. Turn the mixture into an ice tray or shallow rigid container and freeze for 1 hour or until the cream is starting to freeze round the edge of the tray.

Meanwhile, place the sugar and water in a small saucepan and stir over a low heat until the sugar dissolves. Increase the heat and boil for 2 minutes without stirring. Remove from the heat, stir in the breadcrumbs and allow to get cold.

Remove the ice cream, just as it is beginning to freeze, from the freezer and turn into a bowl. Beat until creamy, stir in the breadcrumbs and replace the mixture in the container.

To freeze: Cover, seal and freeze.

To serve: Unwrap and thaw at room temperature for 10 minutes. Spoon into individual glasses and serve with a chocolate sauce.

Serves 4 to 6.

Cakes and Baking

Marble cake
Apple cake

Marble cake

METRIC
175 g. margarine
175 g. caster sugar
2.5 ml. vanilla essence
2 large eggs, beaten
225 g. self-raising flour
50 g. plain chocolate,
  melted
30 ml. milk

IMPERIAL
6 oz. margarine
6 oz. caster sugar
½ teaspoon vanilla essence
2 large eggs, beaten
8 oz. self-raising flour
2 oz. plain chocolate,
  melted
2 tablespoons milk

Grease a 20 cm./8 in. round cake tin and line with greased greaseproof paper. Cream the margarine and sugar together until pale and fluffy. Beat in the vanilla essence and the eggs, the equivalent of one at a time, adding a little flour between each addition. Gradually fold in the remaining flour. Place half the cake mixture into another basin and mix in the melted chocolate and the milk. Put alternate spoonfuls of plain and chocolate mixture into the cake tin.

Bake in a moderate oven (180°C/350°F or Gas Mark 4) for 1–1¼ hours, or until well risen and the cake springs back when lightly pressed. Allow to cool in the tin for 5 minutes, then turn out onto a wire rack and remove the greaseproof paper.

To freeze: When cold wrap in foil or place in a polythene bag. Seal and freeze.

To serve: Unwrap and thaw at room temperature for 3 hours. Decorate with chocolate buttercream if desired.

Apple cake

METRIC
275 g. self-raising flour
5 ml. salt
2.5 ml. ground cinnamon
1.25 ml. ground cloves
125 g. butter
225 g. caster sugar
1 egg, lightly beaten
5 ml. vanilla essence
350 g. cooking apples, grated

IMPERIAL
10 oz. self-raising flour
1 teaspoon salt
½ teaspoon ground cinnamon
¼ teaspoon ground cloves
4 oz. butter
8 oz. caster sugar
1 egg, lightly beaten
1 teaspoon vanilla essence
12 oz. cooking apples, grated

To decorate
5 ml. clear honey
15 ml. toasted flaked
  almonds

To decorate
1 teaspoon clear honey
1 tablespoon toasted flaked
  almonds

Grease an 18 cm./7 in. square cake tin and line with greased greaseproof paper. Sift the flour with the salt and spices twice. Cream the butter and sugar until pale and fluffy. Gradually beat in the egg and vanilla essence. Stir in the grated apple and gradually fold in the flour. Turn the mixture into the prepared tin and smooth the top. Bake in a moderate oven (180°C/350°F or Gas Mark 4) for 1¼ hours or until a skewer inserted in the cake comes out clean. Leave in the tin for 5 minutes then turn onto a wire rack to cool and remove the greaseproof paper. Brush the top of the cake with the honey and sprinkle with the nuts.

To freeze: Open freeze. When frozen, pack in a polythene bag, seal and return to the freezer.

To serve: Unwrap and thaw for 4 hours at room temperature.

Buttercream

METRIC
100 g. butter
225 g. icing sugar, sifted
15 ml. milk

IMPERIAL
4 oz. butter
8 oz. icing sugar, sifted
1 tablespoon milk

Place the butter in a bowl and beat with a wooden spoon until soft. Gradually beat in the icing sugar alternately with the milk and continue beating until light and fluffy.
To freeze: Pack into small rigid containers, cover, seal and freeze.
To serve: Thaw in the container for 5 hours at room temperature.
Makes enough to fill and cover the top of a two-layer 18 cm./7 in. sandwich cake.

Variations

Chocolate buttercream
Melt 50 g./2 oz. plain chocolate in a small bowl over a pan of hot water. Beat into the beaten butter alternately with the icing sugar, instead of the milk. Beat until light and fluffy. Freeze and serve as for basic buttercream.

Coffee buttercream
Beat 15 ml./1 tablespoon coffee essence into the beaten butter alternately with the icing sugar, instead of the milk. Beat until light and fluffy. Freeze and serve as for basic buttercream.

One mix fruit cake

METRIC
225 g. soft margarine
225 g. soft brown sugar
4 eggs, beaten
45 ml. milk
225 g. mixed dried fruit
25 g. walnuts, coarsely chopped
350 g. self-raising flour, sifted
2.5 ml. ground cinnamon
2.5 ml. mixed spice

IMPERIAL
8 oz. soft margarine
8 oz. soft brown sugar
4 eggs, beaten
3 tablespoons milk
8 oz. mixed dried fruit
1 oz. walnuts, coarsely chopped
12 oz. self-raising flour, sifted
½ teaspoon ground cinnamon
½ teaspoon mixed spice

Grease a deep 20 cm./8 in. cake tin and line with greased greaseproof paper. Place all the ingredients in a mixing bowl and beat together for 2–3 minutes, or until thoroughly mixed. Turn the mixture into the prepared tin, and bake in a moderate oven (180°C/350°F or Gas Mark 4) for 1¼ hours or until a fine skewer inserted in the cake comes out clean.

Leave in the tin for 5 minutes, then turn out onto a wire rack to cool and remove the greaseproof paper.
To freeze: When cold, wrap in foil or place in a polythene bag. Seal and freeze.
To serve: Unwrap and thaw at room temperature for 4–5 hours.

One mix fruit cake; Marmalade cake

Marmalade cake

METRIC
225 g. plain flour
5 ml. baking powder
100 g. butter
100 g. caster sugar
2 eggs, beaten
30 ml. firm bitter orange marmalade
Grated rind of 1 orange

IMPERIAL
8 oz. plain flour
1 teaspoon baking powder
4 oz. butter
4 oz. caster sugar
2 eggs, beaten
2 tablespoons firm bitter orange marmalade
Grated rind of 1 orange

Grease an 18 cm./7 in. round cake tin and line with greased greaseproof paper. Sift the flour and baking powder into a bowl, rub in the butter until the mixture resembles fine breadcrumbs, then stir in the sugar. Beat the eggs, marmalade and rind together and add to the dry ingredients. Mix well, and turn the mixture into the prepared tin.

Bake in a moderate oven (180°C/350°F or Gas Mark 4) for 45 minutes or until a fine skewer inserted in the cake comes out clean. Allow to cool in the tin for 5 minutes, then turn out onto a wire rack and remove the greaseproof paper.
To freeze: When cold wrap in foil or place in a polythene bag. Seal and freeze.
To serve: Thaw wrapped at room temperature for 3–4 hours.

Serve plain with butter or ice as for Walnut and brown sugar flan (page 149).

American fudge cake

METRIC	IMPERIAL
75 g. plain chocolate	3 oz. plain chocolate
350 g. caster sugar	12 oz. caster sugar
300 ml. milk	½ pint milk
100 g. butter	4 oz. butter
2 eggs, beaten	2 eggs, beaten
1 teaspoon vanilla essence	1 teaspoon vanilla essence
50 g. walnuts, chopped	2 oz. walnuts, chopped
225 g. plain flour	8 oz. plain flour
1½ teaspoons baking powder	1½ teaspoons baking powder
½ quantity chocolate buttercream	½ quantity chocolate buttercream

Grease 2 × 23 cm./9 in. sandwich tins and line the bases with oiled greaseproof paper.

Place the chocolate in a small pan with 150 g./5 oz. of the sugar and half the milk. Stir over a low heat until the chocolate has melted and the ingredients are blended. Cool.

Cream the butter and remaining 200 g./7 oz. sugar until pale and fluffy. Gradually beat in the eggs and vanilla essence, stir in the chocolate mixture and walnuts. Fold in the sifted flour and baking powder alternately with the remaining 150 ml./¼ pint milk. Divide the mixture between the prepared tins and bake in a moderate oven (180°C/350°F, or Gas Mark 4) for 30 minutes or until the cakes spring back when lightly pressed.

Leave in the tins for 5 minutes, run a knife around the edge of the cakes and turn out onto a wire rack to cool. Remove the oiled paper. When cold, sandwich with chocolate buttercream.
To freeze: Open freeze. When frozen, place in a polythene bag, seal and freeze.
To serve: Unwrap and thaw for 3 to 4 hours at room temperature.

Farmhouse cake

METRIC	IMPERIAL
225 g. butter	8 oz. butter
225 g. caster sugar	8 oz. caster sugar
Grated rind of 1 orange	Grated rind of 1 orange
4 eggs, beaten	4 eggs, beaten
225 g. self-raising flour, sifted	8 oz. self-raising flour, sifted
2.5 ml. nutmeg	½ teaspoon nutmeg
75 g. ground almonds	3 oz. ground almonds
400 g. mixed dried fruit, currants, sultanas, raisins and candied peel	14 oz. mixed dried fruit, currants, sultanas, raisins and candied peel
75 g. glacé cherries, chopped	3 oz. glacé cherries, chopped
50 g. blanched, split almonds	2 oz. blanched, split almonds

Grease a deep 20 cm./8 in. cake tin and line with greased greaseproof paper. Cream the butter and sugar with the orange rind until pale and fluffy. Add the eggs, a little at a time, adding a little flour between each egg to prevent the mixture from curdling. Fold in the nutmeg, ground almonds, the dried fruit and glacé cherries lightly coated with a little of the flour and the remaining flour. Turn into the prepared tin, smooth the top and arrange the almonds over the surface.

Bake in a warm oven (160°C/325°F or Gas Mark 3) for 2¼–2½ hours or until a fine skewer inserted in the cake comes

American fudge cake

out clean. Cover the top of the cake with a double thickness of greaseproof paper if it browns too quickly. Leave in the tin for 10 minutes, then turn out onto a wire rack to cool and remove the greaseproof paper.
To freeze: Wrap in foil or place in a polythene bag, seal and freeze.
To serve: Thaw wrapped at room temperature for 6 hours.

Italian uncooked chocolate cake

METRIC	IMPERIAL
150 g. butter	5 oz. butter
15 ml. sugar	1 tablespoon sugar
15 ml. golden syrup	1 tablespoon golden syrup
30 ml. cocoa powder	2 tablespoons cocoa powder
250 g. digestive biscuits, finely crushed	9 oz. digestive biscuits, finely crushed
25 g. ground almonds	1 oz. ground almonds
10 ml. coffee essence	2 teaspoons coffee essence

Cream the butter and sugar together until pale and fluffy. Place the syrup in a saucepan and warm gently over a low heat. Remove from the heat and add the cocoa, biscuit crumbs, almonds and coffee essence. Allow to cool and stir into the creamed mixture. Press the mixture into a shallow greased foil tray (approximately 20 cm./8 in. square).

To freeze: Cover, seal and freeze.

To serve: Unwrap and thaw at room temperature for 2–3 hours. Melt 75 g./3 oz. plain chocolate, pour evenly over the surface of the cake and leave to set. Cut into squares to serve.

Chocolate cake

METRIC	IMPERIAL
175 g. butter	6 oz. butter
175 g. caster sugar	6 oz. caster sugar
5 ml. vanilla essence	1 teaspoon vanilla essence
100 g. plain chocolate, broken into pieces	4 oz. plain chocolate, broken into pieces
4 eggs, separated	4 eggs, separated
30 ml. milk	2 tablespoons milk
175 g. self-raising flour	6 oz. self-raising flour
25 g. cocoa powder	1 oz. cocoa powder

Grease two 20 cm./8 in. sandwich tins and line the bases with greased greaseproof paper. Cream the butter, sugar and vanilla essence together until pale and fluffy. Melt the chocolate in a basin over a pan of hot water. Beat the chocolate into the creamed mixture, then beat in the egg yolks and milk. Sift the flour with the cocoa powder and fold into the mixture. Whisk the egg whites and gently fold into the mixture.

Divide the mixture equally between the prepared tins and bake in a moderate oven (180°C/350°F or Gas Mark 4) for 25–30 minutes or until golden brown and the cakes spring back when lightly pressed. Leave in the tins for 2 minutes, then turn out onto a wire rack to cool and remove the greaseproof paper.

To freeze: When cold, place the cakes one on top of the other with foil or greaseproof paper between them. Wrap in foil or place in a polythene bag, seal and freeze.

To serve: Unwrap and thaw for 2 hours at room temperature. Sandwich the layers together with buttercream and dust the top with sifted icing sugar.

Farmhouse cake; Italian uncooked chocolate cake; Chocolate cake

German cheesecake

METRIC
Pastry base
100 g. plain flour
Pinch of salt
50 g. butter
15 g. sugar
15–30 ml. cold water

IMPERIAL
Pastry base
4 oz. plain flour
Pinch of salt
2 oz. butter
½ oz. sugar
1–2 tablespoons cold water

Filling
75 g. butter
75 g. caster sugar
2 eggs, beaten
225 g. curd cheese, softened
Grated rind and juice of
  1 lemon
25 g. ground almonds

Filling
3 oz. butter
3 oz. caster sugar
2 eggs, beaten
8 oz. curd cheese, softened
Grated rind and juice of
  1 lemon
1 oz. ground almonds

Sift the flour and salt into a bowl and rub in the butter until the mixture resembles fine breadcrumbs. Stir in the caster sugar and add enough cold water to blend to a firm dough. Knead very lightly for 1 minute then form into a ball, wrap in foil and chill in the refrigerator for 20 minutes.

Roll out the pastry on a floured surface and use it to line a 23 cm./9 in. flan ring, set on a baking tray. Place it in the refrigerator to chill for 20 minutes.

Cream the butter and sugar together until light and fluffy and gradually beat in the eggs, alternating with the curd cheese. When thoroughly blended, stir in the lemon rind and juice and the ground almonds. Pour into the prepared pastry case.

Bake in a moderate oven (180°C/350°F or Gas Mark 4) for 45 minutes or until the filling is set. Allow to cool in the ring.
To freeze: Open freeze. When frozen, remove from the ring, wrap in foil, seal and freeze.
To serve: Thaw in the refrigerator overnight.

Victoria sandwich

METRIC
100 g. butter
100 g. caster sugar
2 large eggs, beaten
100 g. self-raising flour
  sifted with pinch of salt

IMPERIAL
4 oz. butter
4 oz. caster sugar
2 large eggs, beaten
4 oz. self-raising flour
  sifted with pinch of salt

Grease two 18 cm./7 in. sandwich tins and line the bases with greased greaseproof paper. Cream the butter and sugar together until pale and fluffy. Beat in the eggs, the equivalent of one at a time, adding a little flour between each addition. Gently fold in the remaining flour.

Divide the mixture equally between the 2 prepared tins and bake in a moderate oven (180°C/350°F or Gas Mark 4) for 25–30 minutes or until well risen and the cake springs back when lightly pressed. Leave in the tin for 2 minutes, then turn out onto a wire rack to cool and remove the greaseproof paper.
To freeze: When cold, place the cakes one on top of the other with greaseproof paper or foil between them. Place in a polythene bag or wrap in foil, seal and freeze.
To serve: Thaw wrapped at room temperature for 3 hours. Fill and decorate as required.

German cheesecake
Ginger ring cake; Victoria sandwich

Ginger ring cake

METRIC
100 g. soft margarine
150 g. black treacle
75 g. golden syrup
120 ml. milk
2 eggs, beaten
50 g. caster sugar
225 g. plain flour, sifted
5 ml. mixed spice, sifted
10 ml. ground ginger, sifted
2.5 ml. bicarbonate of soda,
    sifted

IMPERIAL
4 oz. soft margarine
5 oz. black treacle
3 oz. golden syrup
4 fl.oz. milk
2 eggs, beaten
2 oz. caster sugar
8 oz. plain flour, sifted
1 teaspoon mixed spice,
    sifted
2 teaspoons ground ginger,
    sifted
½ teaspoon bicarbonate of
    soda, sifted

Orange icing
175 g. icing sugar, sieved
45 ml. fresh or diluted
    frozen orange juice
Grated rind of 1 orange
15 g. butter

Orange icing
6 oz. icing sugar, sieved
3 tablespoons fresh or diluted
    frozen orange juice
Grated rind of 1 orange
½ oz. butter

Grease and lightly flour a 23 cm./9 in. ring mould. Place all the ingredients, except those for the icing, in a mixing bowl and beat for 2–3 minutes or until smooth. Turn into the prepared ring mould and bake in a cool oven (150°C/300°F or Gas Mark 2) for 1–1¼ hours or until the cake springs back when lightly pressed. Leave in the tin for 5 minutes, then turn out on a wire rack to cool.

Sift the icing sugar into a bowl. Place the orange juice, rind and butter in a saucepan and heat gently until the butter has melted. Stir into the icing sugar, and beat until smooth. Coat the ring with the icing and allow to set. If preferred, the cake may be iced after freezing.

To freeze: Open freeze. When frozen, wrap in foil, seal and return to the freezer.

To serve: Unwrap and thaw at room temperature for 2–3 hours.

173

Coffee and walnut cake

METRIC	IMPERIAL
225 g. butter	8 oz. butter
225 g. caster sugar	8 oz. caster sugar
3 large eggs, beaten	3 large eggs, beaten
30 ml. coffee essence	2 tablespoons coffee essence
225 g. self-raising flour	8 oz. self-raising flour
75 g. walnuts, chopped	3 oz. walnuts, chopped
1½ quantities coffee buttercream	1½ quantities coffee buttercream

Grease 2 × 20 cm/8 in. sandwich tins and line the bases with greased greaseproof paper. Cream the butter and sugar together until pale and fluffy. Add the eggs, the equivalent of one at a time, beating well. Add the coffee essence. Fold in the flour and walnuts. Divide the mixture between the prepared tins and bake in a moderate oven (180°C/350°F or Gas Mark 4) for 35 minutes or until the centres are firm and the sides starting to shrink from the sides of the tins. Leave in the tins for 5 minutes, to cool. When cold, sandwich together with a little of the buttercream and coat the top and sides with the remaining buttercream.

To freeze: Open freeze. When frozen, wrap in foil or place in a polythene bag. Seal and freeze.

To serve: Unwrap and thaw for 3–4 hours at room temperature. Decorate with walnuts.

Coffee and walnut cake

Caribbean coffee gâteau

Caribbean coffee gâteau

METRIC	IMPERIAL
6 eggs	6 eggs
15 ml. coffee essence	1 tablespoon coffee essence
175 g. caster sugar	6 oz. caster sugar
150 g. plain flour	5 oz. plain flour
25 g. cornflour	1 oz. cornflour
30 ml. rum	2 tablespoons rum
1 quantity coffee buttercream	1 quantity coffee buttercream
50 g. plain chocolate, grated	2 oz. plain chocolate, grated

Grease 2 × 23 cm./9 in. sandwich tins and line the bases with greased greaseproof paper. In a bowl over a pan of simmering water, whisk the eggs, coffee essence and caster sugar until very thick and creamy. Remove from the heat and gently fold in the sifted flours. Divide the mixture equally between the 2 tins and bake in a fairly hot oven (190°C/375°F or Gas Mark 5) for 25 minutes or until the cake springs back when lightly

Pineapple gâteau

pressed. Leave in the tins for 5 minutes, then turn out and cool on a wire rack.

Sprinkle the 30 ml./2 tablespoons rum over the surface of the cake.

Sandwich the cake together with some of the buttercream and use the rest to cover the top of the cake. Sprinkle the grated chocolate over the surface of the cake.

To freeze: Open freeze. When frozen, wrap in foil or place in a polythene bag. Seal and freeze.

To serve: Unwrap and thaw at room temperature for 4 hours.

Pineapple gâteau

METRIC	IMPERIAL
225 g. butter	8 oz. butter
225 g. caster sugar	8 oz. caster sugar
4 eggs, beaten	4 eggs, beaten
100 g. glacé pineapple, chopped finely	4 oz. glacé pineapple, chopped finely
100 g. glacé cherries, washed, dried and finely chopped	4 oz. glacé cherries, washed, dried and finely chopped
225 g. plain flour	8 oz. plain flour
5 ml. baking powder	1 teaspoon baking powder
25 g. walnuts, roughly chopped	1 oz. walnuts, roughly chopped
50 g. ground almonds	2 oz. ground almonds

Lemon buttercream
175 g. butter
350 g. icing sugar, sifted
Juice and grated rind of 2 lemons

Lemon buttercream
6 oz. butter
12 oz. icing sugar, sifted
Juice and grated rind of 2 lemons

Grease a 23 cm./9 in. round cake tin and line with greaseproof paper. Cream the butter and sugar together until pale and fluffy. Add the eggs, a little at a time, beating well between each addition. Toss the pineapple and cherries in 15 ml./1 tablespoon of the flour and add to the mixture. Sift the remaining flour and baking powder together and fold into the mixture, together with the walnuts and almonds.

Turn the mixture into the prepared tin, smooth the surface with a knife and bake in a moderate oven (180°C/350°F or Gas Mark 4) for $1\frac{1}{4}$–$1\frac{1}{2}$ hours or until the cake springs back when lightly touched. Cover the top of the cake with greaseproof paper if it is browning too quickly. Leave in the tin for 5 minutes, then turn out to cool on a wire rack and remove the greaseproof paper.

Cream the butter and gradually add the icing sugar, lemon rind and juice, beating well to give a spreading consistency. Spread over the top and sides of the cake and whirl up with a knife to give a 'spiked' appearance.

To freeze: Open freeze. When frozen wrap in foil or place in a polythene bag. Seal and freeze.

To serve: Unwrap and thaw at room temperature for 3 hours.

175

Standby cookies

METRIC	IMPERIAL
225 g. plain flour	8 oz. plain flour
5 ml. baking powder	1 teaspoon baking powder
100 g. butter	4 oz. butter
175 g. caster sugar	6 oz. caster sugar
5 ml. vanilla essence	1 teaspoon vanilla essence
1 egg, beaten	1 egg, beaten

Sift the flour and baking powder together and rub in the butter until the mixture resembles fine breadcrumbs. Stir in the sugar, vanilla essence and beaten egg and mix to a smooth dough. Turn the dough out onto a floured surface and knead for 2 minutes. Wrap in foil, then chill in the refrigerator for about 15 minutes. Shape the dough into a long roll, 5 cm./2 in. in diameter.

To freeze: Wrap the dough in foil, seal and freeze.

To serve: Unwrap the dough and thaw for 1 hour in the refrigerator. Cut into slices 1 cm./½ in. thick and place the slices on a greased baking sheet. Bake in a fairly hot oven (190°C/375°F or Gas Mark 5) for 10 minutes or until turning golden. Leave for 2 minutes, then remove and cool on a wire rack.

Makes approximately 40.

Variations

Chocolate cookies

Add 50 g./2 oz. plain grated chocolate with the sugar.

Nuttys

Add 50 g./2 oz. finely chopped walnuts or almonds with the sugar.

Ginger cookies

Omit the vanilla essence and add 10 ml./2 teaspoons ground ginger with the flour and baking powder.

Cherry cookies

Add 50 g./2 oz. finely chopped glacé cherries with the sugar.

Standby cookies and variations

Frangipan tartlets

METRIC	IMPERIAL
Shortcrust pastry made with 200 g. flour, 100 g. fat, etc.	Shortcrust pastry made with 7 oz. flour, 3½ oz. fat, etc.

Filling	**Filling**
100 g. butter	4 oz. butter
100 g. caster sugar	4 oz. caster sugar
100 g. ground almonds	4 oz. ground almonds
25 g. plain flour	1 oz. plain flour
Grated rind of ½ a lemon	Grated rind of ½ a lemon
10 ml. lemon juice	2 teaspoons lemon juice
1 egg white	1 egg white

Topping	**Topping**
30 ml. apricot jam, sieved	2 tablespoons apricot jam, sieved
50 g. toasted flaked almonds	2 oz. toasted flaked almonds

Roll out the pastry thinly on a floured surface and cut out 16 6 cm./2½ in. circles with a fluted pastry cutter. Use these to line 16 individual patty tins and leave to chill in the refrigerator for 10 minutes.

Cream the butter and sugar together until light and fluffy, stir in the ground almonds, flour, lemon rind and juice. Whisk the egg white until stiff and fold into the creamed mixture. Divide the prepared mixture between the pastry cases, and bake in a fairly hot oven (190°C/375°F or Gas Mark 5) for 20 minutes or until the filling is set and golden brown.

Turn the tartlets out carefully onto a wire rack. Warm the apricot jam gently in a saucepan, stirring constantly and brush over the tartlets, then sprinkle with the toasted almonds.

To freeze: Cool completely, then open freeze. When frozen, pack into a rigid container. Cover, seal and freeze.

To serve: Unwrap and thaw at room temperature for 1–2 hours.

Makes 16.

Brandy snaps

METRIC
100 g. butter
100 g. demerara sugar
150 g. golden syrup
100 g. plain flour
10 ml. ground ginger

IMPERIAL
4 oz. butter
4 oz. demerara sugar
5 oz. golden syrup
4 oz. plain flour
2 teaspoons ground ginger

Put the butter, sugar and syrup into a saucepan and stir over a low heat until the sugar and butter have melted. Sift the flour and ginger together, add to the melted mixture and beat well until smooth.

Lightly grease a baking tray and, allowing for spreading, place 6 × 5 ml./1 teaspoons of mixture on the tray. Keep the remaining mixture warm. Bake in the centre of a warm oven (160°C/325°F or Gas Mark 3) for 8 minutes or until pale gold. Leave for 1 minute on the baking tray, then remove with a palette knife and roll the brandy snap round the handle of a wooden spoon so that the smooth side is outermost. Leave for 2 minutes to set, then slide off and cool on a wire rack. Repeat the procedure with the rest of the mixture.

To freeze: Pack carefully into rigid polythene containers, using foil or greaseproof between the layers. Cover, seal and freeze.

To serve: Unwrap and thaw at room temperature for 1 hour. Serve plain or filled with whipped cream.

Makes approximately 36.

Frangipan tartlets; Brandy snaps; Viennese stars

Viennese stars

METRIC
225 g. margarine
175 g. butter
175 g. icing sugar
Grated rind of 1 orange
Pinch of ground cinnamon
15 ml. cornflour
225 g. self-raising flour
225 g. plain flour
15–30 ml. milk

IMPERIAL
8 oz. margarine
6 oz. butter
6 oz. icing sugar
Grated rind of 1 orange
Pinch of ground cinnamon
1 tablespoon cornflour
8 oz. self-raising flour
8 oz. plain flour
1–2 tablespoons milk

Cream the margarine, butter and sugar together until pale and fluffy. Beat in the orange rind, cinnamon and cornflour, then sift the flours and fold into the mixture, beating or kneading well until smooth. If the mixture is very stiff, add a little milk. Place the mixture in batches into a piping bag, which has been fitted with a large rose nozzle, and pipe small stars well apart on greased baking trays.

Bake, in batches, in a moderate oven (180°C/350°F or Gas Mark 4) for 15 minutes or until pale beige in colour. Allow to cool on a wire rack.

To freeze: Pack into a rigid container, using foil or greaseproof to separate each layer. Cover, seal and freeze.

To serve: Unwrap and thaw at room temperature for 1 hour. Serve dredged with icing sugar, or sandwich together with butter cream.

Makes approximately 60.

Rich shortbread

METRIC	IMPERIAL
225 g. butter	*8 oz. butter*
100 g. caster sugar	*4 oz. caster sugar*
275 g. plain flour	*10 oz. plain flour*
50 g. fine semolina	*2 oz. fine semolina*
A little extra caster sugar	*A little extra caster sugar*

Lightly butter and flour 2 × 18cm./7in. sandwich tins. Cream the butter and sugar together until pale and fluffy. Sift in the flour and semolina together and add to the creamed mixture, a little at a time. Gradually draw the mixture together with the fingertips, knead lightly until smooth, divide the mixture in half and press each half into a prepared tin. Prick all over with a fork and sprinkle with the extra caster sugar.

Chill in the refrigerator for 15 minutes, then bake in a warm oven (160°C/325°F or Gas Mark 3) for about 30 minutes, or until pale brown in colour. Leave in the tins for 5 minutes, then while soft cut each shortbread into 8 triangles and transfer to a wire rack to cool.

To freeze: Wrap in foil or place in a rigid container, seal and freeze.

To serve: Unwrap and thaw at room temperature for 2–3 hours.

Makes 16 triangles.

Jammy buns

METRIC	IMPERIAL
225 g. self-raising flour	*8 oz. self-raising flour*
Pinch of salt	*Pinch of salt*
Pinch of mixed spice	*Pinch of mixed spice*
50 g. butter	*2 oz. butter*
50 g. caster sugar	*2 oz. caster sugar*
1 egg, beaten	*1 egg, beaten*
30 ml. milk	*2 tablespoons milk*
30 ml. jam or lemon curd	*2 tablespoons jam or lemon curd*
15 ml. granulated sugar	*1 tablespoon granulated sugar*

Sift the flour, salt and mixed spice into a bowl and rub in the butter with the fingertips until the mixture resembles fine crumbs. Stir in the caster sugar, and add the egg and enough milk to make a firm dough. Knead lightly until smooth. Divide the dough into 12 pieces and roll them into balls. Make a hole in each bun and place 2.5 ml./½ teaspoon of jam in each one, then pinch the opening together firmly and place the buns, jam side down, on a greased baking tray. Sprinkle the tops of the buns with the granulated sugar and bake in a hot oven (220°C/425°F or Gas Mark 7) for 10 minutes or until brown. Cool on a wire rack.

To freeze: Pack in a rigid container or polythene bag. Seal and freeze.

To serve: Unwrap and thaw for 2–3 hours at room temperature.

Makes 12.

Flap jacks

METRIC	IMPERIAL
100 g. margarine	*4 oz. margarine*
100 g. soft brown sugar	*4 oz. soft brown sugar*
75 g. golden syrup or honey	*3 oz. golden syrup or honey*
225 g. rolled oats	*8 oz. rolled oats*
A little cooking oil	*A little cooking oil*

Put the margarine, sugar and syrup or honey into a saucepan and stir over a low heat until melted. Add the rolled oats and mix well.

Brush a shallow tin (20 × 30cm./8 × 12in.) with the cooking oil and spread the flap jack mixture into the tin, smoothing the top with a knife. Bake in the centre of a moderate oven (180°C/350°F or Gas Mark 4) for 20 minutes or until the flap jacks are golden brown. Cool for 5 minutes, then cut into 24 bars. Allow to get cold before removing them from the tin.

To freeze: Pack in a rigid container with foil or greaseproof between each layer. Cover, seal and freeze.

To serve: Unwrap and thaw at room temperature for 2 hours.

Makes 24.

Queen cakes

METRIC	IMPERIAL
100 g. butter	*4 oz. butter*
100 g. caster sugar	*4 oz. caster sugar*
2 eggs, beaten	*2 eggs, beaten*
100 g. self-raising flour	*4 oz. self-raising flour*
2.5 ml. vanilla essence	*½ teaspoon vanilla essence*
50 g. sultanas, chopped	*2 oz. sultanas, chopped*
15–30 ml. milk	*1–2 tablespoons milk*

Cream the butter and sugar together until very pale and fluffy. Gradually beat in the whole eggs, the equivalent of one at a time, adding a little flour between each addition. Stir in the vanilla essence and sultanas. Fold in the remaining flour, adding sufficient milk to make a soft dropping consistency. Divide the mixture equally between 20 paper cases and bake in a moderate oven (180°C/350°F or Gas Mark 4) for 15 minutes or until the cakes spring back when lightly pressed. Allow the cakes to cool on a wire rack.

To freeze: Pack in a polythene bag, seal and freeze.

To serve: Unwrap and thaw at room temperature for 1–2 hours. After thawing the queen cakes can be iced with glacé icing and each decorated with half a glacé cherry.

Makes 20.

Flap jacks; Queen cakes; Jammy buns; Rich shortbread

Chocolate brownies

METRIC	IMPERIAL
100 g. plain chocolate	4 oz. plain chocolate
100 g. butter	4 oz. butter
100 g. caster sugar	4 oz. caster sugar
1 egg, beaten	1 egg, beaten
2.5 ml. vanilla essence	½ teaspoon vanilla essence
150 g. plain flour	5 oz. plain flour
2.5 ml. baking powder	½ teaspoon baking powder
Pinch of salt	Pinch of salt
100 g. walnuts, roughly chopped	4 oz. walnuts, roughly chopped
A little milk to mix	A little milk to mix

Grease a 20 cm./8 in. square tin. Melt the chocolate in a small bowl, over a pan of hot water. Cream the butter and sugar together until pale and fluffy, then gradually beat in the egg and vanilla essence. Sift the flour, baking powder and salt together and fold into the creamed mixture. Stir in the melted chocolate and walnuts with enough milk to make a soft dropping consistency.

Turn the mixture into the prepared tin and bake in a moderate oven (180°C/350°F or Gas Mark 4) for 20–30 minutes or until a fine skewer inserted in the cake comes out clean. Cut into squares and leave in the tin until cold.

To freeze: Remove from the tin and wrap in foil or place in a polythene bag, seal and freeze.

To serve: Unwrap and thaw at room temperature for 2 hours. Serve plain or coat with chocolate glacé icing.

Drop scones

METRIC	IMPERIAL
150 g. plain flour	5 oz. plain flour
10 ml. baking powder	2 teaspoons baking powder
Pinch of salt	Pinch of salt
15 ml. caster sugar	1 tablespoon caster sugar
1 egg, beaten	1 egg, beaten
120 ml. milk	4 fl.oz. milk
25 g. butter, melted	1 oz. butter, melted
A little corn oil	A little corn oil

Sift the flour, baking powder and salt into a bowl and add the sugar and beaten egg. Gradually add the milk and melted butter and beat to a smooth batter.

Heat a heavy frying pan or griddle and grease lightly with a little corn oil. Pour 15 ml./1 tablespoon of the mixture onto the pan or griddle and allow to cook for ½ minute or until the surface is puffed and the underside is golden brown. Flip the drop scone over with a palette knife and cook until the other side is golden brown. Place on a clean, warm tea towel to keep moist and repeat the procedure with the remaining batter.

To freeze: When cold, pack in a rigid container or polythene bag, seal and freeze.

To serve: Unwrap and thaw at room temperature for 1 hour. Serve with butter and preserves, or with maple syrup and whipped cream.

Makes 8 to 10.

Chocolate brownies; Date and walnut bread; Drop scones

Date and walnut bread

METRIC	IMPERIAL
350 g. self-raising flour	12 oz. self-raising flour
2.5 ml. salt	½ teaspoon salt
2.5 ml. mixed spice	½ teaspoon mixed spice
75 g. caster sugar	3 oz. caster sugar
75 g. walnuts, finely chopped	3 oz. walnuts, finely chopped
75 g. sugar coated dates, chopped	3 oz. sugar coated dates, chopped
2 eggs, beaten	2 eggs, beaten
300 ml. milk	10 fl.oz. milk
50 g. butter, melted	2 oz. butter, melted

Grease a 1 kg./2 lb. loaf tin and line with greased greaseproof paper. Sift the flour, salt and mixed spice into a bowl and stir in the sugar, walnuts and dates. Mix the eggs and milk together and add to the dry ingredients. Stir in the butter and beat well for 2 minutes.

Turn the mixture into the prepared loaf tin and spread so that it is level. Bake in a moderate oven (180°C/350°F or Gas Mark 4) for 1½ hours or until a fine skewer inserted in the cake comes out clean. Leave in the tin for 5 minutes then turn out to cool on a wire rack and remove the greaseproof paper.

To freeze: Wrap in foil or place in a polythene bag, seal and freeze.

To serve: Thaw wrapped for 3–4 hours at room temperature.

Chocolate circles

METRIC	IMPERIAL
100 g. margarine	4 oz. margarine
100 g. caster sugar	4 oz. caster sugar
1 small egg, beaten	1 small egg, beaten
Drop of vanilla essence	Drop of vanilla essence
225 g. plain flour	8 oz. plain flour
25 g. cocoa powder	1 oz. cocoa powder
2 × 25 g. chocolate flakes, crushed	2 × 1 oz. chocolate flakes, crushed
175 g. cooking chocolate	6 oz. cooking chocolate

Cream the margarine and sugar together until pale and fluffy and beat in the egg and vanilla essence. Sift the flour and cocoa together and stir into the creamed mixture. Add the crushed flake, turn out onto a floured surface and knead lightly to a smooth dough. Wrap in a polythene bag and chill in the refrigerator for 30 minutes.

Roll out the dough approximately ½ cm./¼ in. thick on a floured surface. Cut into 5 cm./2 in. rounds with a plain cutter, remove the centres with a smaller cutter and place the circles on a lightly greased baking tray. Bake in a fairly hot oven (190°C/375°F or Gas Mark 5) for 15 minutes. Leave on the baking tray for 2 minutes then remove and cool on a wire rack.

Melt the chocolate gently in a small bowl over a pan of hot water. When the biscuits are cold dip the top of each ring, holding it on a fork, into the melted chocolate and place to set on a sheet of oiled greaseproof paper.

To freeze: When the chocolate has set, pack the biscuits in a rigid container with foil or greaseproof paper between the layers. Cover, seal and freeze.

To serve: Unwrap and thaw for 1 hour at room temperature.

Makes approximately 24.

Chocolate circles; Ginger cake

Ginger cake

METRIC	IMPERIAL
150 ml. milk	¼ pint milk
5 ml. bicarbonate of soda	1 teaspoon bicarbonate of soda
100 g. butter	4 oz. butter
100 g. golden syrup	4 oz. golden syrup
100 g. treacle	4 oz. treacle
75 g. soft brown sugar	3 oz. soft brown sugar
15 ml. orange marmalade	1 tablespoon orange marmalade
100 g. self-raising flour	4 oz. self-raising flour
100 g. wholemeal flour	4 oz. wholemeal flour
5 ml. mixed spice	1 teaspoon mixed spice
30 ml. ground ginger	2 tablespoons ground ginger
Salt	Salt
2 small eggs, beaten	2 small eggs, beaten

Grease a 20 cm./8 in. round cake tin and line with greased greaseproof paper. Pour the milk into a saucepan, add the bicarbonate of soda and heat gently until tepid. Place the butter, syrup, treacle, sugar and marmalade in another saucepan and heat gently, stirring until the ingredients are combined and the sugar dissolved.

Place the flours, mixed spice, ginger and a pinch of salt in a bowl and mix together thoroughly. Stir in the treacle mixture, then the warmed milk and beat well to a smooth batter. Beat in the eggs.

Pour the mixture into the prepared tin and bake in a warm oven (160°C/325°F or Gas Mark 3) for 1 hour or until a fine skewer inserted in the cake comes out clean. Allow to cool in the tin for 10 minutes then turn out onto a wire rack to cool completely and remove the greaseproof paper.

To freeze: Wrap in foil or place in a polythene bag. Seal and freeze.

To serve: Unwrap and thaw for 3 hours at room temperature. Serve plain or iced and decorated with pieces of crystallised ginger.

Continental fruit plait

METRIC	IMPERIAL
½ kg. strong flour	1 lb. strong flour
50 g. caster sugar	2 oz. caster sugar
25 g. fresh yeast	1 oz. fresh yeast
90 ml. lukewarm water mixed with 180 ml. lukewarm milk	3 fl.oz. lukewarm water mixed with 6 fl.oz. lukewarm milk
5 ml. salt	1 teaspoon salt
5 ml. mixed spice	1 teaspoon mixed spice
5 ml. ground cinnamon	1 teaspoon ground cinnamon
50 g. chopped mixed peel	2 oz. chopped mixed peel
50 g. sultanas	2 oz. sultanas
75 g. currants	3 oz. currants
50 g. butter, melted	2 oz. butter, melted
1 egg, beaten	1 egg, beaten
30 ml. honey	2 tablespoons honey

Sift 100 g./4 oz. flour into a warm bowl and add 5 ml./1 teaspoon of the sugar. Blend the yeast with a little of the milk and water and stir, with the remaining liquid, into the sifted flour. Beat well, and leave for about 20 minutes or until frothy. Add the rest of the flour sifted with the salt, the remaining sugar, the mixed spice and cinnamon, the mixed fruit and melted butter to the yeast mixture and stir in the beaten egg. Mix to a soft dough, then turn out and knead on a floured working surface until smooth and elastic. Place in a clean, greased bowl, cover with a damp cloth and leave in a warm place until the dough has doubled in size.

Turn out onto a floured surface and knead lightly for 2 minutes. Divide into three and roll each third into a sausage shape, 30 cm./12 in. long. Plait the 3 lengths together. Dampen the 3 ends of each plait with a little water, pinch together to seal and tuck underneath the loaf. Place the plait on a greased baking tray. Cover with a greased polythene bag and leave to prove in a warm place until it has nearly doubled in size. Remove the bag and bake the plait in a hot oven (220°C/425°F or Gas Mark 7) for 25–35 minutes. Transfer to a wire rack to cool and brush with the honey to glaze.
To freeze: Pack in a polythene bag, seal and freeze.
To serve: Thaw wrapped at room temperature for 3–4 hours. Serve with butter.

Doughnuts

METRIC	IMPERIAL
225 g. strong flour	8 oz. strong flour
5 ml. salt	1 teaspoon salt
10 ml. sugar	2 teaspoons sugar
15 g. fresh yeast	½ oz. fresh yeast
120 ml. lukewarm milk	4 fl.oz. lukewarm milk
25 g. butter, melted	1 oz. butter, melted
30 ml. raspberry jam	2 tablespoons raspberry jam
Oil for frying	Oil for frying

Sift the flour, salt and sugar into a warm bowl, dissolve the yeast in the warm milk and add to the flour together with the butter. Mix to a smooth dough and knead on a floured surface until smooth and elastic. Place the dough on a clean, greased bowl, cover with a damp cloth and leave to rise in a warm place for 1 hour.

Turn the dough out onto a floured surface and knead lightly. Divide into 12 pieces, form into balls and flatten. Place a little jam in the centre of each, fold edges up and over to enclose the jam, press together firmly to seal and gently roll into a ball shape. Place on a greased baking tray, cover with a greased polythene bag and prove in a warm place for 20 minutes.

Fry the doughnuts a few at a time in a frying basket in hot deep fat (175°C/350°F) until golden brown and puffy. Lift out and drain on absorbent kitchen paper.
To freeze: When cold, pack into polythene bags, seal and freeze.
To serve: Place the frozen doughnuts on a baking tray and reheat in a fairly hot oven (200°C/400°F or Gas Mark 6) for 6–8 minutes or until heated through. Toss in caster sugar and serve straight away.
Makes 12.

Continental fruit plait; Scones; Doughnuts; Scofa loaf

Scones

METRIC	IMPERIAL
½ kg. self-raising flour	1 lb. self-raising flour
5 ml. salt	1 teaspoon salt
100 g. margarine	4 oz. margarine
100 g. caster sugar	4 oz. caster sugar
300 ml. milk	½ pint milk
Beaten egg or extra milk for glazing (optional)	Beaten egg or extra milk for glazing (optional)

Sift the flour and salt into a bowl, cut the margarine into small pieces and rub it into the flour with the tips of the fingers, until the mixture resembles fine breadcrumbs. Stir in the sugar and add enough milk to make a soft but not sticky dough.

Turn the dough out onto a floured surface and knead lightly, then roll it out to about 1 cm./½ in. thickness and stamp out rounds with a 5 cm./2½ in. plain cutter. Place on a lightly floured baking tray and brush with the beaten egg or milk, if used. Bake in a hot oven (220°C/425°F or Gas Mark 7) for 10–15 minutes or until well risen and golden brown. Cool on a wire rack.

To freeze: When cold, place in a polythene bag, seal and freeze.

To serve: Reheat from frozen in a moderate oven (180°C/350°F or Gas Mark 4) for 15–20 minutes. Serve warm, with butter.

Makes approximately 20.

Scofa loaf

METRIC	IMPERIAL
2½ kg. scofa flour	3 lb. scofa flour
5 ml. salt	1 teaspoon salt
10 ml. baking powder	2 teaspoons baking powder
10 ml. sugar	2 teaspoons sugar
50 g. lard	2 oz. lard
450 ml. sour milk	¾ pint sour milk
450 ml. cold water	¾ pint cold water

Sift together the flour, salt and baking powder. Stir in the sugar and rub in the lard. Add the sour milk and cold water and mix to a soft dough. Turn out onto a floured surface and knead for 1 minute or until smooth. Divide the dough in half, shape each half into a round loaf and flatten slightly with the palm of the hand. With a knife, mark out 6 triangular shapes on each loaf. Place on a floured and greased baking tray and bake immediately in a hot oven (220°C/425°F or Gas Mark 7) for 25–30 minutes or until the bread is brown and crusty and sounds hollow when tapped. Remove from the oven and cool on a wire rack.

To freeze: Wrap in a polythene bag, seal and freeze.

To serve: Unwrap and thaw at room temperature for 4–5 hours.

Croissants

METRIC	IMPERIAL
½ kg. strong flour	1 lb. strong flour
5 ml. salt	1 teaspoon salt
5 ml. sugar	1 teaspoon sugar
15 g. fresh yeast	½ oz. fresh yeast
120 ml. warm water mixed with 120 ml. warm milk	4 fl.oz. warm water mixed with 4 fl.oz. warm milk
100 g. butter	4 oz. butter
1 egg, beaten with a little milk	1 egg, beaten with a little milk

Sift the flour and salt into a warm bowl. Add the sugar. Blend the yeast and a little of the warm liquid together and stir into the flour with the remaining liquid. Mix to a fairly stiff dough and knead lightly on a floured surface for 8 minutes or until smooth. Place in a greased bowl, cover with a damp cloth and leave to rise in a warm place until it has doubled in size. Turn out and knead the dough lightly on a floured surface until smooth and elastic.

Roll out the dough into a rectangle approximately 50 × 20 cm./20 × 8 in. Divide the butter into three and dot one portion of butter over two-thirds of the dough. Fold the dough into three, bringing the bottom, unbuttered third up and folding the top third over. Give the dough a quarter turn and seal the folded edges with the rolling pin. Repeat the process twice more, rolling out, folding over and turning the dough, with the rest of the butter. Place the dough in an oiled polythene bag and chill in the refrigerator for 30 minutes. Roll out the dough and repeat the rolling, folding and turning process, without butter, three more times. Replace the dough in the polythene bag and chill in the refrigerator for at least 1 hour.

Roll out the dough again to a rectangle approximately 50 × 20 cm./20 × 8 in., divide in half lengthwise and cut each strip into 10 cm./4 in. squares, then divide each square into 2 triangles. Roll each triangle up, starting at the longest edge, and rolling towards the point. Tuck the end underneath, bend iinto a crescent shape, and leave to prove in a warm place on a greased floured baking sheet inside an oiled polythene bag for 15–20 minutes.

Remove the bag, brush with beaten egg and milk and bake in a hot oven (220°C/425°F or Gas Mark 7) for 15–20 minutes, or until puffed and golden brown. Cool on a wire rack.

To freeze: When cold, pack into a rigid container, cover, seal and freeze.

To serve: Thaw wrapped at room temperature for 2 hours, or reheat from frozen in a moderate oven for 10 minutes or until heated through.

Makes 20.

Basic white bread

METRIC	IMPERIAL
½ kg. strong flour	1 lb. plain strong flour
10 ml. salt	2 teaspoons salt
25 g. butter	1 oz. butter
15 g. fresh yeast	½ oz. fresh yeast
300 ml. lukewarm milk and water, mixed	½ pint lukewarm milk and water, mixed

Sift the flour and salt into a warm bowl and rub in the butter. Blend the yeast with a little of the lukewarm liquid and stir into the dry ingredients with the remaining liquid. Mix to a firm dough which leaves the sides of the bowl clean. Turn out onto a floured surface and knead for 8 minutes until the dough is smooth and elastic. Place the dough in a clean, greased bowl, cover with a damp cloth and leave to rise in a warm place for 1 to 1½ hours or until doubled in size.

Knead the dough again for 5 minutes on a floured surface then either shape into a loaf and place in a greased 1 kg./2 lb. loaf tin, or divide into 12 pieces, shape into rolls and place on a greased and floured baking tray. Cover and prove in a warm place until doubled in size.

Bake in a hot oven (220°C/425°F or Gas Mark 7) for 30–40 minutes for the loaf, or for 15–20 minutes for the rolls, or until the bread sounds hollow when tapped. Cool on a wire rack.

To freeze: Place in a polythene bag, seal and freeze.

To serve: Thaw wrapped at room temperature for 3–4 hours for a loaf or for 1–2 hours for rolls.

For speed the bread or rolls may be wrapped in foil and heated from frozen in a fairly hot oven (200°C/400°F or Gas Mark 6) for 30 minutes for a loaf or for 15 minutes for rolls.

Malt loaf

METRIC	IMPERIAL
225 g. wholemeal or strong white flour	*8 oz. wholemeal or strong white flour*
5 ml. salt	*1 teaspoon salt*
15 g. butter	*½ oz. butter*
50 g. currants	*2 oz. currants*
50 g. sultanas	*2 oz. sultanas*
25 g. chopped candied mixed peel	*1 oz. chopped candied mixed peel*
25 g. soft brown sugar	*1 oz. soft brown sugar*
15 g. fresh yeast	*½ oz. fresh yeast*
120 ml. warm milk	*4 fl.oz. warm milk*
30 ml. malt extract	*2 tablespoons malt extract*

Sift the flour and salt into a warm bowl, rub in the butter and add the dried fruit, mixed peel and brown sugar. Blend the yeast with the milk, add to the dry ingredients, together with the malt extract and mix well.

Turn out onto a floured surface and knead the dough for 3 minutes or until smooth and elastic. Place in a clean, greased bowl, cover with a damp cloth and leave to rise in a warm place until it has doubled in size. Turn out onto a floured surface and knead once more for 2 minutes, then shape into a loaf and place in a ½ kg./1 lb. greased loaf tin. Cover and prove in a warm place until the dough rises to the top of the tin.

Bake in a very hot oven (230°C/450°F or Gas Mark 8) for 10 minutes, then reduce the heat to fairly hot (190°C/375°F or Gas Mark 5) for 25 minutes or until the bread sounds hollow when tapped. Turn out and cool on a wire rack.

To freeze: Place in a polythene bag, seal and freeze.
To serve: Thaw wrapped at room temperature for 3–4 hours.

Croissants; White rolls; Malt loaf; Speedy brown loaf

Speedy brown loaf

METRIC	IMPERIAL
225 g. brown flour	*8 oz. brown flour*
225 g. strong white flour	*8 oz. strong white flour*
10 ml. salt	*2 teaspoons salt*
10 ml. sugar	*2 teaspoons sugar*
25 g. lard	*1 oz. lard*
15 g. fresh yeast	*½ oz. fresh yeast*
300 ml. lukewarm milk and water, mixed	*10 fl.oz. lukewarm milk and water, mixed*

Topping
Salted water
Rolled oats

Topping
Salted water
Rolled oats

Sift the flours, salt and sugar into a bowl and rub in the lard. Blend the yeast with a little of the lukewarm liquid and add to the dry ingredients with the rest of the liquid. Mix to a soft dough. Knead on a floured surface for 8 minutes or until the dough is smooth and elastic.

Divide the dough in half, shape and place each half in a greased ½ kg./1 lb. loaf tin. Brush the tops with the salted water and sprinkle with the oats.

Place the tins in a greased polythene bag and leave to rise in a warm place until the dough has doubled in size. Bake in a very hot oven (230°C/450°F or Gas Mark 8) for 30–40 minutes or until the bread sounds hollow when tapped. Turn out and cool on a wire rack.

To freeze: Pack in polythene bags, seal and freeze.
To serve: Thaw wrapped at room temperature for 3–4 hours.

Index

Acknowledgments

The publishers would like to thank Bejam Group
Ltd., for the loan of the freezers, and the
following companies for the loan of accessories
for photography:

Best of British
Elizabeth David Ltd.

General Trading Company (Mayfair) Ltd.,
Sloane Street
David Mellor, Ironmonger, Sloane Square
Royal Worcester China
Josiah Wedgwood and Sons Ltd.